THE CITY OF GOD

AND

THE CHURCH-MAKERS:

AN EXAMINATION INTO STRUCTURAL CHRISTIANITY, AND CRITICISM OF CHRISTIAN SCRIBES AND DOCTORS OF THE LAW.

BY

R. ABBEY.

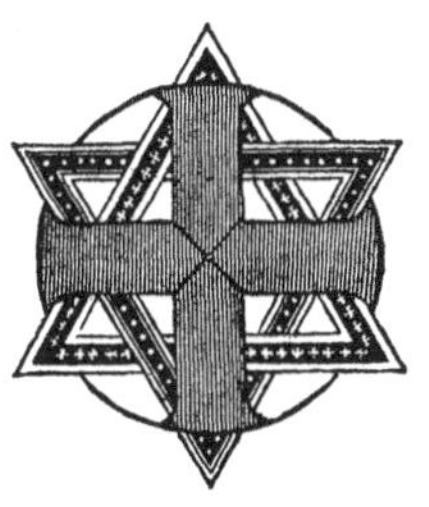

NEW YORK:
PUBLISHED BY HURD AND HOUGHTON.
Cambridge: Riverside Press.
1872.

RIVERSIDE, CAMBRIDGE:
STEREOTYPED AND PRINTED BY
H. O. HOUGHTON AND COMPANY.

NOTE.

Everybody knows that some of the greatest hindrances to the spread of Christianity are found in the Church. Among the foremost of these may be named the dissensions and animosities among the several denominations. And this is consequent on the diversity of view and opinion as to the legal character of the "Primitive Church," so called. The great question is held to be, How did Jesus Christ organize the first Church? Did He do it this way, or that way? Did He place it under the rule of a Pope, or Bishops, or Elders, or the suffrages of all the members? If a Pope, what powers did He give him, either absolute or contingent? If Bishops, what limitations, if any, were prescribed to them? If ministerial parity was the primary law, then how was the body of Elders governed? And if the first Church was "republican," then what? How was power reached, wielded, etc.?

Beginning with the unnatural and mythical error that Jesus Christ formed a new Church at all, the strife begins; and nine tenths of all our Church troubles is the natural result. The trouble is not the existence of different denominations. That is natural and harmless. The damage is in the lessening, or the unchurching of each other, because of the supposed non-conformity of Christians to this fabulous model. The strife is about a myth, a fact that never happened.

Ecce Ecclesia, as also *Church and Ministry*, and *Ecclesiastical Constitution*, which preceded it a number of years, were more feeble attempts to set forth *The City of God*, the natural and spontaneous association of Christian people, as the Church is frequently called in Scripture, in contrast with the multitudinous Church of the *Church-makers.*

If this book is not wofully wrong, then the work of the Church-makers is the most astonishing feature in the history of the Church, or in any other history. That such errors have not been before pointed out and cured is astounding. But I have no more wonder for others than for myself, for I have long drifted in the same channel, and labored in Church-making as honestly and industriously as others. "I verily thought with myself," that the Church was a corporation, working under a charter prescribed "at the first," by Jesus Christ. This was the teaching of my youth, and the sum of the unbroken lessons of my riper years. With no other reading, no other teaching, it formed in me, as in others, the staple of a religious education. In some form or other I read it in almost every book I read, and heard it in almost every sermon I heard. It was the unquestioned predicate of all arguments, the basis of all exhortations, and the axiom of all doctrines. "Jesus Christ made a totally new religion and new Church," was the sum of the Christianity we have been taught. Nothing but the very power of God could sustain the Church under such a load of error. I thank God I have lived long enough to correct some of my own participations in them!

More than twenty years ago, I thought leak-holes were discoverable in this popular Church notion. From that day to this present, it is neither presumption nor egotism to say that, to get rid of these shackles, "I labored more abundantly than they all."

I am not unmindful of the responsibility of such a publication as this, but, of course, without ability to measure it. Books, and prayers, and midnight hours, and foolscap written and burned, and public lectures, and pulpit labors, and private consultations, have at least borne witness to an honest industry in the premises. This book was written and carefully examined by the best and soberest counsel known to me, several years ago. But nerve faltered, and responsibility hesitated and drew back. The fancied iron in a will, not yet well tested, proved insufficient. The thoughtful reader may perceive the cause of this shrinking. He who deems it an easy thing, or pleasant, or agreeable to human feelings, or can calculate about the novelty of appearing original, in such a publication as this, has sounded the depths of social life and pious feeling to little purpose. A little less than threescore and ten years of varied and active life have, it is hoped, been sufficient to cure any risings of green ambition, that may have lurked around the fond anticipations of younger manhood. I dreaded the publication. With as clear a view in it of the *City of God*, as ever of the sun seen in the heavens, my heart and flesh recoiled before the gaze of mistaken judges, and the accredited scribes. Meanwhile friends urged and wrote, — "Publish it! publish it! Why do you not publish it? Write on! The Church needs it; God calls for it; duty, not feelings, must govern. Publish; feed the lambs, and challenge the doctors to read!"

I am somewhat aware of, though I cannot account for the principle, that declares war to the knife against the man who dares to disturb opinions or teachings regarded by such belligerents as settled. Secretly he is declared an outlaw. Innovation is the unpardonable sin. Galileo is not the only man who has been imprisoned. Men will die at the stake rather than give up a stereotyped lesson, or even a long-accustomed mode of teaching it. The law has long since gone forth from the high halls of power and folly, that the man who dares to question "standard authority" is the enemy of his race; and if he cannot be reached by the siege guns of reason and argument, he must at least be pestered, teazed, and annoyed to death by the scribbling million.

The man who holds this pen has sometimes almost nerve enough to question whether there is any "authority" in theology or ecclesiastical science outside the Bible, that is absolutely standard. But while he does so he yields to no man in deference to the opinions, the learning, or the teachings of the talented, the wise, and the good. With a proper respect, as he thinks, for the authors he criticises, but with a far higher regard for the Church and the subjects treated, he has, after some trial, and under the urgings of duty, keyed up a nerve sufficiently to enable him to hand this little manuscript to the printer. God and the Church will take care of it!

CONTENTS.

INTRODUCTORY ADDRESS.

APPEAL is earnestly and affectionately made to Christian people, of all names and tenets, in behalf of the things herein presented. That they are important in a high degree to the simple understanding and practice of Christianity by the common people, as well as by scholars, none will probably question. They certainly underlie nearly all the great questions of Christianity. The author is not raising questions for debate, nor has he any party, school, sect, or denomination to oppose or to support. The reader will find nothing herein that he will consider debatable, or from which he will dissent, when fairly understood.

It is claimed, nevertheless, that many of our best authors, with most surprising inconsistency, and blind following of each other, frequently contradict some of the most important and well settled principles of both theology and ecclesiastical science. These erroneous teachings are radical, fundamental, and belong as well to the primary lessons of the nursery and the Sunday-school, as to the higher classics. They misguide us every day in our nurseries, our pulpits, and our studies. By them Church exclusiveness, intolerance, and bigotry are fostered; denominational strife is enkindled, and worse still, Romish and High Church superstition and error are furnished with all the apparent plausibilities they claim to possess.

Appeal is made to the urgency and stress of the case. It does not admit of mere questions of finesse, and party successes and advantages. Religious truth is suffering. It is a wonder the Church lives and thrives, under such a load of error and misteaching.

A large number of our books are seriously defective. We take religious writers too much on trust. Denominational support is greatly injuring us. The greatest compliment paid to *Ecce Ecclesia* is, that it could not be discovered to what Church the author belonged.

Some will complain that I make an indiscriminate onslaught upon the authors. A more important inquiry would be, whether their truths or their errors are objected to. Do blunders and misstatements become true by prescription? Or is their value added to by the mere force of names?

Others may object that the author is arrogant, dogmatic, and peremptory in his criticism. That may be very likely; but who cares anything about the author? The book is the only thing presented to the public. It is a wonder such objections, so utterly unimportant, should be thought of. Perhaps the printer was unamiable. Another may object, that the authors are made to teach what they did not intend. That is also quite likely. But who cares anything about the intentions of authors? We are concerned only in their teachings. The only question with us is, What do they write? What is actually understood from their lessons? And even if a more or less strained explanation would relieve them, what care the people for that? The responsibility of authors attaches not to a defensive criticism, or perhaps hypercriticism, but to their plain, simple lessons, unexplained and undefended. It is a miserable author who needs explanation, and defense. Theological teachings, especially such as are intended for popular use, must carry an obvious meaning on their face. Children, and some grown people, do not always carry critics with them.

In the following pages, two hundred authors shall speak for themselves. Care has been taken to give their language its plainest, simplest, and most obvious meaning. Let any man read, and then say if I controvert doctrines not taught. We then proceed to inquire, What do these authors teach? The following is a brief summary of some of the things they inculcate. They are generally understood as I state them. Strange as it may seem, on reflection, the following glaring and dangerous errors do form a large amount of the common creed of the Church, especially the more unintelligent portions of it. Let the reader read slowly and note carefully.

First. There are two separate and distinct systems of religion in Scripture, one in the Old Testament, and one in the New. The former is called the Law, and the latter the Gospel.

Second. This first system, generally called Judaism, was a mere temporary system, not designed for mankind at large, but for a special people, the Jews only.

Third. The condition of salvation under the law, Judaism, or the Old Testament, was the performance of certain religious rites and ceremonies, particularly the killing of certain animals by way of atonement for sin.

Fourth. The ceremonial slaying and offering of animals in sacrifice under the law was a real, proper, and true sacrifice.

Fifth. When Christ appeared, He, by his supreme authority, abrogated this system of Old Testament religion, or Judaism, and forever discontinued all ceremonial worship.

Sixth. The Saviour at the same time ordained and established for all mankind forever, a wholly new religious system, called Christianity, or the gospel. This new system was so thoroughly novel, that not a principle or doctrine of it ever existed before.

Seventh. This new religion, and the salvation it introduced, rests upon the atonement of Christ, was not restricted to Jews, as the old religion was, but was for all men. It rested not on external observances, as did the old, but on the new principle of faith in Christ.

Eighth. Christ invited, entreated, and commanded the Jews to abandon their old religion, and embrace the gospel; but they all refused except a very few, perhaps twelve or twenty or so.

Ninth. All the Jews, except those very few, being very wicked, and accustomed to their formal religion of the Old

Testament, refused the gospel, and their descendants still adhere strongly to the old religion of the Old Testament.

Tenth. The whole Jewish people, therefore, became very much incensed against the Saviour for attempting to destroy their religion, and they unanimously sought and procured his death.

Eleventh. When Pilate sought to release Jesus, the whole body of the Jews cried out, "Crucify Him! His blood be on us and our children!" and this imprecation was answered by the destruction of the Jewish temple, and the dismemberment of the Jewish state.

Twelfth. At and prior to this time, all worship in the old Church was confined to the temple at Jerusalem; but now, in the new Christian Church, permission was given to worship anywhere.

Thirteenth. The Saviour not only abrogated the religion of the Old Testament, but the Church also. He opposed, cursed, and abandoned the old Church, and set up a new and different one in its stead.

Fourteenth. This new Church was set up in Jerusalem with entirely new laws, new conditions of membership, new officers, new government, new ritual, and new principles of every kind. It began with a few members, perhaps twelve or twenty.

Fifteenth. The Saviour also instituted a new ministry, on an entirely new basis, the old being dissolved and the ministers all being deposed.

Sixteenth. This new ministry of the new Church was at the first composed of the eleven or twelve apostles, others being added after.

Seventeenth. This new ministry was violently opposed by all the old ministers and members of the old Church. So when they began to preach the gospel in Jerusalem, the entire world was against them.

Eighteenth. At the first meeting of note of the new Church, three thousand people were converted, and joined the Church, renouncing wholly the religion of the Old Testament; the Holy Ghost being now for the first time introduced among men.

Nineteenth. The Lord also established new sacraments in the new Church, they being a kind of mystery, and sign of existing grace.

Twentieth. This new Church and religion were not a reform of the old. Both the religion and Church of the Old Testament were so utterly defective and unsuited to mankind, that they were both wholly destroyed.

Twenty-first. Some of the first Christians apostatized from the new faith, and lapsed back into the religion of the Old Testament. This gave the apostles great concern, and Paul wrote several epistles, cautioning the Church against the religion of the Old Testament.

Twenty-second. The Jews at the birth of Jesus were all the lineal descendants of Abraham; and the Jews of the present day are their descendants, constituting their entire posterity, and holding their religion, that is, the religion of the Old Testament.

Twenty-third. The two systems of salvation called respectively the Law, and the Gospel, sustaining a chronological relation to each other, cannot coexist.

Twenty-fourth. So Jesus Christ being divine, and the head of the Church, its founder and the framer of its charter and laws, the test of a Church's identity must be the original model. This model we gather from various descriptions of it in the New Testament. A true Church now must be the same, in succession, as the original, with the same prescribed laws and same government.

Now I will not say that every one of these twenty-four articles, just as written, is taught by every one of the authors here quoted; but it is said that they are held and taught in terms by a large number of them, and that they all teach all these errors in some form, by fair implication. And further, that great masses of Christians in all the churches understand the Scriptures that way, through the misteachings herein complained of.

Instead of these errors the following theses are not only true, but will probably be held incontrovertible.

First. Scripture knows but one system of religion. The Old and New Testaments teach the same.

Second. There was never any temporary system for Jews or for anybody else. The only religion known to any part of Scripture was for all mankind.

Third. The law knows no salvation. The supposition is absurd. Ceremonies are modes of worshipping and of inculcating truth. They have the same place in religion now that they always had.

Fourth. Sacrifice for sin was always exactly the same in all ages of the world. There was never any other than Christ, our Saviour. In the early age the slaying of animals was a mere instrumental mode of teaching the doctrine, as books are now.

Fifth. The Saviour never abrogated or changed any system of religion or doctrines, but always maintained and enforced the doctrines of the Old Testament. He never abrogated ceremonies. There are probably as many in use in the Church now as there ever were. Nevertheless, a number of religious ceremonies ceased forever at that time. But those that ceased did so, not by any means because of any authoritative command, but because of the absolute and natural necessity of the thing. These particular ceremonies shadowed forth the incarnation; then how could they continue afterward? No other ceremonies ceased but those of that class, and for that reason. When a thing is seen it is no longer adumbrant.

Sixth. The Saviour never ordained, established, or taught any Christianity different from the religious doctrines of the Old Testament. The gospel of the New Testament is the gospel of the Old. They differ not in doctrines or principles, but merely in modes of teaching.

Seventh. All religion of all Scripture was always plenary as to all mankind. It was never restricted as to Jews or anybody else. It always rested on faith in Christ, and never on external observances.

Eighth. The Saviour entreated and commanded all the Jews to adhere strictly to their old religion, and not depart from it; and great multitudes, probably one half or more, did so; and their successors, afterward called Christians, have continued to do so, at least nominally, to this day.

Ninth. About a full half or more of the Jews in the time of the apostles were among the most noble, pious, and self-sacrificing Christians known to the history of the Church. For about ten years after the death of Jesus they constituted the entire Apostolic Church, apostles and all. It is not known that they or any of them ever opposed the Saviour in the least, or in any way. The people known as Jews now are descendants, not by any means of the Jews in general of that age, but of those only who in that age apostatized from their religion by denying Jesus as the Christ, and who thereby constituted themselves a new and false Church, with a new and false faith unknown to Scripture.

Tenth. Very few of the Jews, probably not more than one or two hundred, if so many, out of all their millions, had, or could have had, anything to do with the crucifixion. They could not even know of it until afterwards. So far as their sentiments are known, they were, with very few exceptions, the friends of the Saviour and in favor of the Messiahship of Jesus, at the time of his death, or at least were not opposed to it.

Eleventh. The cry "Crucify Him!" was the reckless exclamation of a little handful of rabble at the governor's door, where there could have been only a few persons, perhaps twenty or fifty. Its connection with the siege of Jerusalem, forty years after, is mere fancy.

Twelfth. At, and for hundreds of years prior to, the time of Christ, congregational worship, as now, was common among the Jews everywhere. So far as we know, it never was confined to the three great temples, much less to that at Jerusalem.

Thirteenth. Jesus Christ never, so far as there is the least intimation, entertained a sentiment unfriendly to the Church of his fathers. On the contrary He loved and supported it to the hour of his death. A new Church was not dreamed of in that age. It is the invention of a far later period. Besides being historically untrue, it is philosophically impossible. The supposition destroys the very idea of the Church.

Fourteenth. Neither did the Saviour prescribe any government for the Church, either in whole or in part. Nor did He institute a new ministry, or depose old ministers.

Fifteenth. There was no time within a hundred years of the apostolic age, in which we are allowed to infer that there existed in the true Church, less than thousands of true, divinely accredited ministers of the gospel.

Sixteenth. The gospel, all the gospel known to Scripture — that is, the tidings of salvation by Christ — was preached in the days of Abel and the prophets.

Seventeenth. On the day of Pentecost, as it is called, the three thousand spoken of were all in the Church, and we are obliged to infer that at least many of them were pious. So we are not at liberty to suppose that they were all then converted, though some may have been. They did not join the Church, for they were already in it.

Eighteenth. The establishment of new sacraments in the Church, at any time, would be an impossibility, because it would imply a new religion, which implies a changed duty, or a new human nature, or both. Sacrament is religious obligation. This grows out of the natural relation of man to his Maker. So Jesus did not appoint sacraments, but the modes of administering the sacraments. The two things are widely different.

Nineteenth. The divine abrogation or disannulment of a divinely recognized Church is not simply impossible, it is more; it is an absurdity. The repeal of any divine law is impossible.

Twentieth. For Christians, at any time, to lapse, or backslide, into the religion of the Old Testament, is an absurdity, because the Old Testament enjoins the highest style of Christian piety. You might as well suppose one to lapse into the religion of the New Testament.

Twenty-first. The Jews, in the days of Jesus, as the Church in that period is generally called, were not probably, one in a thousand, descended from Abraham lineally, Both the law and the practice was, that they mix by intermarriage with all people everywhere, who could be induced to join them. They were probably more nationally mixed than other peoples of that age. The people known as Jews, since that age, are by no means the descendants, either nationally, religiously, or ecclesiastically, of the mass of Jews living in the time of Jesus; but only and exclusively of those who apostatized by denying the Christship in Jesus. This apostate offshoot from the Church was probably less than half the number.

Twenty-second. Christians, at and since the apostolic age, are lineally the regular, straightforward descendants and successors of the Jews as seen at the birth of Jesus, religiously and ecclesiastically, though much mixed by intermarriage with others. This must be so on supposition that Christianity is the true religion as contrasted with modern Judaism.

Twenty-third. The Law, as that term is used in juxtaposition to Gospel, is not a system of salvation, but of absolute obedience, before salvation was either known or necessary. The law still exists in all its force; but Christ, with salvation, assists us in meeting its demands. So the two systems form themselves into one, and coexist, since Christ was furnished to the world in the days of Adam. The term law is also used in Scripture to mean various things. Frequently it means the ritualistic rules prescribed through Moses. These are mere instrumental modes of teaching and enforcing the principles of salvation.

Twenty-fourth. The supposition that the Christian Church must have been organized with a prescribed law of government, at some particular time, because it now exists, is a great error. No such event ever happened, or could have happened. Such a religious corporation would not be a Church. Religious people from the very first associated together as such, naturally and necessarily, because they were religious. Association necessitates rules, and all churches make their own rules. Christ is the Head of the Church, therefore, in its spiritual and religious aspects, but not as referring to external government.

If the Saviour organized the twelve apostles into a corporate society for the propagation of Christianity, then, — because that means that He prescribed a law of government for it to be in perpetual force — then the very form of the government was divine. It is a revelation, and then, nothing can be a Church that varies from that form. The society has omnipotent power of perpetuity. The outward identity must be maintained. Then I see not how the doctrine of Infallibility is so easily avoided — not personal, but official infallibility; not human, but divine infallibility, conferred upon the corporation, not on the individual members. Whether that infallibility is to be found in the decisions of the president — call him Pope, if you will — or on some board or council, is a very different and very incidental question.

This doctrine of the Church's corporate formation is the only fundamental principle, that underlies all Romanism, and all High Churchism, of every grade and kind. Let that be conceded, and Romanism is at least plausible, if not necessary. Then ministerial, if not prelatical apostolic succession follows; and then Church exclusiveness, Campbellism, exclusion of children from the Church, and a train of pestiferous evils and disadvantages follow, which, to say the least, hang heavily as clogs upon the Church.

The doctrine of the corporate formation of the Church also furnishes logical infidelity the greater portion of its support; indeed it is the most formidable enemy the Church has, or ever had. It is, one way or another, in many more ways than a casual observer would suppose, the fountain, the father, of almost all our religious troubles, theological and ecclesiastical.

In the above twenty-four theses, the reader is shown at a glance the blunders in brief outline, which are exposed more fully in the following pages. Blunders, I say, for the statements cannot be believed. Opinions and blunders are different things.

The erroneous teachings herein controverted, besides the support they give to Romanism, to prelatical and Campbellitish High Churchism of a more direct kind, have largely taught the people almost, and sometimes wholly, to repudiate the Old Testament Scriptures as a rule of life; and by many they are held only as a sort of historic prelude to the real Scriptures. And so, how often has it been gravely inquired whether this or that has been "reënacted," in the New Testament! There are many and grave authors among them, who hold that Old Testament Scripture, to be binding, must be reënacted.

The scholarly reader will be likely to find too much repetition herein. He will be pleased to bear in mind that the essay is intended for the masses. Many extracts similar to those published are passed over, while some pains has been taken to give them a range pretty wide, over most of the field of the science of the Church, as well as some glances into theology.

The reader is again requested to bear in mind, because it is important, that it is no part of the author's business to criticise the authors, merely to point out their errors. What good would it do to show that a certain man, who wrote a book, was right, or was wrong, in this or in that? That might be a legitimate business for critics, or reviewers; but these criticisms are of a very different sort. They are about books, not men. The inquiry is, What do the books teach, as they are actually understood? What do the people — the masses, the children, not scholars — believe on these subjects, after reading the passages herein quoted? And what boots it, though more extensive readers find out that the author believed the reverse of what is stated? The poison has gone forth, and is lodged in ten thousand places, where the antidote does not reach.

Care has been had to quote in convenient form for clear inspection. Brief passages are selected for brevity. The same things are often found in more voluminous passages. Infringement on the context is carefully avoided. Hypercriticism is neither indulged in, nor allowed in others.

Perhaps it may not be amiss again to caution the reader against supposing these criticisms set up opinions, or matter of belief, different from the authors criticised. Strange as it may seem, there is and can be but little, if any difference of opinion here. With a few exceptions, if indeed there be any, the errors pointed out are mere blunders, not statements of belief. With a few exceptions of Roman

Catholic and other High Church, and a very few semi-infidel writers, it is well and abundantly known, that the authors themselves believed no such things as they themselves have so plainly written. They are for the most part pure blunders, not opinions. It is my business to point them out for the Church, but not mine, more than others, to account for them. This, it must be confessed, would be difficult.

But there are a few things of which we might be reminded. In the first place, authors, and especially religious authors, are more likely, unconsciously, to follow file-leaders, than almost any other class of men. Again, it is seen at a glance that the fundamental ideas of a new Church and new religion are absolutely necessary to the existence of Romanism and all other forms of High Churchism. And hence the necessity in that quarter, that the belief be kept up. Thirdly, since the Lutheran reformation, the question whether Jesus and the apostles did or did not organize a new Church, and teach a new religion, has not been brought prominently forward and debated at all, that I am aware of. Strange as it may seem, it has been suffered to pass without inquiry.

The reader is now introduced to about two hundred authors.

THE CITY OF GOD

AND THE

CHURCH-MAKERS.

I.

ERRORS OF AUTHORS.

1. RUTER'S *Gregory*, p. 23, tells us that "The greater number of the first converts to Christianity were of the Jewish nation."

This gives a wrong impression. All the first converts, if he chooses so to call it, to Christianity — that is, to Jesus as Christ, before the preaching to Cornelius, about ten years after the crucifixion — were Jews, without exception. At this time the belief in Jesus, that He was Christ, had spread into almost all countries, and the Christians must have amounted to many thousands, if not to millions. But these persons were in no proper sense converts. They were merely persons who continued steadfastly to adhere to their former faith.

2. *Nevins's Biblical Antiquities*, p. 414, says: "It may be remembered also, that the Lord's Supper, which was regularly celebrated in the Christian churches every week, was an institution altogether peculiar to their worship, to which there was noth-

ing that corresponded in any way whatever in the services of the synagogue."

So far from this being true, the Lord's Supper was the identical passover itself, and so expressly declared and denominated by the Saviour himself. Only the mode of administering it was new.

3. Dr. George Smith (*Elements of Divinity*, p. 167) says the Old Testament was "specially made to the elect people;" and that the New was "intended for the world." Then what right have we to use it as Scripture, and farther to thwart the divine intention by continually publishing it to the world?

4. On page 193, he says the Gospel of John "describes the rise and progress of the Christian Church in Judea."

This is likely to make a wrong impression, because it is unquestionably true, that there was then, and had been for many centuries in Judea, a regular Church, divinely recognized, and which was essentially Christian.

5. Schaff, in his *Church History*, p. 39, says: "Christianity, at the first, had to sustain a mighty conflict with Judaism and heathenism."

In other words, Christ and the apostles, in teaching true religion, set up and waged a mighty conflict against the revealed religion of Scripture, and also against heathenism!

6. On page 172, Schaff says: "The Jews were split at the time of Christ, into three sects — the Pharisees, Sadducees, and Essenes."

This statement is directly against all the reliable history there is on the subject. First, the Pharisees, Sadducees, and Essenes were not sects at all, as we use that term. They were sects in philosophy, not religious sects. Secondly, it cannot be said that the Jewish Church was split into these three societies, when the former numbered many millions, and the latter, at the highest estimates, never numbered over about ten or eleven thousand. You might as well say that the Christian Church, in the nineteenth century, was split into three classes of lecturers in the Smithsonian Institute.

7. Dr. Schaff (*Church History*, p. 214) tells us that the Old Testament "ordains circumcision for all time."

But Paul certainly understood the Old Testament differently. He understood circumcision to be the mode of administering the initiating ordinance for the period of the Church anterior to the death of Christ exclusively, and as anticipating that event. And a greater than Paul so understood the Old Testament. Did our Saviour, in administering that ordinance as we do now, violate the law of the Old Testament? Did He ever, in one jot or tittle, to use his own words, infringe upon any rule of Scripture? Such ceremonies as were ordained for that period alone, were so recognized and so disposed of. Did the Saviour, or any inspired New Testament writer, ever depart from the rule, "Thus it is written"?

8. Dean Milman, in his *History of Christianity*, first paragraph of Preface, says that Christianity is "the new relation established between man and the Supreme Being."

This cannot be, because that would necessitate a change in the character of God, or the nature of man, or both; either of which is out of the question. The relation between God and man is not a subject of prescription or legislation at all. It results spontaneously and necessarily from the character of God and the nature of man.

9. Dean Milman says: "About this point of time Christianity appeared." That is, at the time of the preaching of the Saviour.

No, sir! Christianity is as clearly written by Isaiah, Ezekiel, and Daniel, as by Matthew, John, and Paul. And Dean Milman himself so teaches us in more than a hundred places.

10. At page 28, Dean Milman says that "God is *power* in the old religion; He is *love* under the new."

And the book says that God is without variableness, or even the shadow of turning.

11. At page 90, Milman says, speaking of the morality of Jesus, that, "It was morality, grounded on broad and simple principles, which had hitherto never been laid down as the basis of human action."

And yet, with all other theologians, he teaches that all conceivable human morals, in their simple principles, are laid down as the basis of human action in the twentieth chapter of Exodus, beginning at the third verse.

12. Again, he says: "Christian morality was not that of a sect, a race, or a nation, but of universal man."

And yet he teaches that the precepts of the decalogue are, and always were, binding on all men.

13. At page 145 we are told: "The resurrection of Jesus is the basis of Christianity; it is the groundwork of the *Christian* doctrine of the immortality of the soul."

That is all very true, except the italicizing of the word "Christian." This makes the whole sentence teach erroneously. It is true that the resurrection of Jesus is the basis of Christianity, and the groundwork of the doctrine of the immortality of the soul. But it is also true that this was always the Christian doctrine, as well in the days of Abel and Isaiah as of Peter and Paul. Has the doctrine of the immortality of the soul been changed?

14. Macknight (*Epistles*, p. 20) says: "It is the Apostle Paul, chiefly, who, by proving the principal doctrines of the gospel from the writings of Moses and the prophets, hath shown that the same God who spake to the fathers by the prophets, did in the last days speak by the Son."

That sentence is rendered very defective by the insertion of the word "principal." Paul did not thus prove the principal doctrines of the gospel, but every one — every one, without exception, and so repeatedly it was declared by himself. Which one did he not prove from the writings of Moses and the prophets?

15. Dr. Clarke tells us, in his Preface to the Gospel of Matthew, that, "The term New Covenant, as used here, seems to mean that grand plan of arrangement or reconciliation which God made between Himself and mankind, by the death of Jesus Christ, in consequence of which all those who truly repent and unfeignedly believe in the great atoning sacrifice, are justified from their sins and united to God."

I think this fails as a particular definition, for the reason that, most undoubtedly, thousands of years before this, there existed a great plan of arrangement or reconciliation which God made between Himself and mankind, by the death of Jesus Christ, in consequence of which all those who truly repent and unfeignedly believe in the great atoning sacrifice, are justified from their sins and united to God. This, and nothing more nor less, is the precise condition of salvation, written in a hundred places, in various forms of expression, all through the Old Testament. And it is unquestionable, also, that many in Old Testament times were actually saved under these conditions.

16. Dr. Clarke says: "The Jews were the first and most inveterate enemies the Christians had."

No; not *the* Jews, but Jews; for it is also certain that Jews were the first and most pious and heroic friends the Christians had. For about ten years after the death of Christ, until the preaching to Cornelius, the entire Apostolic Church — as we call the Church at that time, apostles and all — were all Jews. By this time, those who acknowledged Jesus as Christ must have amounted to many thousands, and were spread almost over the known world.

17. *Buck's Dictionary* says: "Christ was despised and hated by the Jews without a cause."

This expression conveys a very incorrect idea; and it has been so very frequently repeated, by so many, and in so many forms of expression, that it has become a commonplace and a settled matter with many, to the great injury of Biblical truth. The simple truth is that many, and for a very short time perhaps most of the haters of Christ, were Jews; but it is also true, that at the same time all the friends and followers of Christ were also Jews. And it is also certain that these Jews, so faithfully and heroically devoted to the cause of Christ, were numbered by their three thousands, and five thousands, and multitudes, great multitudes, often repeated, and by countless myriads all over the land. So that the Jews were never haters of Christ.

Let any one look carefully into the New Testament, and he will find that in every place where the Jews are spoken of, as opposed to the person or teachings of Christ, it never refers to the Jewish people at large. In a few places it refers to the nation or government, that is, to the Sanhedrim, or officials; but mostly it refers locally to certain or a very few Jews who chanced to be there present, where some local occurrence is narrated. Now examine every place carefully.

18. In *Jahn's Biblical Archæology*, p. 390, we read of "the conversion of the Jews to the Christian system." And in very many other places in this and many other books it is clearly supposed that the Jews, as such, needed to be converted to some other system, or religion, called Christianity.

The reply is, that there is no such other religion as is supposed known to divine revelation. 1st. There is no doctrine of religion — no, nor not even a rule of morals — in the New Testament that is not in the Old. They are only more fully explained and elaborated in the New. 2d. The Jews, before the apostasy of such as did apostatize after the death of Jesus, and indeed those who remained in the Church — and to the present day, all of us — needed instruction in their religion, and a more close conformity to it, but certainly not conversion from it. How can anybody be converted from divine revelation? The apostate Jews, like any other apostates, need to be converted from their apostasy to their former faith. But do pious men need conversion? They need more enlightenment, but they are already converted. Many millions of the most pious as well as the most wicked men that ever lived were Jews.

A misuse of the word *remnant*, as seen in Rom. ix. 27, xi. 5, has had a strong tendency to mislead or confirm the misleadings of many. "A remnant shall be saved," is understood to mean a very small portion, a very few, as compared with the whole. The Jews, therefore, who were not cut off through unbelief, were but the smallest fraction of the whole. And so Burkitt says, "The greatest number of these would be passed by for their unbelief, and a remnant only be saved." But this reading very widely misapprehends the meaning of the word *remnant*. Remnant means the portion which remains after a part has been removed. But it has no more signification of a small than of a large portion. The remnant of anything may be one fourth, or one half, or nine tenths of the former whole. This is the proper meaning of the word. It is used about seventy times in the Old Testament. I readily acknowledge, however, that remnant is frequently used in the Old Testament to mean a small portion; and even if that were the meaning in the texts quoted from the prophets as above, it would not relieve the difficulty. The reference is to the destruction of Jerusalem, and it is certain that the number who fled and escaped that destruction was quite small as compared with the number of unbelieving Jews who perished. Most of the Christian Jews are not taken into this account at all, because they had already, some time before, left the city.

19. Lord King, formerly High Chancellor of England, and author of a most excellent ecclesiastical classic, calls his work "An Inquiry into the Consti-

tution, Discipline, Unity, and Worship of the Primitive Church, that flourished within the first three hundred years after Christ."

This most valuable work, which is made up entirely of laborious historical research, is an argument going to prove that its title, "Primitive Church," is a misnomer. Primitive means first, original, beginning. And if the history of the Church in that period be correctly stated, then, beyond all question, it was not first, original, nor beginning, but was, as Mr. Richard Watson, in making the same kind of an argument, says it was, "the very same that was before the coming of Christ." The extensive republication of Lord King's book, and polemical use of it by Methodist and other presbyterial writers, is to show that the Christian Church, after Christ, was by no means primitive; that, as Mr. Watson says, "the Christian Church is not another, but the very same," which was previously called Jewish.

20. Dr. Bangs writes a most valuable treatise, proving, by many forms of argument, that no form of Church government was prescribed to the Church at the time of the Christian era; that is, that a Church was not then made, but that the one Church continued uninterruptedly. And then he makes a most fatal admission against his whole argument, which otherwise would be an unanswerable one, by calling his book "An Original Church of Christ." Both things cannot possibly be true.

21. Dr. Clarke frequently speaks of the Jews, at and before the coming of Christ, as though they were not Christians, but the religious opponents of Christians.

If any one doubts that this is a mistake, I ask

him, first, Did they hold the Old Testament as Scripture, and confess its faith? Second, Does the Old Testament contain or tolerate any religious doctrine, precept, or sentiment, which is not wholly based on, and inherent in, our Saviour Jesus Christ, as He is presented in all the Scriptures? Then what is a Christian?

22. "For the law was given by Moses, but grace and truth came by Jesus Christ." (John i. 17.)

This is oftentimes misunderstood. These two states of things have no relation to the order of time, but to the natural order of sequence, the beginning and development of religious principles in the soul. To suppose the two things chronologically related, would imply that during four thousand years salvation was offered upon conditions utterly impracticable, *i. e.*, was not offered at all; and that afterward God became merciful and offered salvation by free grace. Salvation was always offered on the same conditions.

23. "For the original faith of the Christian Church, the Scriptures of the New Testament, are certainly the only competent authority." (*Ruter's Gregory*, p. 24.)

By the original faith, I suppose, is meant the faith actually entertained by Christians in the early ministry of the apostles. And it will be remembered that the faith of these persons was taught them, explained to them, and inculcated exclusively by arguments and considerations drawn from the writings of the Old Testament. Then, while that faith is more fully and elaborately explained in the New than in the Old Testament, it cannot be said that the latter is absolutely incompetent to describe it, since, as above intimated, it was once taught and described exclusively from these writings.

24. "From the very first, therefore, we find in the Church of Christ a regular chain of authority and subordination." (*Ruter's Gregory.*)

First of what? I inquire. He alludes to the ministry of the apostles and of the seventy. But surely no one will say that Isaiah did not minister in the regular Church of Christ. Then, I repeat, how was it first, at a period several hundred years later?

25. "For if the several books differ, the difference is in precise agreement with the known circumstances of the authors; whilst in every respect the peculiarities prove that the writers of them were what they professed to be—Jews converted to Christianity." (*Smith's Elements*, p. 31.)

The objection I make here is, that there was never any such confession as is here stated, nor, indeed, was there any such conversion. Of the most of these writers there is, in the historic Scriptures, not the least intimation about their conversion. The inference is, therefore, that they were converted before they became acquainted with the Saviour. And I know of no conversion which a pious man needs. Paul was converted afterward, but he was converted to the written religion of his own Scriptures, which he had for several years so misunderstood.

26. "In most of the early Christian communities a portion of the Church had been Jews by birth." (*Conybeare and Howson's St. Paul.*)

So far from this being a correct description of the times, it is true that for about eight or ten years after the crucifixion—until the preaching to Cornelius—not only a portion, but all the members of the Church, without a single exception, who acknowledged the Christship of Jesus, not only had been Jews, but continued to be Jews so long as they lived. Certainly, in that period at least, all the Christians were Jews; and so far from their ceasing to be Jews, the only way they could possibly continue to be Jews was to confess Christ according to the Scriptures. Those who denied Christ ceased to be Jews — true Jews. They called themselves Jews, but did lie. (Rev. iii. 9, ii. 9, and other places.)

27. "The Jewish believers had renounced the righteousness of the law." (*Conybeare and Howson.*)

Then they were apostates from the divine faith. How can revealed religion require a renunciation of some righteousness, revealed in Scripture, or of anything revealed? I know of no apostasy that does not consist in a renunciation of something revealed; nor can I conceive of a renunciation of anything revealed that is not apostasy.

28. "The festival of the Passover was instituted for the purpose of preserving among the Hebrews the memory of their liberation from Egyptian servitude, and the safety of their first-born on that night when the first-born of the Egyptians perished." (*Jahn's Biblical Archæology.*)

There is no doubt that the first and most primary and immediate object of the Passover was as is here stated. But it is equally clear that its great object was to teach typically and symbolically the doctrine of our great Passover, the Shiloh to come. And in the third place, the Passover was, and still is, one of the two sacraments of religion. But to denominate the Passover a festival merely, is to overlook the thing itself, and have régard only to the mere form of exhibiting it. It was celebrated in a festive manner, it is true, but the thing itself is a sacrament. The same sacrament, performed in a different mode, is in the Church now.

29. "His blood be upon us and our children." (Matt. xxvii. 25.) Dr. Kitto, speaking of the destruction of Jerusalem, says: "Thus was inflicted the doom which was impiously invoked when the inhabitants of Jerusalem cried out, 'His blood be upon us and our children.'"

And when did the inhabitants of Jerusalem cry in that manner? Some attribute the expression to the whole Jewish people. The simple facts are in a nutshell. A few priests and officials, members of the Sanhedrim, not the people, were urging the conviction of Jesus before Pilate, in or around the door of his court-room, where it was physically impossible there could have been more than few — perhaps twenty, or fifty, or so — present, in the hearing of the governor, and participating in the trial. They, these priests, officers, and the little rabble around them, cried, "His blood," etc. But there is no pretense that they spoke on the behalf of any but themselves. Indeed, the whole history shows plainly that the great mass of the Jewish people of the city were very much in favor of Christ, and strongly inclined to favor his Messiahship. And the trial and execution were hurried forward very precipitately for fear of the people.

30. Dr. Kitto says of the people he calls Jews, forty years after the death of Christ, that "they were ready in crowds to rally round the standard of their ancient faith."

He is under a great mistake. The people who at this period were ready to rally round the standard of their ancient faith were now called Christians. They began to be called Christians at Antioch, several years before this time; and the people who at that time were called Jews were a part of the former Jewish Church, who apostatized from its religion, and who then and now hold a very different religion from their ancient faith.

31. Dr. Taylor — quoted by Dr. Clarke — paraphrases Rom. ix. 27, thus: "But a small remnant of the Jews shall be taken into the Church."

In this short sentence there are two manifest and very important errors. The first is, in considering the remnant small — small as compared with the other portion. The word *remnant* does not always imply that the remaining portion is either smaller or larger than the other portion which was taken away. Remnant means that which remains, be it much or little, after a portion, much or little, has been removed. And in very many places in the first ten or twelve chapters of Acts, and elsewhere, it is stated and unmistakably explained, that the Jews who remained true to Christ were "thousands," and "multitudes," oft repeated, and "many ten thousands," meaning myriads; but what proportion of the whole, is not particularly stated.

The second error is in supposing that this remaining portion had to be taken into the Church. Taken into what Church? Were they not already in the Church? Are we not told almost everywhere, in and out of the pulpit, that there was never but one Church and one religion? Are we not a thousand times taught that the one Church which was instituted at an early period, continued uninterruptedly to the present day? And likewise, that the one true religion was uninterruptedly continued?

Now, it is the one way or the other. It cannot be both ways. If the men of true religion and true faith who held firmly to their principles and the true Church had to be taken into the Church again, or into some other Church, then be it so. And if they were already in the Church, and did not leave it, but remained in it, holding firmly to its faith, then be it that way.

If Drs. Clarke and Taylor are right, then Paul and his coadjutors are wrong. The case is a plain one, and leaves no room for argument except as between these parties.

32. Dr. Abel Stevens says that one of the reasons why the Saviour and the apostles frequented the synagogues in their ministry was, "because it allowed them considerable freedom of speech, by which they could address their new doctrines to the people."

I ask, What new doctrines? The point is important. There is a sense in which the above statement is true, but I do not know whether that was or was not the Doctor's meaning. The doctrines preached by the apostles were new to many who heard, just as the same doctrines we preach now are new to many who hear, and who are ignorant of the doctrines they nominally profess. But they were certainly not new to the Church — new to religion. There is not a doctrine in the New Testament, nor was there one taught by the apostles, which they did not find in, and teach out of, the Old Testament.

And the Doctor himself says, that they always found in the synagogues "the Old Testament Scriptures, by the reading and exposition of which they could prove their doctrines." That is exactly right. They proved every doctrine they preached by the reading and exposition of the Old Testament.

33. Stillingfleet verges so closely upon the truth as almost to touch it: "We have the same orders for prayers, reading the Scriptures according to occasion, and sermons made out of them for increase of faith, raising hope, and strengthening confidence. We have the discipline of the Church answering the admonitions and excommunications of the synagogue. And last of all, we have the bench of elders sitting in the assemblies, and ordering the things belonging to them."

Or, in fewer words, we have the same identical, continuous, unchanged Church. The Church relates to the two periods, before and after the coming of Christ, just as it relates to any other two periods.

34. Schaff, in his *History of the Apostolic Church*, tells us that "Christianity at the first had to sustain a mighty conflict with Judaism and heathenism." (Page 39.)

Now, it is matter of moment to inquire what this false and wicked thing is which held such a mighty conflict with true religion. Schaff gives us this information on page 139, when treating on a differing point: —

"Judaism is the religion of positive, direct revelation, in word and action; a communication not only of divine doctrine, but also of divine life."

Then how could Christianity have a conflict with revelation? Surely there can be no conflict between divine doctrine and divine life on the one hand, and Christianity on the other.

35. Coleman's *Biblical Atlas*, speaking of Paul, says: "Toward the Christians, as a new religious sect, apostates from the faith, regardless of the law and the sacred institutions of Moses, he entertains the most implacable hatred. As the new religion spreads, and gathers daily fresh accessions, his zeal for his religion rises to the most ungovernable fury against the new sect."

Now it is matter of very considerable importance in Biblical theology, which was the new sect — which set up the new religion — the followers of Christ, or the Jews who denied Him? That one or the other did, is very certain. A short time previously they were all together, in one Church, in one common fellowship, and all professing the same religion. And now they are separate, widely separate, in different and opposing churches, with different and opposing religions, and are indeed very hostile to each other.

So it is certain that either one or both abandoned their old religion and the old Church. Now, which were the apostates? Mr. Coleman says the Christians are the apostates, that they set up the new religion. And it is certain the rejecting Jews charged this boldly upon them. It is, however, a question stoutly held, on this side and on that, to this day.

Now, how are you going to determine? I answer, with the simplest and most infallible certainty. If Jesus was the Christ, then the rejecting Jews apostatized; and if He was not, then Mr. Coleman, and I would not like to say how many more with him, are correct, and Christianity is a falsehood and an apostasy.

Mr. Coleman tells us plainly that the Christians

did repudiate utterly and wholly the Old Testament, its teachings, its morals, and its religion. Listen again: "The Christians, as a new religious sect, apostates from the faith, regardless of the law and the sacred institutions of Moses"—

No apostate Jew, in denying Christ, ever said or need say more than that against Christianity. No one ever held, or attempted to hold, more than that in order to prove modern Judaism the true, and Christianity a false, religion. Indeed, I can conceive of no facts which would more conclusively prove Christianity to be heresy, and modern Judaism to be the true faith of God. Brethren! Christian brethren! these errors must be arrested.

Now, if that argument can be jostled, then we have no farther use for human logic nor human reason.

36. Our Lord and Saviour, Jesus Christ, is frequently spoken of as the Founder of our religion. This is most certainly true; but in what sense is it to be understood? Certainly not in the sense that eighteen hundred years ago He set up, established, ordained, originated, or founded a system or some doctrines of religion. This He did not do. He is the founder of Christianity in the sense that, as the Jehovah, the Omnipotent, He is the maker and founder of all things. He is the founder of religion in the sense that, in the days of Adam, He revealed to mankind the Christian religion, which system of recovering grace and salvation from sin was taught from time to time to man, by farther and still farther revelations, the whole closing with the teachings of the apostles; but in no other sense.

37. "The belief in a future state may be said to

have been an open question among the Jews when our Lord appeared." (*Conybeare and Howson's St. Paul.*)

Yes, it might perhaps be called an open question, but just precisely as it is an open question now with us. Then, as now, it was a closed question so far as the religion of the Church was concerned. But, as is the case now, there were then persons who did not understand the Scriptures in this as well as other respects.

38. "Such were the Pharisees. And now, before proceeding to other features of Judaism, and their relation to the Church, we can hardly help glancing at St. Paul." (*Ibid.*)

Here it is strangely assumed that the religious errors of some or all of the Pharisees were a feature of Judaism. Just exactly in the same sense it might now be said that the religious errors of some Universalists, for instance, are a feature of Christianity.

39. "The odium incurred by adopting the new doctrine might undermine the livelihood of some who depended on their trade for support" (referring to Paul). (*Ibid.*)

There was no new doctrine adopted in those days by anybody, so far as we read, except by the unbelieving Jews. Paul was thus often accused by his enemies of adopting a new doctrine; but he stoutly denied it everywhere, on all occasions. And it is remarkably strange indeed, that his panegyrists now should suggest, or rather indeed affirm, the same thing of him which he himself so loudly complained of then, as a false and injurious accusation.

40. "First the Samaritans, and then the Gentiles,

received that gospel which the Jews attempted to destroy." (*Ibid.* p. 79.)

The propriety of that statement may be judged of from the unquestionable fact, that at the time it is located (Acts viii. 1), and for several years thereafter, the entire Church in association with the apostles — call it by what name you will, amounting most certainly to many thousands — was composed exclusively of Jews, without a single exception.

Nevertheless, it is true that Jews, some Jews, were attempting to destroy it. At that time the contest was among Jews exclusively, Jews on the one side, and Jews on the other.

41. "The festivals observed by the Apostolic Church were at the first the same as those with the Jews." (*Ibid.* p. 440.)

And when, and by what authority, were they changed? Excepting those which obviously and naturally belonged to the period before Christ's appearance, they were never changed, but remain to this day, saving incidental modifications, such as always occur from time to time.

42. "It appears that they remained some considerable time at Antioch, gradually insinuating, or openly inculcating, their opinion that the observance of the Jewish law was necessary to salvation." (*Ibid.* p. 210.)

I understand the very reverse. The reference is to the false brethren mentioned in Gal. ii. 4. They sought to inculcate, not the observance of the Jewish law, but a departure from it. The Jewish law, or the Old Testament, as is here meant, restricts circumcision to the period before Christ, as fully explained heretofore. And these false brethren wanted to continue it afterward, as though Christ had not come.

Surely that was violating the Old Testament provision. And Paul wanted to conform to it by discontinuing that ceremony.

43. "They" (the Christians) "were a new and singular party in the nation, holding peculiar opinions, and interpreting the Scriptures in a peculiar way." (*Ibid.* p. 67.)

They were the regular Church party, interpreting the Scriptures correctly, for they had the Saviour and the apostles to assist them in doing so, if that can be called peculiar. They interpreted them just as everybody did who did it properly. As to the nation, most of the officials, who in those days were generally spoken of as the nation, interpreted the Scriptures so peculiarly as to carry themselves, and many others with them, out of the Church.

44. "All parties in the nation united to oppose, and if possible to crush, the monstrous heresy" (*i. e.*, the Christians). (*Ibid.* p. 67.)

No, sir! there was one party who did not oppose them. And what party was that? The true Jews, who held firmly to their religion, and who alone for several years constituted the entire Church under the ministry of the apostles.

45. "We can imagine Saul, then the foremost in the Cilician synagogue, disputing against the new doctrines of the Hellenistic Deacon." (*Ibid.*)

What would the reader generally understand by the word *new*, in the above sentence? Not probably what is really true. The doctrines preached by Stephen were certainly not new to the Church, to religion, to those who understood the doctrines of the Church, to those who looked for no other Christ than Jesus, for it seems He was the Christ of their old religion; though they were regarded as new by such novices and mistaken men in religion as Saul. Men who looked for some other Christ, and repudiated Jesus, would certainly regard Stephen's preaching as new. Such preaching would be regarded as new by such persons now. But if Stephen's preaching was really new, new to the settled religion of the Church, then it was necessarily false for that very reason, and ought to have been disputed against. All new religion is necessarily false.

And then Stephen himself declares, and argues at length, that his doctrines were not new. He proves, or certainly attempts to prove, every doctrine and every sentiment he advances, by reference to the then existing Scriptures, the Old Testament. (Read the seventh chapter of Acts.)

46. "The modern Jews still adhere as closely to the Mosaic dispensation as their dispersed and despised condition will permit them." (*Religious Ency.*, p. 692.)

Then it is logically and infallibly certain that theirs is the true religion, and Christianity is a heresy. It is hard to hold our patience under such monstrous teaching.

If Jesus is the true and identical Christ of the "Mosaic dispensation," using that expression as the writer does, then no condition in life, dispersed or despised, will authorize, much less necessitate, his rejection. To reject Christ, Jesus Christ, He being the Christ of the Mosaic dispensation, is, most certainly and palpably, to reject all the religion of that dispensation. Will any man say that the Old Testament contains any religion with its Christ wholly excluded?

47. "The Jews had such an opinion of this prophet's sanctity, that they ascribed the overthrow of Herod's army, which he had sent against his father-in-law, Aretas, to the just judgment of God for putting John the Baptist to death." (*Relig. Ency.*)

This is most certainly true and well stated. But then, how comes it that at this very time these same Jews were so violently opposed to these very principles of religion, as is so repeatedly and unqualifiedly stated by this same writer and others? Both things cannot be true.

48. "Judaizing Christians — those who attempted to mingle Judaism and Christianity together." (*Hend. Buck's Dict.*)

That is, those who held that the Old Testament was Scripture, and mingled the common Scripture of revelation in the teachings of religion!

49. Macknight (Preface to Gal., p. 280) says that Christians are not bound at all by the precepts of the Old Testament. "But their obligation to abstain from their vices doth not arise from their having been forbidden to the Israelites and proselytes by Moses, but from their being expressly forbidden by Christ and his apostles. At the death of Christ the law of Moses was abolished in all its parts, to all mankind, as a religious institution."

And again, on Col. ii. 14, he explains, in the most unqualified language, that we are not bound by anything written in the Old Testament; but to whatever laws or precepts we are bound, it is exclusively because we find them written in the New.

Well, as this issue lies fairly between Dr. Macknight and the apostles, I shall certainly not interfere with any feeble views of my own. It is very certain that the apostles, as well as the Saviour himself before them, urged every duty they enjoined, and enforced every precept they advanced, on the sole and exclusive ground that that was the written law of religion in the Old Testament.

50. Mr. Coleman says: "In the Old Testament everything relating to the kingdom of God was estimated by outward forms, and promoted by specific external rites. In the New everything is made to depend upon what is internal and spiritual."

I cannot account for such language. As a simple matter of fact, it is notoriously true, and questioned neither by Mr. Coleman nor anybody else, that the Old Testament estimates no religious principle nor duty by outward forms, but that internal and spiritual graces, emotions, and feelings, are enjoined everywhere therein, and that it never offers salvation on any other conditions. In these respects there is no difference whatever between the Old Testament and the New.

51. Dr. Abel Stevens (*Hist. Meth.*, vol. i. p. 17) says: "For generations the primitive Christians had no temples, but worshipped with familiar simplicity in private houses or in the synagogues of converted Jews, which were scattered over the Roman Empire."

In the synagogues of converted Jews? Why, my dear sir, they were the very Jews themselves, who, like anybody else, worshipped in their own synagogues, as churches were then generally called, where they and their fathers had always worshipped. They all continued to worship where and as they had always done, except the rejecting Jews, who went out of the Church. They had to go somewhere else and worship, unless they could convert the whole synagogue, or the majority of it, to their heresy, which they frequently did.

52. I am not able to see either the force or the propriety of Keith's reply to Celsus, where the Epicurean philosopher undertakes to ridicule the doctrine of morals as put forth by our Saviour, when He said, "Whoever shall smite thee on thy right cheek, turn to him the other also." Keith refers it to his "ignorance of the difference between the dispensations of the law and the gospel."

After claiming to know at least as much about the law and the gospel as a heathen philosopher could be reasonably expected to know, I confess myself, with Celsus, quite ignorant of any such difference as Keith supposes. So far as I am able to read, the Saviour had no reference to any difference between dispensations. He merely explained and repeated the law as it was and is, but not as the mistaken men around him understood it.

53. Olshausen (Preface, p. 37) says: "They remarked rightly that in the Old Testament the divine justice was most prominently exhibited in the revelation of a rigorous law; while the New most fully displayed the divine mercy in the revelation of a forgiving love."

All that is mere fashionable theological rhetoric, which some learned men think they have a right to indulge in, and possibly some of them do not know any better; but surely men who will reflect a moment, can but see that there is not a word of truth in it. There is no divine justice nor rigorous law revealed in the Old Testament, and not explained and commented on in the revelations of the New Testament; nor is there any divine mercy, nor forgiving love, in the New Testament not revealed in the Old. If there are, they can be specified.

54. Olshausen opens his Introduction to his Commentary on the New Testament with this remarkable declaration: —

"As the revelations of God to man assume two principal forms, namely, the law and the gospel; so the Scriptures are divided into two parts, of which the first relates to God's covenant with man in the *law*, the second to the covenant in *grace*."

I confess I do not know what to make of such a declaration. Its meaning is seemingly plain and unmistakable; and as to the principal fact stated, everybody half informed must know it to be wholly untrue. It is impossible the author can mean what he so plainly states.

There is no mistaking what is meant by God's covenant with man in the law. There need be no debate where there is nothing debatable. There are some things about the Scriptures which everybody knows. The Scriptures set forth two entirely different systems of divine administration with man. The first regards him merely as an intelligent moral being, a subject of moral control, and it supposes him to obey promptly and precisely all God's rules of conduct. This is the law — preëminently THE LAW. Nor is there anything else in Scripture which without express or implied qualification can be so called. It says, "Do these things, and you shall live by them." This would give the highest possible happiness to man, regarding him as a mere moral and intelligent agent. And it is all the rule there ever ought to have been, because there ought not to have been a necessity for any other.

But alas! there was. Man became a sinner as well as a free, intelligent moral agent. And now, what? Why, one of two things is inevitable: either a gospel, a system of grace, or total and inevitable ruin. God in his mercy ordained the former, and so provided a Saviour and a system of salvation, not mere happiness, by faith. This system is called the gospel, and most appropriately is it named.

And now we are told that the Old Testament reveals the former, and the New Testament the latter, and that this is their Scriptural relation.

No, it is not so; they have no such relation. A more palpable error could not be stated. Everybody knows that the Saviour, the system of grace, the being saved from sin by and through Christ, salvation, was introduced into the world thousands of years before the New Testament had an existence. And I present the open Old Testament in proof that the system of grace is offered in it to all mankind in perhaps a thousand places. And it is well known that by and in this covenant of grace, a good many persons, or at least some, were actually saved.

The simple truth is, that the two systems, Law and Grace, are contained in both Testaments, and all over both everywhere; at least, both relate to both.

Moreover, it is known to all theologians that not only is this the case with the written Scriptures, but that the very person of the Saviour appeared in different kinds of manifestation, occasionally, to the

Old Testament saints. That our Saviour began to exist about eighteen hundred years ago, and that then, and not till then, the covenant of grace began to operate, is a mythical, mystical, fashionable fable, which, though perhaps taught in, is disbelieved by, every Sunday-school in the land. And why such doctrine is tolerated in the books, is a strange thing to me.

55. The objection raised against the apostles and their followers, and the only objection I know of in these times or ever, was, that their religion was new, and therefore false. This was the question. And on all hands it was, as it must have been, acknowledged, that the party who had the old religion had the true religion; and those who had introduced new tenets, had, in the very necessities of the case, introduced false ones. That is to say, in other words, one party held that Jesus was Christ, according to the Old Testament Scriptures, and the other that He was not. And so each party charged the other with introducing a new religion, the one for receiving, and the other for rejecting, Jesus as Christ.

And so we see Celsus, who was one of the first to put infidelity into logical form, take this same ground. "It is but a few years," he says, "since He who is now reckoned by the Christians to be the Son of God, delivered this doctrine."

And a little later we hear Porphyry say: "If Jesus Christ be the way of salvation, the truth and the life, and they only who believe in Him can be saved, what became of those men who lived before his coming?" And you will see the same objections, and indeed no others, raised by Tacitus, Trajan, Julian, etc.

This is precisely what might be expected. But then it is strange indeed that Keith, in endeavoring to refute these very charges, should acknowledge that Jesus was "the author of the *new religion of the Christians*."

Then the other party is right, and Christianity is false.

56. Macknight (Gal. iii. 22) says the law of faith was "made known obscurely in the first promise, Gen. iii. 15; and afterward in the covenant with Abraham."

How does Macknight know that religion was communicated to the world obscurely at the first? This is drawing pretty heavily upon the imagination. There is not, I believe, the slightest intimation of such a thing in Scripture. And it would seem to require very strong proof to induce one to believe that God would teach the conditions of salvation in an obscure way. Obscure means, as used here, not easily understood or made out; not clear or legible; abstruse or blind; or dim and of uncertain meaning.

Macknight mistakes the words of the historian for those of divine teaching. Gen. iii. 15, is what Moses tells us about the teaching. What the teaching itself was, in its actual details, is another thing. We are in the same condition here as in any other instance of exceeding brief, synoptic history. What occurred, is one thing; how much the historian tells future generations about it, is quite another. Perhaps, in this instance, it was not necessary that very much should be explained to us about the religious teaching of those very distant ages. The religious teachings in the days of Adam might have been explained in eleven volumes, as well as in eleven words; or those of the present age might be alluded to in eleven words.

57. Olshausen says of the Ebionites: "They denied the real divinity of our Lord, and regarded him as the son of Joseph; thus seceding wholly from the true Church." (Vol. i. p. 37.)

That is exactly right. Denying Christ is seceding from the Church. But then, why does not the writer apply this rule to the hundreds of thousands of Jews who a few years before did that very same thing? By failing to assert their secession from the Church, Olshausen runs into the dilemma of supposing and admitting that the apostles and their followers left the Church. The apostles affirmed that Jesus is the Christ, and the other party of Jews denied Him. Then, which party left the Church?

58. Mr. Henry (Gal. ii. 4) speaks of the two different modes of salvation as "by the works of the law, or by the faith of Christ."

The evident drift and meaning of his teaching is, that back yonder a few years, the former was the mode of salvation; and now, the latter is the rule which was recently adopted by Christ. And if this be the way commentators teach, what may be expected of us learners?

59. On Gal. v. 1, Mr. Henry says: "Since, then, we can be justified only by faith in Christ, and not by the righteousness of the law; and that the law of Moses was no longer in force, nor Christians under any obligations to submit to it; therefore he would have them to stand fast in the liberty wherewith Christ hath made us free," etc.

I ask Mr. Henry if any persons were ever justified in any other way, or on any other conditions, than by faith in Christ? And again I ask, if any law of Moses, or any other divine law, was ever in force, and not now in force? And again: Was ever anybody under any obligations to submit to any divine law which is not now binding on all mankind? Paul says the righteousness of the law is fulfilled in us.

Mr. Henry's mistake is the common one of supposing that the law, the inexorable law which says obey and live, stands related to the milder terms of the gospel, which says, believe in the Lord Jesus Christ, in the order of time; that the one preceded the other chronologically. That is not the way of it: the two systems have no chronological relations. They relate to each other in the order of sequence. Our Saviour was just as much of a Saviour, and saved men in the same way, a thousand years before Mary had a son, as in the days of his flesh, or at this day. He never was anything short of the great Jehovah. His incarnation was a mere manifestation of the Godhead to human senses.

60. Mr. Henry, on Gal. iii. 24, says: "In the foregoing verse the Apostle acquaints us with the state of the Jews under the Mosaic economy; that before faith came, or before Christ appeared, ... they were kept under the law."

Here this great error about when faith came, or when the law ceased and the gospel began, is apparent. "In the foregoing verse the Apostle acquaints us with the state of the Jews under the Mosaic economy."

No! Right there is the error. He makes no allusion to any chronological period whatever. In the twenty-third verse Paul acquaints us with the state of man, as man, without a gospel, that is, without a Saviour. He says: "But before faith came we were kept under the law." And now Mr. Henry tells us that before faith came means before Christ appeared. No, sir! I understand it to mean precisely as it says — "before faith came." And when did faith come to man's rescue? Ask Abel; or ask Paul to ask him; or ask Abraham or the prophets.

Before faith came we were under the inexorable law. But I beg pardon of Paul's interpreters, when they make him acquaint us that this thing happened to mankind about three years before he was converted. No! that event happened four thousand years before Paul was born.

61. Dr. Lardner (*Credibility of the Gospel History*, vol. i. p. 179) in speaking of Acts v. 26, where it is said of the officers who were sent to apprehend Peter and John, that they feared the people lest they should have been stoned, says: "This may seem a surprising change in the people, considering the eagerness with which they demanded that Christ should be crucified."

I see no evidence whatever of any such change in the people as is here supposed, because I do not see that they, the people, demanded that Christ should be crucified. I see that the Jews — the government, the Sanhedrim, the officers, priests, Pharisees, and a few followers — demanded that Christ should be crucified. But the people were opposed to it. Moreover, there was no time for any such change to take place. The two things spoken of were in the same year, and likely within a few weeks or months of each other.

62. Dr. Eadie, in his most excellent *Analysis*, makes one section as follows: "Prophecies having special reference to the Gentiles as successors to the Jews in spiritual privilege."

But in the Scriptures ranged under this caption, we do not see any allusion to any successors to Jews. We see scriptures which merely predict the universal spread of religion everywhere; and of course the Church is always the successor of those who have just passed away. Matt. xxi. 43 refers not to the Jewish people as a people, but to the persons to whom the Saviour was speaking, namely, the chief priest and elders.

63. Bloomfield says the word "trouble," in Gal. i. 7, means "harass your minds with vain doubts whether the Mosaic law is to be retained in the gospel of Christ."

I do not see how this can be possible. What can the learned Doctor mean by the Mosaic law, else than some or all of the doctrines of religion or rules of ethics written in the Old Testament? And all these are in the gospel of Christ. So he certainly does not mean the Mosaic law.

His statement would be true if he had said the false teachings of the Mosaic law; not what the Mosaic law was and is, but false teachings of what it was not. The question was, whether false teachers of the Scriptures should prevail, or how far they might prevail in inculcating, instead of the written law, that which it was not. Paul was not afraid the law of Moses would be received by Christians, for it was to do that he so incessantly labored. It was misrepresentations of the law he feared.

64. The Rev. E. P. Murphy, D. D., of Kentucky,

in a sermon in *Sermons for the College*, says: "Two methods of salvation have, at different times, been proposed to mankind. . . . . The gospel proposes to save them in another method, and on peculiar terms; it introduces a new idea — the principle of faith."

Into such terrible extravagances unthinking Christians are led by the notion of two religions, the Jewish and the Christian. And it passes, in Christian lands and among Bible readers, for theology.

65. Even Dr. Chalmers, who is so very seldom in error, speaks of "the purer morality of Christ," as compared with that of the Old Testament.

But this cannot be so. No morality can be purer than revelation. The mind of God cannot be purer at one time than at another. The same Mind of immaculate purity is the author of all the morality revealed in all Scripture. In the New Testament morality is more widely elaborated than in the Old, that is the difference.

66. "Are we not told in profane records that Christianity was first propagated in Judea?" — meaning in the days of Pontius Pilate. (*Keith's Evidences*, p. 174.)

Yes, we are told so in profane records, *i. e.*, by Tacitus, Pliny, Trajan, Julian, and others. This is precisely the charge brought against the Christians in those days, by all their enemies, that their religion was then first propagated; that it was new, and, therefore, false. And if the fact charged had been true, then their complaints would have been just, for a new religion must necessarily be false.

But there are no other records than those of the enemies of Christianity and of mistaken theologians, which acknowledge the charge to be true, that the Christian faith was first propagated in those days. The divine records everywhere maintain that this faith is precisely that of the prophets of old.

67. "Having given you a short account of the sacraments of the Jewish Church, I proceed to observe that they have been superseded by the Christian sacraments. This is plain with respect to the passover, for we have already seen that immediately after the celebration of it the Lord's Supper was instituted." (*Dick's Theology*, p. 466.)

I think the author misses the point clearly. There cannot be two sets of sacraments in human religion, because sacrament is the obligation which religion imposes, and not a matter of changeable legislation. passover and the Lord's Supper were not two different sacraments, but two different modes of administering the same obligation. I see no sort of warrant in the language to justify the belief that "the Lord's Supper was instituted immediately *after* the celebration of the passover." The book says the Lord's Supper was the passover. The thing then instituted was the Lord's Supper, not the sacrament. The nature of things required this change. The author fails to notice the very wide distinction between the sacrament and the mode of administering it.

68. "It appears to have been less from an intolerant disposition, than from a wish to please the Jews at all hazards, that Herod Agrippa persecuted the Christians." (*Kitto's History of Palestine*, p. 397.)

This persecution was that which arose on the death of Stephen. These two opposing parties, the persecutors and the persecuted, were, therefore, at the first, all, and throughout nearly all, Jews. When this persecution began, and for several years after, every Christian was a Jew. Some others came into the Church, but not many, before the death of Herod; but from the language here used by Dr. Kitto, the uninformed reader would suppose that the persecuted Christians were some different kind of people, and not Jews.

69. In the beginning of the Preface to *Owen's Questions*, we read: "In the ancient temple service, under the Mosaic dispensation, there were various orders of priests, to each of which an allotment of duty was made; and all of these, in their several spheres, bore an honorable part, because subservient to the great end for which that service was instituted. So, under the Christian dispensation, 'the glory of which is greater than of the former,' there are divers ministrations, all of which are honorable, because promotive of the glory of God and of human weal. And, though all of those who perform these ministrations do not wear sacerdotal garments, or burn incense, or enter the holy of holies with 'the Urim and Thummim,' and the breastplate of judgment, nevertheless, they are recognized by the great Head of the Church," etc.

From this language the Sunday-school scholar would infer that under the Mosaic dispensation, that is, before the time of Christ, the worship, as prescribed and practiced, was the temple service, as here described. And then, what will he do with this information when he comes to be informed that then, and for many hundred years previously, the worship of the people was indeed but very little of it in or near the temple, but was performed in congregations, as it is now, all over the city of Jerusalem, all over Palestine, and all over the known world?

The worship of those times, almost all of it, was in small congregations, as it is now; and instead of its being performed in sacerdotal garments, burning incense, entering the holy of holies, etc., it was performed almost precisely as our Sabbath service is now. Our Sunday-school books ought to teach more correctly.

70. Macknight says: "It is the Apostle to the Gentiles who hath set the Sinai covenant, or law of Moses, in a proper light, by showing that it was no method of justification."

Secondly, therefore, "And beginning at Moses and all the prophets, he expounded unto them in all the Scriptures," or law of Moses, how that there was no justification by its provisions!

71. Macknight (Preface to Hebrews) says: "And on all these considerations the unbelieving Jews were exhorted to forsake the law of Moses, and embrace the gospel."

And now we will see what Paul says about it. Paul said, "For the hope of Israel I am bound with this chain." And again: "I stand and am judged for the hope of the promise made of God unto our fathers. Unto which promise our twelve tribes instantly serving God," etc. And again it is said, Search the Scriptures, the Old Testament, if you wish to know what Christianity is.

72. Macknight (Preface to Hebrews) says: "Most of the Jews adhered to the law of Moses with the greatest obstinacy, because God had spoken it at Sinai by the ministry of angels, in the hearing of their fathers, accompanied with great thunders and lightnings, and tempest, and darkness."

Most devoutly might it be wished that this were

true; and not only that most, but that all had done so. Certainly the reason assigned is the very best that could be. Show that God has spoken it, and very few Christians will wish to inquire any farther.

73. Dr. Belcher says the twelfth Article of the faith of modern Jews is, "that the Messiah is to come, though He tarry long." And again, that "the modern Jews adhere as closely to the Mosaic dispensation as their present dispersed condition will allow."

Both these things cannot be true, because the Mosaic dispensation, *i. e.*, its religion, declares Jesus Christ to be the Messiah. Then, supposing this to be true, it follows that, to hold that Messiah is to come, is to depart as widely from the Mosaic dispensation as it is possible for any one in any condition, dispersed or otherwise. The modern Jew departs wholly and fundamentally from all the religious faith of the Old Testament, because the Old Testament teaches no religious faith save in Jesus Christ.

74. Dr. Stuart, in his essay on the *Peculiarities of Christianity*, among other statements somewhat similar, says our Saviour was to "entirely change the whole face of the Jewish religion;" and that "He proposed to teach a new religion."

By the Jewish religion I presume he intends to be understood the official, written, established religion of the Church at that time. Or perhaps he would include in the word religion the actual external worship practiced at that time. In either view, was it entirely changed? Was it changed generally? Was it changed at all, beyond such modifications as are occasionally seen in the history of the Church? It was not! The history is plain.

"He proposed to teach a new religion." This new religion is several times spoken of by Dr. Stuart. Beyond all question there was no new religion in those times that the Saviour had anything to do with. The only new religion known in those days, that I know of, was the new faith set up by the rejecting Jews, in opposition to the Saviour.

To "entirely change the whole face of the Jewish religion" is a mere fancy, utterly unsupported by truth or reason.

75. Dr. Stuart says: "It was a bold undertaking to come out against the whole Jewish people, and especially the priesthood, on the subject of their religion."

But this the Saviour did not do. I ask Dr. Stuart for the evidence that the whole Jewish people, or even a majority of them, ever offered the Saviour any opposition in any matter of their religion. I undertake to say there is no such testimony.

76. "Who among them all ever knew or taught what a holy life is, and the necessity and importance of it?" (*Dr. Stuart, of Andover.*)

I will mention the names of a few: Moses, Joshua, Samuel, Ezra, Nehemiah, Job, David, Solomon, Isaiah, Jeremiah, Ezekiel, Daniel, Hosea, Joel, Amos, Obadiah, Jonah, Micah, Nahum, Habakkuk, Zephaniah, Haggai, Zechariah, Malachi, and many others incidentally mentioned in Scripture.

77. It is apparent that Dr. Stuart does not hold the Jewish religion, the religion of the Church before Christ, responsible for the errors of its mistaken advocates. He understands that point pre-

cisely, because he says: "If tyrants, claiming the name of Christians, have persecuted and oppressed in order to extend the domain of Christianity, or religion, which absolutely forbids this, then the Christian religion is not answerable for it." And of course, just so of the religion of the Church at any time.

78. Dr. Stuart, in his *Commentary on Romans*, commences his Introduction thus: "History affords no certain evidence respecting the individual who first preached the gospel at Rome. The Romish Church, indeed, maintain that Peter was the founder of the first Christian community in that city."

Allow me to suggest that both he and the Romish Church, in this dispute, are requiring history to perform impossibilities. History cannot point out a thing which never happened. In the nature of the thing there could have been no such event, nor any such individual. What does he mean by first preached the gospel? Revealed religion was certainly preached, more or less perfectly or correctly preached, in the city of Rome, long before the death of Jesus. There was a church there before that time. We learn thus much, at least, from Acts ii. 10. Now, who first preached in that church, among those persons professing faith in Christ, and in accordance with their general belief, that the man Jesus was the Messiah of their faith, is a very different question from that debated by Dr. Stuart and the Romish Church. That question is: Who first preached the (new) gospel at Rome? and, What individual was the founder of the first Christian community in that city? In the sense here meant, no such things ever happened.

I respectfully suggest that Dr. Stuart would have been a hundred-fold more successful in this argument, if, instead of joining issue with the Romanists on the mythical question they raise about a fact which never had an existence, he had asked his opponents to show that a Christian church, some church different from that which had existed of old, was founded at all at Rome, either by Peter, or by any one else. The admission by Dr. Stuart, that some person, after the death, or after the birth, of Jesus Christ, first preached the gospel at Rome, meaning by the word gospel some doctrines of religion, is, first, the admission of that which is historically untrue; and secondly, if not absolutely fatal, is greatly embarrassing to his argument with the Romish Church. Strange that he makes it; and stranger still that a thousand others do the same thing.

79. "It is certain that great numbers of Jews and devout proselytes were converted at first to Christianity." (*Horne's Introduction*, vol. i. p. 134.)

No; that is a transparent blunder; and in the mouth of a Christian it is a contradiction of his faith. It is certain that great numbers of persons then in the Church, known as Jews, were, at first — the first day, week, year, or several years, of the preaching of the apostles after the resurrection — found in church association with the apostles. Indeed, they, and they alone, composed the entire Church, in association with the apostles, for ten years or so after the death of Jesus. Of this there can be no doubt. And it is equally certain that they must have amounted to hundreds of thousands, and most probably to several millions, including all the countries where the apostles and their friends preached. But to say these persons were converted to Christianity, is to say that they were converted from their present faith, the written faith of Scripture, and to a different faith. This was the very thing, and the only thing, charged against the Christians by their unbelieving brethren. To say they were converted to Christianity, is a very different thing from saying they were taught a better understanding of their own religion, and a closer comformity to it. I suppose nobody would call that conversion. To be better instructed in our own religion, is a different thing from being converted to another.

Jews at the present time, or since the apostasy, may be converted to Christianity, because they never professed it; but the Jews here spoken of could not be so converted until they should first apostatize, and then be converted from the apostasy. This was the case with some, I should presume, but it could not be at first, because with these multiplied thousands there is not the slightest pretense of evidence that they had ever apostatized at all. Indeed, in the nature of the circumstances, it was impracticable. *Horne's Introduction*, saving these blunders, one of the best and most useful books in any language, teaches in hundreds of places, plainly and square out, that Christianity is a totally foreign religion, new and unknown prior to its introduction by Jesus Christ and his apostles. Strange that the learned author did not see, not only that this proves Christianity a false religion, but that it is the only point relied upon by the unbelieving Jews, from the apostles' days to this day, to sustain their position. That conceded, of course, proves that they are right. The Introduction must be written over again.

80. In the *New Biblical Atlas*, a Western publication, generally received as a text-book, at page 31, we read: "The gospel was preached to the Samaritans by Philip, and the first Christian church out of Jerusalem was formed in the city of Samaria, within one year of our Lord's death." And *Coleman's Biblical Atlas*, p. 211, makes the same remark.

For proof they refer to Acts viii. 5–8, where there is not — nor is there anywhere else in the New Testament — the slightest allusion to such an occurrence as they relate. Let us look at the unquestionable facts.

Long before this time there had been in Samaria large numbers of Samaritan Jews, with their churches, or synagogues, if any one prefers the term. They could not believe in Jesus until Jesus lived, nor have faith in Him as the Messiah until He died and rose. Immediately on the occurrence of these things we see Philip, in Samaria, preaching in the synagogues. Preaching what? What did Philip preach that had not always been preached there? I answer, Nothing additional, but that Jesus was Christ. "And the people, with one accord, gave heed unto those things which Philip spake," etc. "And there was great joy in that city."

Now, that is all that took place, all that anybody pretends took place. The people received Jesus with one accord at the very first opportunity. The churches were already there, and suffered no change in anything, so far as we are informed. No doubt, however, they were greatly instructed and informed in their faith. They acknowledged Jesus, and fully received Him as the Christ they had always received, so soon as the nature of things rendered it possible. Was that the formation of another Church? As well might you call it the formation of another city, another language, another civil state, or another religion, as another Church. It was palpably and notoriously neither.

81. *Reason and Revelation* is a recent publication by Milligan, Carrol & Co., Cincinnati. Throughout this whole philosophical treatise, as its title indicates it to be, the religion we call Christianity is held to be one wholly new to mankind in every essential respect. At page 358, he follows the blunders of others, in making Paul persuade his Hebrew brethren to repudiate every religious lesson they had received. "There was nothing in the old covenant that could take away sins."

By old covenant, he is understood to mean Old Testament. Who believes that? Did anybody ever believe it, except the millions of children and unreflecting persons thus imposed upon?

"But under the new covenant the sins of Christians are remembered no more."

As if there was any other covenant, that is, arrangement for salvation, ever made by the Almighty with his creatures, since the first sin of Adam.

82. *Ecce Deus Homo*, p. 28, says of John the Baptist, "Suddenly, and without any warning, he appears before the people of Judea with the startling message, 'Repent ye, for the kingdom of heaven is at hand.'"

Startling? Surely not. The Christian doctrine of repentance had been in their Scriptures abundantly, and read and preached in their churches every Sabbath day for at least over a thousand years.

Neither is this kingdom any new doctrine. It is expressly stated that John told them it was not. (Matt. iii. 3.)

83. Again, he tells us, page 33, about what John did "before the dispensation of ceremonies passed away."

Have ceremonies, religious ceremonies, passed away? What do men mean by such expressions? There were some ceremonies before the incarnation, which cannot apply since; they discontinue. But that was not certainly a dispensation of ceremonies. Ceremonies continue as before.

84. Again, "He gave it" (the Church) "a written constitution, under which it exists."

No; the only thing I know of in Scripture, at all savoring of the character of an ecclesiastical constitution, is written in Genesis and Exodus. There is not a hint of such a thing in the New Testament.

85. Again, "Jesus hath revealed a doctrine, and inspired holy men to commit the same to writing," etc.

No; I do not think that Jesus revealed a doctrine.

86. "God segregated them" (the Jews) "from the other nations of the earth, and by the most rigid enactments prevented them from mixing with other people." (Page 144.)

On the contrary, everybody knows He did the very reverse. He commanded all men to be religious, and required the Church to receive everybody that would come in, forbidding that there should be a difference between those already in and those coming in. Nevertheless, religious people of course segregate. This must always be so without any enactments, so long as a part of the people remain irreligious.

87. *McClintock and Strong's Cyclopædia*, vol. i. p. 3, teaches that Aaron, as high priest, offered sacrifice for sin. This clear, simple proposition, is plainly stated and elaborated. The reader understands the teaching in its simple and natural sense, namely, that in those days, sacrifice for sin, by way of atonement to an offended God, was really offered by Aaron and his successors, and accepted by Jehovah. Whereas the truth is, that Aaron never offered any sacrifice, really, any more than those gentlemen did. He only acted the visible forms of offering, as a mere mode of teaching the doctrine of atonement, just as we do now by other instrumentality.

88. On page 10 we are told about "the vicarious offering of animal sacrifice" by Abel.

Surely there was no such offering. Abel's animals were no more vicarious than McClintock and Strong's "Cyclopædia" is vicarious. The two are but different modes, in different ages of the world, of teaching the doctrine of one only vicarious Sacrifice.

89. "In the New Testament *adoption* appears not so much a distinct act of God, as involved in and necessarily from justification." (*Ibid.* p. 78.)

In the New Testament? Why exclude the Old? And why write a chapter about a New Testament doctrine which is common to all revelation?

90. In art. "Apostasy," same book, p. 307, we read, "The primitive Church distinguished several kinds of apostasy; first, those who went entirely from Christianity to Judaism," etc.

What! That is most surprising. What you call the primitive Church was Judaism; that is, it was composed of those persons exclusively who stood firm by the Old Testament, as Jesus and his apostles taught and exhorted; who maintained the doctrine and principles enunciated by the prophets, as men do now. And the first and only apostasy we know of in that age, was those who went away from Judaism, the Old Testament, by denying Jesus as the Christ. It is most remarkable that McClintock and Strong, in their treatise on apostasy, do not even mention what is by far the greatest and most important one known to the history of religion, namely, that of those Jews who repudiated their Christ, and then and there left the Church.

91. On page 310 we are told that the apostles "created themselves into a community at Jerusalem," which was "the mother Church."

On the contrary, is it not palpable they did nothing of the sort? The question of Church was never raised or discussed by or between anybody in those times. The apostles and those acting with them never changed their ecclesiastical relations, or thought of doing so; but lived, preached, and died in the Church of their fathers. As to the mother Church, the pope might be inquired of about that. He may know; I do not. Did any but the apostates leave the Church?

92. Neander's *Planting and Training of the Christian Church*, the history of something that never happened, opens thus: "The Christian Church, as a community proceeding from the new principle that was to transform the world, and destined to introduce this new principle into humanity, presupposes, as the basis of its existence, the person who was Himself, in his whole being and manifestation, that world-transforming principle without whom the existence of the Church itself would be a monstrous lie."

Neander is not only a theologian, but a teacher of theologians, and this is one of his books of instruction. And I ask, what new principle, in either religion or morals, was then introduced? There is manifestly no historic truth in the statement. It might as well be said that a new world-transforming principle of mathematics, or of architecture, was then introduced into humanity. Neither was done. And so, Neander's *Planting and Training of the Christian Church* is a romance. There is no such Church.

93. "It was the boundary line between the Old and the New." (*Ibid.*)

Old and new what? Can any man answer? Modes of teaching were old and new. Nothing else was.

94. "It is true that Christ, during his ministry on earth, laid the foundation of the outward structure of the Church." (*Ibid.* p. 6.)

I open the broad face of the New Testament, where any man may see the utter erroneousness of this whole statement as a mere matter of fact. I see not in it the slightest appearance of such a historic thing, but the reverse.

95. "The vital principle of this community, which once in existence, should become the imperishable seed for the propagation of the Church in all ages, had not yet germinated." (*Ibid.*)

That is, in other words, religion did not yet exist in the world!

96. Dr. Whedon, of New York, in his Commentary, in most respects a most excellent one, quotes in the Introduction, from Tacitus, Pliny, and other heathen writers, to show the existence of a "new religious sect" at the time of the apostles; and so he regards

their testimony as proof that Christianity was then a "new religion," and thus he shows "the origin of Christianity."

Of course. This was the very ground of their opposition to it, and that of the rejecting Jews. It is a new religion, they say, and therefore false. If new, it certainly was false, and that is the proof of it. But it is strange Dr. Whedon should say so, because he is a Christian, and therefore supposed to be on the other side of this question. His assent that Christianity is new, is unaccountable.

97. On the 5th page of the Introduction, Dr. Whedon tells us that the Church in that age bears testimony that they were "primitive Christians," "a holy Church," etc.

It seems to me this testimony is the very reverse, that they were primitive only as to their general name; but that their religion was as old as the prophets.

98. On page 7 the Doctor speaks of the Saviour's "bringing his religion into existence."

What! Bringing his religion into existence? Then it was necessarily false. The best possible proof of the falsity of any religion is that it was brought into existence. This is the case with Mohammedanism, Mormonism, etc.

99. I hoped that Dr. Whedon's Introduction was not a very good index to his book; but on page 46 we are told that the mission of John the Baptist was to "bring the people to the moral standard of the Mosaic law, in order to fit them for the gospel."

That is strange. Bring the Church up to the divinely prescribed standard of morals, in order to prepare them for some other morals. Are there any better morals taught in the New Testament than in the Old?

100. On Matt. iv. 23, we read that "Our Saviour and the apostles found the synagogues most eligible places for the first preaching of the gospel."

And this suggests the inquiry, What was it they first preached? Any new doctrines, new morals, or new principles of life, or salvation, or religion? The answer is, No. Then why write in a way to induce the belief that all these things were new? The synagogues were churches, and of course, as is the case now, were very eligible and appropriate places for preaching, as well in that day as any other. Churches used to be called synagogues.

101. Dr. Whedon says, "The synagogues resembled the Christian churches."

Yes, — if a thing can be said to resemble itself. They were Christian churches.

102. "Christianity therefore is not the destruction, but the completion of Mosaicism." (*Whedon*, Matt. v. 17.)

How can a religious system be the completion of some other system of religion? I do not know what the expression means. What is meant by religion being completed? If wrong, it could be righted; but what is completed? Can truth be completed?

Much is said to this effect by many authors, and no one that I have met with has attempted to explain what was completed or finished. Surely there could be no finishing or completing of the incarnation of Christ. That occurred wholly at the time it did, though it was anticipated from the beginning. And as doctrines of religion or rules of moral conduct, how can they have a beginning and a completion? Modes of teaching are always improving. They are merely instrumental. They are not by any means completed yet. I think this whole thing of the Mosaic religion being completed in Christianity, is a sort of convenient myth, and grows out of the great, monstrous untruth of a new religion. And these quotations only show how our very best theologians are led astray by the introduction of a radical but undiscovered error.

103. On Matt. xxvi. 20, Dr. Whedon makes this remark: "Then occurs that part which our Lord transfers to the new dispensation."

It has been a very nice point to decide, with those theologians who find it necessary to do so, when was the exact time of the close of the old dispensation, and the beginning of the new. In many respects the exactness of this time, to a day or an hour, is vastly important. Dr. Whedon draws this important line in the history and chronology of the world, through the middle of the ceremony of the last passover. Others fix other periods. One difficulty in finding it is, that the Scriptures make not the most remote allusion to it in any way whatever.

104. McClintock and Strong (*Ency.*, vol. i. p. 517) say, "The effect of the atonement thus wrought is, that man is placed in a new position, freed from the dominion of sin, and able to follow holiness," etc.

And so, previously to this new law of saving men, there was no freedom from sin, and no holiness in the world! This is taught as a lesson in theology! Then the atonement applies to man personally in this chronological way. Only those who lived subsequently to the time of the crucifixion have any interest in it!

105. Again. "The victory of the death of Christ

over the power of the devil begins now to play a prominent part in the idea of atonement."

No, not begins now. It began ages previously.

106. "Baptism is one of the sacraments of the Christian Church." (*McClintock and Strong's Cyc.*, vol. i. p. 639.)

Rather, it is the mode of administering one of the sacraments. A wide difference.

107. Whedon (*Com.*, Matt. xxvi. 29) says, "We may first remark, that the passover was a true sacrifice: for the victim was a true substitute for the sinner, dying in his stead, and showing by his death that the sinner ought to die."

Then the writers of the New Testament but very poorly understood the Old, for they everywhere teach that Jesus Christ was the only sacrifice for sin ever known to true religion. What! a dumb animal a true sacrifice, making a real atonement? A true substitute for the sinner? Then indeed we have had a dispensation in which an animal was as good as a Saviour! A book, or a sermon, might show that a sinner ought to die; but a book is not therefore a true sacrifice; it is only an instrument used to teach the doctrine of sacrifice. I suppose it was to prevent such blunders as this that Paul said, "It is not possible that the blood of bulls and goats should take away sins;" though before the true and only Sacrifice was slain, it might be used to teach the doctrine of vicarious sacrifice.

108. "The vocation of the Gentiles therefore is an eminent illustration of the superior excellence of the New Testament above the Old."

Then God is much more kind and mild to his people than formerly! But who is this that judges and decides of the superior and inferior excellence among the works and teachings of Jehovah? And so the lessons of Matthew are greatly superior to those of John, and Paul, and inferior to Mark, Isaiah, and Peter! Who constituted these judges? Is not all revelation absolutely perfect?

109. "Paul compares the Jews to children, and the Christians to youths." (*Ibid.* p. 367.)

Where? Certainly not in the New Testament. I find Paul (Rom. ii. 28) teaching that Jews, true Jews, are Christians.

110. In hundreds of places Calvin teaches in his *Institutes*, in the clearest and most unqualified manner, that both the Church and religion of Christianity began — not merely the name, but the thing — began absolutely in the time of the apostles.

And yet the ministers of that school, on direct inquiry, will hold that they both began thousands of years before. Are they both true? The theory supports Romanism, but the practice repudiates it.

111. "I grant indeed that whatever promises we find in the law concerning the remission of sins, are accounted part of it." (*Ibid.* vol. i. p. 335.)

And yet I suppose nothing is better understood in theology than this, that the law is a simple requisition of absolute and unconditional obedience, knowing nothing whatever of remission of sins, of pardon, of gospel, or anything of the sort.

112. "Here we have to inquire in what respect the legal covenant is compared with the evangelical, the ministry of Christ with that of Moses." (*Ibid.* vol. vi. p. 359.)

And so, the faith of thousands has been led astray by this supposed difference between Moses' religion and Christ's, as if the Bible contained two kinds.

113. "The Old Testament contains nothing perfect." (*Ibid.* vol. vi. p. 360.)

Was plainer infidelity ever written? And yet Calvin was a Christian. This is probably a misconstruction, and if so, certainly a very great one, of Heb. vii. 19. The word "law" here means the primitive constitution, not the law of salvation as taught in the Old Testament. The law of absolute obedience was not perfect, complete, or sufficient, in its adaptation to man in his fallen condition.

114. "The Old Testament is the revelation of death." (*Ibid.* p. 362.)

The Old Testament offers full and free salvation to all mankind, and on the simple condition of faith and obedience in and to its teachings.

115. On page 362, in contrasting the Old and New Testament, we read, "The former is the ministration of condemnation, because it convicts all the children of Adam of unrighteousness; the latter is the ministration of righteouness, because it reveals the mercy of God."

This is so plainly erroneous that it is strange any one can fail to see it. And yet, because Calvin wrote it, it passes, century after century, for halfway theology.

116. "The Scripture calls the Old Testament a covenant of bondage, because it produces fear in the mind." (*Ibid.* p. 363.)

No; the remark alluded to is not about the Old Testament, but a very different thing, namely, the law, the primary law, requiring absolute and unconditional obedience. This knows no pardon, no salvation, no Saviour; and is the same in the New Testament as in the Old. But the Old Testament offers salvation and a Saviour the same as the New. It is strange that a theologian should make such a blunder.

117. "Now the whole may be summed up thus: that the Old Testament filled men's consciences with fear and trembling; but that by the benefit of the New Testament they were delivered and enabled to rejoice." (*Ibid.*)

And yet every man ought to know that there is not a doctrine of religion, nor offer of salvation in the New Testament which is not first written in and taught out of the Old.

118. "The new covenant is placed in opposition to the old." (*Neander.*)

The Word of God opposing the Word of God! Who can believe it?

119. *History of Doctrines by Hagenbach*, Am. ed., Sheldon & Co., 1866, p. 44: "With the incarnation of the Redeemer, and the introduction of Christianity into the world, the materials for the History of Doctrines are already fully given."

And yet it is well known that both the religion of Christianity and the Redeemer, with all the doctrines of religion known to Scripture, were in the world, to the salvation of millions, many hundred years before the incarnation.

120. "Jesus is not the founder of a school, but in the most exalted sense, the founder of a religion, and a Church." (*Ibid.*)

But neither Jesus nor the apostles ever said a word, or did a thing, so far as we read, about a new Church or a new religion. And we do read that they all belonged to the old Church, and practiced the old religion to the end of their lives.

121. "Our Saviour indeed adopted many of the

current opinions, especially the Mosaic doctrine of *one* God, and also the prevailing opinion of and expectations of the age concerning the doctrine of angels, the kingdom of God, etc.; but to consider Him merely the reformer of Judaism, would be to take a very narrow view of his work." (Page 45.)

This error has spread itself very wide over our literature, and it is not too much to say that immense harm has grown out of it. It makes the system of salvation that we call religion, as taught in the Old and New Testaments, to be two separate and distinct systems, not only radically and fundamentally different, but radically opposed to each other. The Old Testament and its teachings being wholly wrong, the Saviour did not attempt to improve it, but set it aside entirely by a wholesale abrogation and repudiation of it!

On the contrary, the plain truth is, that He did not attempt to either reform or change the religion, the written and well known religion of the Church, one iota; He only taught and enforced a better understanding of it, and a closer conformity to it. What else did, or could, the nature of things require? Was not the Old Testament, every word in it, taught by the very same Christ who inspired and thus dictated every word of the New?

122. "There are two errors which the new-born Christianity had to guard against." (Page 54.)

One of these errors was that committed by the Almighty in the revelation of the Old Testament, namely, Judaism; and the other was idol worship! And if that is profanity, it is Hagenbach's, not mine.

123. *Character of Jesus*, by Schenkel, 1866, p. 72, says: "In the light of the gospel, the last shad-

ows of the old covenant still cast by John, soon melted away."

There are perhaps no words of Scripture so generally misunderstood as old covenant and new covenant, as used in our version. There never were any such covenants as are frequently explained and understood by these expressions. These covenants were not different modes, or conditions of salvation, as is here supposed. Salvation was always offered on the same conditions.

What was new in the new covenant was not its religion, but superior facilities for teaching it. The scenes presented by Christ now in the person of Jesus, being visible, historic, sensible, and no longer adumbrant, are more easily taught and understood than before.

124. "Was not Moses then appointed by God as the mediator of his covenant people?" (*Ibid.*)

He was no more a mediator than Isaiah or Paul.

125. "Was not a chosen priesthood divinely instituted for Israel?" (*Ibid.*)

That depends upon what is meant by priesthood. If a real, atoning priesthood is meant, then No! But if a moot, symbolic priesthood, in mere appearance, used instrumentally to teach the doctrine, to inculcate and enforce it, is meant, then there was.

126. "Change of heart and faith, He represented as the two indispensable conditions of participation in the kingdom of God." (*Ibid.* p. 92.)

Certainly; the very same conditions always prescribed. "Create in me a clean heart, O God, and renew a right spirit within me."

127. Liddon, in his *Bampton Lectures*, says: "The early assaults upon Christianity were uniformly di-

rected against the person of our Lord. The earliest were for the most part, from outside the Church." (*London Christian Remembrancer*, Jan. 1868, p. 142.)

The first statement is certainly true, because the person of Jesus was the only question in dispute. But the other is not true, because, for a number of years the only opponents of Jesus and the apostles, save a very few Roman soldiers, who merely assisted about the crucifixion, were all in the Church. But their opposition to Jesus necessarily carried them out of it.

128. "Theologians are not yet agreed how far the period of the *ancient* Church ought to be extended." (*McClintock and Strong's Cyc.*, vi. p. 367.)

That is strange! Why, most assuredly you must extend it as far back as religion reaches. What is the Church but the external association of religious people, as such?

129. Again, same page, "The New Testament of course gives the beginnings of the most important Christian usages, such as Baptism, the Lord's Supper, Ordination, Prayer, etc."

I think that prayer, at least, to say nothing of ordination, etc., was previously known. I think that is taught in more than a thousand places in the Old Testament.

130. "Though Peter had been so long a convert to Christianity, he keeps clear of the customs of the Jews." (*Patrick, Lowth, and Whitby's Com.*, Acts x. 2.)

And so there is a belief abroad that Peter was a convert to Christianity, and so he undoubtedly was, but not in the sense here meant. He was a convert just as all other religious men are, before or since the age in which he lived. So far as we know, he may have been a convert to Christianity ten or twenty years before he saw the Saviour. But that he ever changed his religion as is here intimated, there is not the slightest suggestion in or out of Scripture, but everything proves he did not.

131. Paul is made to say, "I should not have left Judaism to embrace Christianity," but for so and so. (*Ibid.* Gal. i. 11.)

There is a sense in which it may be said of Paul, though it cannot be said of any of the other apostles, that he left Judaism. But unfortunately that is not the meaning here. Before his conversion he left Judaism, and went off with the apostate Jews after the new and false Judaism. And this Judaism he left, and returned to his old faith, which he now embraced, not only theoretically, but spiritually.

132. In F. W. Farrar's *Critical History of Free Thought*, the second lecture is, much of it, built upon the idea that "the doctrine of an atoning Messiah" was absolutely new in the world in the time of Jesus.

And yet the Old Testament is full of the doctrine. It is strange that so many embrace the notion.

133. *Calmet's Dictionary*, art. "Sacrifice:" "Adam and his sons, Noah and his descendants, Abraham and his posterity, Job and Melchizedek, before the Mosaic law, offered to God real sacrifices."

Then it may no longer be said that Christ is the only sacrifice. These patriarchs offered not a real, but only an apparent sacrifice; not to atone, but to teach the doctrine of atonement.

134. Barnes's *Evidences of Christianity in the Nineteenth Century*, Harpers, 1868, p. 111: "There are two forms of religion in the world which owe their

present existence and influence to the fact that they were at first propagated by direct effort. They are Christianity and Mohammedanism. In this respect they stand by themselves. The religion of the Jews had its origin with their own nation, and grew up with themselves, and identified itself with their legislation, municipal and military regulations, — a growth among themselves, and not an accretion from surrounding nations. They indeed sought to make proselytes, but they never sought or expected to make their religion a universal religion. Moses labored to make the Jewish people a religious people, but not to correct the surrounding nations; and at no period of their history did the Hebrews ever conceive the idea of converting the whole world to their faith. It was the religion of the Jewish nation, not the religion of the world."

I do not see how a greater amount of plain error and misteaching could be crowded into so small a space. Can Mr. Barnes point out the constituents of this new faith? Can he specify one item? One single doctrine, or phase of a doctrine? Mr. Barnes could not say directly that revelation has two religions. Then why mislead and bewilder? If any religious people who ever lived, never sought or expected to make their religion a universal religion, which is a possible thing with regard to any individual persons, in any age of the world, it is because they misunderstood their religion. Many, — we know not how many, — three thousand or two thousand years ago, may have as much misunderstood their religion as Mr. Barnes does now. But that the law of their religion, written then and written now, contemplated all mankind, is so palpable as not to admit of question. What did the prophets teach? There is not a hint in Scripture that its religion is restricted in any wise, to any nation; but on the contrary, its universality is apparent and notorious. If there was a question involved here, Isaiah lv., or lii. 10, or hundreds of passages in Psalms, and all the prophets, might be cited; but it is not in good taste to cite proof of that which is notorious. The blunder is apparent.

135. Van Doren's *Suggestive Commentary on Luke*, Introduction: "It is uncertain whether he (Luke) became a Jewish proselyte before his conversion."

Or, in plainer words, whether he was converted before he was converted!

136. "They looked for Jesus to restore the ancient religion." (*Ibid.* Luke iv. 43.)

And He did so.

137. "Jewish prayers were chiefly praise and benedictions." (*Ibid.* vol. i. p. 10.)

I do not know that human language has uttered prayers more rational, devout, or evangelical, than those read of in the Old Testament.

138. Luke i. 19: The glad tidings were, "First, a gospel. Second, blessings promised in the Old Testament. Third, new doctrines." And the reference is to Gal. i. 6–8.

The Epistle to the Galatians would be a strange place to look for new doctrines.

139. Part II. of *Butler's Analogy*, which treats of revealed religion, assumes, in the entire argument, in every part of it, as an unquestioned and unquestionable fact, that Jesus Christ, by his divine power, revealed to mankind an entirely new system of

religion, previously unknown, especially in its great leading and fundamental doctrines. This "new religion," as he frequently calls it, to distinguish it from that revealed in the Old Testament, is what he always means by "Christianity." He distinguishes it as "the Christian in particular," in contrasting it with "a revelation in general."

The revealed religion, therefore, the analogy of which to nature he so ably and so logically traces, is essentially and constitutionally dualistic. This will not be questioned by any one who will look at the argument.

And yet one dispensation of religion for one age of the world, and another for another, is certainly not known to Scripture. And although Bishop Butler says, "It is an acknowledged historical fact that Christianity offered itself to the world" at the period alluded to, and demanded to be received upon the testimony of the miracles of that age, he will not pretend, on cross-examination, that it was Christianity, any doctrines, or any system of religion that was thus offered to the world, or that indeed it was anything more than an incident pertaining to religion, namely, the advent of the Saviour, and such of his mediatorial and sacrificial acts as were intended for human eyes, that was thus offered. And even this, he will further acknowledge, always pertained to, inhered in, and was part and parcel of the religious system revealed to mankind four thousand years previously.

And although he says that Christianity, so introduced, was proven to be a true system by those miracles, yet, under cross-examination, no man will pretend that they tested, or were calculated or intended to test anything but a simple, single fact in regard to the personality of Jesus, namely, that He was Christ.

And although he says that Jesus Christ "founded a Church," he would be absolutely compelled, on a moment's suggestion, to say He did not, because it is palpable He did not.

140. In *Analogy*, Part II. chap. i., we read as follows: —

"As Christianity served these ends and purposes, when it was first published, by the miraculous publication itself, so it was intended to serve the same purposes in future ages, by means of the settlement of a visible Church; of a society, distinguished from common ones, and from the rest of the world, by peculiar religious institutions; by an instituted method of instruction, and an instituted form of external religion. Miraculous powers were given to the first preachers of Christianity, in order to their introducing it into the world; a visible Church was established, in order to continue it, and carry it on successively throughout all ages."

I will not suffer any one to mistake me so far as to suppose I am debating questions with any one. I am trying only to point out blunders and oversights which do not admit of serious difference of opinion. And so I ask, What was first published and attested by the miracles referred to? Certainly it was not Christianity. Christianity is the name of the system of religion revealed in all Scripture. The theory then first published, and so attested, was the fact of the Christhood of religion in the man Jesus.

The "settlement of a visible Church" is the

necessary result of individual religion. The two things are naturally coinherent, or necessary parts or aspects of the true religion. It has no instituted form of external religion. By this must be meant ceremonial or ritualistic modes of worship. Miraculous powers were given to the first preachers of Christianity, in order to their introducing what into the world? That God would save sinners on condition of faith and repentance? Certainly not. Abel and all the prophets knew and taught that. These miracles attested the identity of Christ and Jesus; that is, that Christ had now appeared in the person of Jesus.

141. "Miraculous powers were given to the first preachers of Christianity in order to their introducing it into the world." (*Ibid.*)

And if the Bishop were asked to specify what it was that these first preachers thus preached and introduced into the world, that he calls Christianity, the question could not be answered. It is palpable they introduced nothing.

142. On page 222, Bishop Butler speaks of "other obligations of duty unknown before."

What were they? Will any man answer? Religious duty then, as now, was unknown to those who did not know their duty, but to none others.

143. Page 256: "There is then no sort of objection from the light of nature, against the general notion of a mediator between God and men, considered as a doctrine of Christianity, or as an appointment of this dispensation."

Then a mediator between God and men, that is, Christ as mediator, is to be considered, exclusively, as an appointment of this dispensation. Strange!

144. Page 266: "He founded a Church."

Most certainly He did not.

145. Page 291: "In them" (Paul's Epistles) "the author declares that he received the gospel in general, and the institution of the communion in particular, not from the rest of the apostles, or jointly together with them, but alone from Christ Himself."

Paul was undoubtedly acquainted with the gospel in general, before he saw the Saviour.

146. Page 292: "But before anything of this kind, for a few persons, and those of the lowest rank, all at once to bring over such great numbers to a new religion, and get it to be received upon the particular evidence of miracles; this is quite another thing."

But there was no new religion, nor any bringing over.

147. Page 328: "Let us then suppose, that the evidence of religion in general, and of Christianity, has been seriously inquired into by all reasonable men among us. Yet we find many professedly to reject both, upon speculative principles of infidelity."

Then revelation contains a religion in general, and a Christianity in particular!

148. Bishop Tomlin remarks, "It is certain the apostles, immediately after the descent of the Holy Ghost, preached the gospel to the Jews with great success."

This, though literally true, makes a wrong impression, because it is explained and understood to mean that the gospel so preached, embraced new religious doctrines and principles not previously known to revelation.

149. Jimeson's *Notes on the XXV. Articles*, p. 153, heads Section 4 thus: "Laws of Moses not binding on Christians."

He can hardly mean the laws and principles of religion as taught by Moses, for these are the purest and best Christianity known to mankind to-day. He probably means those peculiar modes of teaching and inculcating religion before Christ's appearance, and which always pointed forward to his incarnation, commonly called Jewish ceremonies. Then his mistake is, that no binding obligation has been removed by legislation; but from innate necessity they cease to be used now because they adumbrated, or pointed forward to that which had occurred. Adumbration, or forward pointing, ceases, of course, by its own nature, when the thing so pointed to transpires. Adumbration points forward, history points back to the same event. All other laws of Moses are as binding now as they ever were.

150. The doctrine of dualistic revelation is very clearly stated by Dr. Ebrard, who continued Olshausen's Commentary after the death of the author. He says, "The death of Christ was a perfect sacrifice once offered in opposition to the Old Testament animal sacrifices."

The context shows that the opposition means antagonism, because the latter was bad, defective, and imperfect. But there is not known to revelation any two sacrifices, or two systems or doctrines of sacrifice. Only the modes of teaching were different.

151. Robbins' *World Displayed* is a book of history, for families and schools. In his section on "Antediluvian Religion" he says: "In regard to the religious rites of the primeval race of men, it can

only be affirmed that they offered sacrifices both of animals and the fruits of the earth."

That tells us about religious rites — modes of inculcating religious belief; but of the religion itself it does not inform us. The children who receive these teachings of Robbins' understand that the Jews who rejected Christ, and of course who still reject Him, do so in pursuance of, and according to, the written religion of the Old Testament. Then, when they become old enough to reason on the subject, they find it difficult to understand why the Jews were cursed for following the Scriptures; and why we, who do receive Christ, incorporate these same Scriptures into our Bible. This is hard to understand.

152. Dr. Dwight (*Theology*, vol. ii. pp. 93–95) speaks of "the things which the Saviour taught," and then specifies, *seriatim*, the leading doctrines of religion.

The clear understanding here is, that this was the very first teaching of these things to mankind. But the truth is, that each and every one of these doctrines was previously taught in many places in the Old Testament.

153. "Fifthly," the Doctor goes on, "Christ established his Church in a new form." Everything in it was new; "new ministers," "new discipline," "new peculiar duties," etc.

Now, how is it possible for religion and theology to prosper greatly under the influence of such teachings? And then if the Saviour so established his Church, was it not a perfect Church? Why, then, do we complain of the Papist for holding that it continued infallible?

154. "We have seen the foundation of our holy religion laid in the history of our blessed Lord and Saviour, its great Author, as related and left on record by the four several inspired witnesses." (*Henry's Com.*, Pref. to Acts.)

We need not inquire what construction might be possibly forced upon this language; it is sufficient to know it is generally understood to mean that the entire system of religion in the New Testament has its absolute origin in the writings of the evangelists. Could a greater untruth be stated? Could anything better support the fundamental principles of Romanism?

155. "And in this book we find the rise and original of the Church vastly different from the Jewish Church, and erected on its ruins." (*Ibid.*)

Are not such teachings absolutely marvelous?

156. Dr. Clarke says (Acts iii. 22), "Peter evidently gives them to understand that Christ was a legislator, giving a new law, the gospel, to supersede the old."

Then Peter's teaching was evidently untrue. That is certainly untrue. The gospel superseded the law, or came to its relief, four thousand years before Peter was born.

157. *Nelson on Infidelity*, p. 80, says of "the early Christians," they "were almost uniformly either Jews or pagans before their conversion, and even hated the name of Christ."

How much pagans knew or cared about the name of Christ is another question, but we are not informed of any Jews who ever hated that name except those who repudiated Christ by denying Jesus. And of these we are informed of the conversion of but one, namely, Paul, though there very likely were others.

158. Mr. Owen (*Comp. Com.*, Heb. iv. 14) says, "The writer now proceeds to the consideration of a subject introduced chap. iii. 1, where he calls Christ the *High Priest* of the Christian religion."

This is a clear error. Turn to the text and see.

159. "The fault of the first covenant was, that it made nothing perfect." (*Williams in Comp. Com.*, Heb. viii. 17.)

When infidel writers tell us about the imperfections of inspiration, we resent it as sacrilegious; but I am utterly unable to comprehend the meaning of such teachings in the hands of a Christian.

160. On the above remark of Mr. Williams, Prof. Stewart says, by way of salvo, "The meaning is not that the Mosaic economy had positive *faults*, namely, such things as were palpably wrong, or erroneous; but that it did not contain in itself all the provisions necessary for pardon of sin, and the rendering the conscience peaceful and pure, which the gospel does effect."

Better let it stay as it was. The mending only makes it worse. The faults of the Old Testament are, that it is merely worthless! What a sentiment! My pen trembles while I copy it. No provision for the pardon of sin! Nothing to pacify the conscience in the Old Testament! Reader, I exhort you, do not believe it! Let such sentiments be scouted from the Church. Every word that has proceeded out of the mouth of God is a word of mercy, of truth, a perfect word, offering salvation, intended to pacify the conscience, and is pure gospel, and only gospel, from beginning to end. And those men who would set themselves up as judges in matters of the merciful administration of Jehovah, are but poor, miserable, short-sighted creatures like you and me. Who are they, to set down this work of God as faulty, this as a little better, and that as not palpably wrong! What blindness! It was but an incidental remark of an inspired Apostle, that it was all profitable, very profitable. Heb. vii. 19, and other texts, are misunderstood.

The difference between the Old Testament and the New, is not in the moral quality of their teachings, nor in the things taught. On these points I suppose it is enough to say, they are both divine revelation. The difference is in their modes and facilities of teaching. In the one case you stood before the advent of Christ — before his visible work became historic; and so you had to teach it by adumbration. In the other case, you stand and teach after these facts are seen and understood. So here were far superior facilities for teaching, but not superior things taught.

161. Jacobus (*Notes on the Gospels*, Matt. ii. 4) says, "The Jews looked for Christ, at this time, but as a temporal king."

It is common enough to say so, but I know of no evidence of it. There are a few glances of history that would seem to indicate that some few persons, at that time, entertained such notions of the Messiah, but they are very few, and the glances very indirect. But as to this being the settled opinion of the Church, that is out of the question.

162. Again, Matt. iii. 6: "Baptism was known as an initiatory rite. Proselytes to the Jewish religion were received in this way. Hence they understood the ordinance as signifying an espousal of a new religion; and so, it was a mode of public profession."

And so our children and people are mistaught. Scores, and even hundreds, of such errors could be quoted from the same author.

163. On Matt. iii. 9: "The Jews boasted in Abraham. They were his descendants according to the flesh."

Not one in a hundred of them. Perhaps not one in ten thousand. See the arguments on this subject. Pure blood descent, which is understood, is out of the question.

164. "It is, I believe, an unquestionable fact, that before the end of the second century, Christianity had been more widely disseminated over the face of the earth than any other religion, true or false." (*Greyson Letters*, p. 188.)

This is a common sentiment, but made upon data very illusive and untrue. It supposes that the whole number of Christians, at the end of the two hundred years, was increased in that period. But most of those called first Christians were Christians before. They did not now profess a new faith, but only a fact pertaining thereto, and now for the first time existing, namely, that Jesus was the Christ. The dissemination of religion is another thing. There was no period within a hundred years of the Saviour's life, that the true Church did not number hundreds of thousands, if not millions. The probability is, the Church, by the end of the second century, had not gained as much as it lost by the defection of those who repudiated Christ. But history does not inform us.

165. Doddridge closes Section 15 thus: "Let us learn to reflect how necessary it was that the law should thus introduce the gospel."

I presume, on a moment's reflection, any one would regard it a simple absurdity to suppose that the law introduces the gospel. The term law, when used in contrast or in juxtaposition to gospel, means the primary rule of absolute obedience. How can that introduce a gospel? It can have nothing to do with a gospel. If we have a gospel, it was introduced by divine mercy, over and above, and irrespective of the law, meeting its requirements vicariously on our part, the law standing firm. I suppose it would hardly be understood that the law of religious ceremonies introduced the gospel. The gospel existed long before the ceremonies did. And if not, how could ceremonies introduce a gospel?

166. Doddridge, on Galatians i. 6, speaks of "this method of salvation," explaining himself to mean a method different from "the works of the Mosaic law."

By this the learner understands that the works of the Mosaic law, whatever that may mean, was once a method of salvation; and that on the appearance of Christ, He instituted a different and better method. Now, I ask any man if that is theology? And I ask a question a thousand fold more important: How can sound practical religion prosper in a land where such theology interpenetrates the early teachings of the people? There are hundreds of such blunders all through Doddridge's exposition.

167. I have not, in the course of my reading, chanced to see *Tappan's Lectures;* but from an extract, pages 116, 118, in *Horne's Introduction*, vol. ii. p. 120, Carter's ed., 1860, I incline to regard it an excellent book. The extract referred to treats of the

Jewish Sacrifices, so called metonymically, and his account of the character of these symbols is so rational, and so radically dissimilar from the untrue teachings of scores of authors I could easily name, that I recommend the extract to the reader. He will soon discard the strange notion of these animals being real sacrifices, as so many teach, mistaking a symbol for a reality.

168. Dr. Mosheim speaks of "the Church founded by the ministry and death of Christ," discourses largely upon it, and in many places explains and repeats the idea that the existing Christian Church and religion had both their absolute origin in the world in the time of the Saviour's advent, entirely distinct from the Jewish religion and Church. I hold it possible that some things may be clearly stated in the English language, critics or no critics. Then if there never was but one Church, Dr. Mosheim was in error on this point.

169. Suppose it to be true, as stated by Mr. R. I. Wilberforce, that there was a "time when the Church existed in its embryo form in the college of the apostles," a Romish supposition often assented to by Protestants, then what must necessarily follow?

If that is true, then that was the beginning of a new corporation, or religious society, with a new government in the form of a charter, of course providing for legislation, judicature, and execution, for this is what government means, and is. And as it was invested with the powers of perpetual succession, how can the succession deviate even a hair's breadth from the original constitution? Then if this same Church exists at all, now, there can be but one true, divine Church. The descending or perpetuating authority, as originally created, must inhere strictly in the succession. Then Protestant or non-prelatical writers need not insist that a " succession of doctrine " is sufficient to identify the Church. The predicate is not about doctrine, but about legal, external authority to govern a corporation under a prescribed charter. The inquiry then relates to successive, personal investiture, and incumbency. The question is not about the Church's doctrines of religion, but is personal as to appointment to office, like a contested election. The case as stated by Mr. Wilberforce, and strangely assented to by Protestant writers, necessarily supposes one distinct, exclusive line of succession of legal investitures. And thus, of course, the question now arises, Which, among the several existing Church governments, is the true one ? This may be good policy for Papists ; but it is strange Protestants assent to it.

170. " The doctrine of salvation taught by Jesus Christ is called gospel, or good tidings, in several passages of the New Testament." (*Bishop Percy.*)

That is literally very true, but the implication that it was then first taught, is not true, for the prophets taught it also.

171. D'Aubigné says, " Christianity and the Reformation are two of the greatest revolutions known in history."

That depends upon what he calls a revolution. They were great events, but reformation would describe them far better.

172. " The new religion had two features, among many others, which especially distinguished it from all human systems which fell before it. One had reference to the ministers of its worship, and the other to its doctrines." (*D'Aubigné.*)

He who sets out with the idea that Christianity is a new religion, will of course drift into the next errors of new ministers and new doctrines, and kindred illusions.

173. "His disciples, beginning at Jerusalem, travelled over the Roman empire and the world, everywhere proclaiming their Master the author of everlasting salvation." (*D'Aubigné.*)

And the prophets, and all other true ministers of religion, hundreds and even thousands of years before, travelled less extensively perhaps, everywhere proclaiming the same thing of the same Master.

174. "The Church was in the beginning a community of brethren." (*D'Aubigné.*)

Yes, we are told so in the last verse of the 4th chapter of Genesis, which is the first historic mention of the Church in Scripture.

175. "Paul of Tarsus, one of the chiefest apostles of the new religion, had arrived at Rome." (*D'Aubigné.*)

No, not when he arrived at Rome, on the occasion referred to. Now he had left the new, false religion, then set up by the repudiators of Christ, and had returned to the old religion of Scripture.

176. "Now that none of these motives could influence Paul to profess the faith of Christ crucified, is manifest from the state of Judaism and Christianity, at the period when he renounced the former and embraced the latter." (*Horne's Int.*, vol. ii. p. 322.)

Did Paul renounce the former faith, as is here stated? He everywhere insists, most rigidly and peremptorily, that in embracing the crucified Jesus as Christ, he did so because he was now convinced that that was the only way to hold fast to Judaism;

thus holding them to be one and the same thing from the beginning. The thing he renounced was not Judaism, in any proper sense, but the new, false Judaism which denied that Jesus was Christ. If Paul renounced the Old Testament teachings, how could he be a Christian?

177. On the next page Horne says, "Shortly after his baptism and the descent of the Holy Spirit upon him, Saul went to Arabia, and during his residence in that country he was fully inducted, as we may reasonably think, by special revelation, and by the diligent study of the Old Testament, in the doctrines and duties of the gospel."

Just so. He learned the doctrines and duties of the Gospel by the "diligent study of the Old Testament." How else could he learn them?

178. Dr. Lovick Pierce, speaking of baptism, says, "It being at best only an outward rite, valuable as a testimonial of an inward grace, but perfectly worthless in itself."

What, I beg to inquire, is it which is thus spoken of as at best only an outward rite? Surely not the sacrament commonly called baptism. The obligation of fidelity to the Church, acknowledged and made potent in baptism, can hardly be called a rite. The rite is the manner in which we acknowledge and promise the fulfillment of the obligation, the sacrament. But the sacrament itself is nothing less than our duty to be religious.

179. Dr. Means, in a sermon on the birth and divinity of Christ, says, "The mystery is now solved. I understand its lofty import. *The infant Messiah breathes.* The merciful God incarnate enters upon his mission of mercy to the world." Again, "The promised redemption has come."

The things here stated can hardly be meant. It is very true that at this time the divine personality became incarnate; but it is certainly not true that in the person of Jesus, He, at this time, enters upon his mission of mercy to the world. They are two very different things, chronologically separate four thousand years. And that the promised redemption has just now come, would mean that in all the four thousand years before, the redemption was merely promised, and is now provided in pursuance of the promise; whereas the redemption was furnished as well as promised at the first. The thing previously promised was not the redemption, but only a concomitant of it, a thing subsidiary to the redemption, namely, the fleshly presence and visible work of the Saviour.

180. M. Renan, in his *Life of Jesus*, proceeds upon the doctrine of a wide and total distinction between the religion of the Bible, before the coming of the Saviour, and the Christianity by which it was superseded. So you hear him speak of "the new worship," "the infant sect" — that "it breaks its last connection with Judaism," and many such expressions.

This view is very comfortable for such writers as Renan. It serves well to distort Christianity, but is embarrassing if you want to elucidate it.

181. On page 196 we are told by Renan, that the last journey of Jesus to Jerusalem was that He might "attack Judaism in its strong hold, Jerusalem."

The very principles the blessed Saviour spent his life in teaching, in inculcating, and enforcing with far more than human power, He went to Jerusalem to attack! It was a religion "with which He had not yet broken!" Historic falsehoods more palpable or more dangerous could scarcely be uttered. A caricature of Christianity is the very thing for such writers as M. Renan. If sound Christian writers had never presented Christianity in these distorted and unnatural features, there would have been far less license for such semi-plausible infidelity as is given us by such writers as M. Renan, the author of "Ecce Homo," and the German infidels of the present day.

182. Dr. Henderson says, "Nine tenths of the mistakes which have beclouded and injured Christianity have arisen from the introduction into it of Jewish principles, practices, and errors." (*Relig. Ency.*, p. 465.)

Errors, Jewish, Romish, or Christian, introduced into Christianity, make up the injury it receives. But I know of no principle it possesses other than such as were formerly called Jewish.

183. Dr. Campbell, in *Comp. Com.*, Acts viii. 26, etc., says the Ethiopian eunuch "became first a proselyte to Judaism and then a convert to Christianity."

This is a strange way to become a Christian, to pass through some other and false religion to reach it. The history, in effect, says he was a Christian. The Scriptures were his Bible, and he went to Jerusalem to worship according thereto. Nevertheless, the Christship of Jesus was not generally promulgated at that time, and that fact could not be believed by him until he had good evidence of it. And so, like all other Christians of that age, he was baptized into that belief.

184. Mr. Henry says (Acts viii. 26): "Here is the story of the conversion of an Ethiopian eunuch to the faith of Christ."

I see no evidence of this. Then what was his faith before? Certainly it was Christ. But there were in that day thousands and millions who had the faith of Christ, but who, in the nature of things, could not have faith in Jesus until they received the necessary information. Nobody could have faith in Jesus until He rose from the dead; and then those who did not see Him must be informed of it.

185. On Acts xiv. 1, Mr. Henry says: "In the close of the foregoing chapter, the gospel was preached, first to the Jews, and some of them believed, and then to the Gentiles, and some of them believed."

That is a cloudy expression with a truth in it, but told in a way calculated to mislead. Surely they did not preach first to the Jews exclusively, and then to Gentiles exclusively. The preaching was, as it is now, to promiscuous assemblies — all who would hear. Nevertheless, this offering of the gospel first to the Jew and then to the Greek was natural, necessary, and unavoidable, easily seen if you look at the then existing state of things. The Jew was already a Christian — never professed any other religion; but in the necessities of the case, without a knowledge of Jesus up to this period. But now, at this precise juncture, it becomes necessary for him to do what could not be done before, namely, receive and believe in Jesus as Christ. So that the preaching of Jesus, in connection with the general preaching of Christ, presented to the Jew nothing but a fact which could not be known before; while as to the Greek, a heathen, one not a Christian at all, he must needs receive not only Jesus, but the whole system of religion. The Jew has only to continue to be a Christian by receiving Jesus, while the heathen must be converted to the religion itself. So that if every congregation had been part Jew and part Gentile, as we might readily suppose, there is apparent propriety in saying the gospel was preached first to the Jew and then to the Greek.

186. *Conybeare and Howson's St. Paul*, Int. p. 10, says: " Then we must study Christianity, rising in the midst of Judaism, we must realize the position of its early churches, with their mixed societies, to which Jews, proselytes, and heathens had each contributed a characteristic element."

What these authors call Christianity, is this: Between eighteen and nineteen hundred years ago the religions of the world were Judaism, proselytism, and heathenism. The first of these had, or once had, a divine oversight or authorship, in some unexplained way, connected with it, but was now wholly false and worthless. The second was a kind of mongrel, superstitious faith, ranging between it and heathenism, and the last was that general mass of idolatry and corruption known as heathen. And Christianity was a new religion, in the formation of which each of these three had contributed a characteristic element. But each of these three systems of faith must needs be repudiated in order to become a Christian. The Jews, as well as the others, were by virtue of their ancient faith the natural enemies of Christianity. This is clearly their outline; but it is clear to me that no such system of religion is known to revelation.

187. *Christian Theism* is an English prize essay by Robt. A. Thompson, M. A., published a few years ago, and republished in this country; page 329: " When or where did man, from the study of himself or nature, assure himself of the truth that the Creator is Infinite Love, till it was enunciated by the Living

Word; till He, by whom the worlds were made, came forth from the bosom of the Father, in the fields and tents of Palestine, proclaiming the sublime truth of Eternal Love from God to man?"

In this extract, and many similar ones that might be made from this same book, the entire religious teaching of the Old Testament is not only ignored, but expressly repudiated. The simple answer to the above is, that centuries before the time here spoken of, the same truth here described was not only annunciated, but reiterated and preached in every conceivable form of expression by the prophets, and was also written in the holy oracles, and read every Sabbath day to the people.

188. Among the most formidable infidel objections to Christianity I know of, is one summed up and quoted in *Chris. Theism* from Mr. Theodore Parker, p. 385, as follows: "The leading nations of the Caucasian race have thus far outgrown, first, the savage's rude fetichistic worship; then classic heathenism; then patriarchal deism; then the Mosaic worship of Jehovah; and now the most enlightened portion thereof come to what is called Christianity."

I do not say that this argument, as it is stated, is beyond the reach of logical argumentation; though I would not like to encounter it as Mr. Thompson does. The argument, to say the least, is grounded wholly upon a great untruth in Christian Theism. And if it had not been assented to by theologians, the argument never could have been raised by infidels at all. Christian writers have put this falsehood into the mouths of infidels. Were I to reply to Mr. Parker, I would not, as Mr. Thompson does, be cajoled into the admission of the Hebrew and Christian religions; but would contend at the threshold, that the Theism of revelation knew but one religion. I would require him to prove his progressive development, and decline furnishing him any material with which to do it, especially false ones. The progressive development theory rests wholly upon the doctrine of dispensations, following along and improving upon each other as they proceed. If "the present dispensation stands in a peculiar relation to the covenant made with Israel at Sinai, which it has entirely superseded," and if "God appeared chiefly in the character of a lawgiver" in a former dispensation, and if "the present dispensation supposes that there may have been one or more past dispensations, and that there may be a dispensation yet to come," then, if these things be so, as we are told, I inquire what is the objection to the theory of progressive development? Infidels may not state it exactly right, but the thing is admitted. Mr. Thompson in his argument with Mr. Parker, admits it; and many other authors admit it. The doctrine of different, rising, improving, better and better dispensations is the doctrine of development, for the doctrine applies as well to God's moral as to his natural providences, though I suppose Mr. Parker would carry it farther than some others do.

189. The learned Dr. Cave must, I think, bear some portion of the responsibility of the errors of later teachers on these points. In his discourse on the evangelical dispensation (*Lives of the Apostles*, p. 101), he says, "The last instance I shall notice of the exalting of this above the Mosaic dispensation, is the universal extent and latitude of it, and that both in regard to place and time."

Was religion ever confined to Palestine? Was it ever geographically circumscribed at all? Certainly it never was. Then why build an argument upon the assumption that it was? And how was it circumscribed in regard to time?

190. Dr. Cave tells us that Jesus Christ "planted the Church and its religion in the days of his humanity."

This is as bad as Neander's "Planting and Training of the Christian Church." What was planted?

191. Dr. Cave says (*Lives Apos.*, p. 194), that "The apostles had been lately converted from their Judaism."

I am at a loss to know what the learned Doctor means by Judaism, so as to make his statement agree with known and well settled history. If he means the religious errors which so plentifully existed in the Church in these times, the answer is, that there is no intimation in the New Testament, that any of the apostles excepting Paul, ever entertained these errors, or any of them. So they could not be presumed to be converted in that sense. And if he means the religious faith and doctrines of the Old Testament properly understood, then the reply is, that that is the true religion which they professed and taught to the end of their lives, which we call Christianity. He could hardly say the apostles were converted from true, revealed religion. I think the Doctor makes a clear mistake.

192. "'Even so hath the Lord ordained that they which preach the gospel should live of the gospel,' is the law of the New Testament." (*Bp. Morris' Church Pol.*, p. 47.)

No; most assuredly this is not the law of the New

Testament, particularly as is here understood. It was ordained in the Old Testament, and elaborately taught there, and in the usual way further taught and explained in the New.

193. Longking, in *Notes*, John iii. 3, says, "The words 'kingdom of God' denote, first, the spiritual kingdom which Christ was about to erect in the world by the preaching of his gospel."

This is either very erroneous or very ambiguous. Ordinarily, it would be understood that at that time Christ was about to preach some new doctrines, or system of religion, which would bring men into some relation to God hitherto unknown, and essentially different from the ordinary religion of the Old Testament. But when we see the Saviour's preaching, we see no doctrine advanced, or precept enjoined, beyond what is already written in the Old Testament. The preaching of his gospel, therefore, was only the enforcement and elaboration of the then written religion of the Church. This error is frequently repeated in various ways in Longking's *Notes*, and the damage thereby to Sunday-schools must be immense.

194. Longking (*Notes*, John iii. 4) says, "Nicodemus appears to have rightly understood our Lord as intimating that he, and any other Jew who would enter that 'kingdom of God,' of which Christ spake, must be born again, as well as any proselyte from heathenism."

Here the great error we are looking at, is very apparent. It is certain the Saviour neither stated nor meant anything of the kind. While it is certain that all men enter the kingdom of Christ, or true religion, in other words, by being born again, it is equally certain that a Jew, as such, needed no conversion. Being a Jew, that is, being in the Church, would imply, *prima facie*, that he was converted in the kingdom, though many of them as it is now, were not. Being born again implies conversion from irreligion to religion; and so applies to all apostate Jews; but it is nowhere intimated that Nicodemus ever departed from the true religion of the Bible, though it is clearly intimated that he was not as well versed in its doctrines as he should have been. The Saviour did not tell Nicodemus that he, because he was a Jew, must be born again.

195. Dr. Hook says, "We will commence with an indisputable fact. In this country there is at this time a religious society known by the name of the Church. The question is, Where, and by whom, was this society instituted?"

The best and most direct answer the history of the world affords to this question is this: "Then began men to call on the name of the Lord." (Gen. iv. 26.) Or, as it would perhaps be more properly read, "Then (about this time) men began to call themselves by the name of the Lord." That is, men began to separate from the wicked, and claim openly to be the Lord's people; to associate as religious people, congregate, segregate for avowedly religious ends and purposes. The Church was not instituted like a mere human society, but is the natural and necessary confluent result of individual religion.

But this is a vital point with Dr. Hook. There is no other possible way by which his prelatical doctrines can be supported than by regarding the present Church as having been instituted *de novo* at the period of the advent.

196. Bishop Hobart says, "The Christian Church was founded by bishops, because the apostles, who were bishops, were the first preachers of the gospel, and planters of the churches."

The objection to this is, that the Christian Church was not founded at all, in the sense here meant. The expression supposes that before the apostles began to preach, there was no Church, and that it was by their labors that it was brought into existence. All this is clearly untrue. It is useless to debate how the Church was then founded, since it was most certainly not done at all. The Church continued. Let this error be corrected, and a vast amount of controversy about the Church will abate. Logical popery will cease, and all forms of High Churchism will find themselves utterly without foundation.

197. The controversy about Episcopacy, three orders in the ministry, and what is sometimes called the apostolic succession, rests entirely on the supposition that Jesus Christ formed his Church; that in the formation of the Church, in the Church as organized by Christ, such and such principles of government were adopted. Take away this supposition, and there can be no such questions as those which enter into these debates. But let it be admitted that Jesus Christ formed his Church, and then the question arises, how He formed it.

In a tract before me of the Protestant Episcopal Society, written by William Hey, Esq., F. R. S., etc., of England, it is said: "We may therefore fairly conclude that the directions which are given in Holy Writ, for the formation of the Church in the time of the apostles, are to be applied to the same society in all ages."

Now, the objection is, that no directions are given at all, in the time of the apostles, or at any other time, for the formation of the Church. Where are any such directions? There are indeed many directions about the morals and religion of the Church, etc., but as to its formation, or government, no such thing is hinted at. There could be no such directions, because there was no formation.

198. Dr. Clarke says (Gal. v. 1.), "Hold fast your Christian profession; it brings spiritual liberty. On the contrary, Judaism brings spiritual death."

Well, I know of no fairer way to dispose of such a statement, than to give it an unqualified denial. His context makes us understand by Judaism, the precepts and the religious doctrines of the Old Testament. On the contrary, I believe that there is not, and never was, anything in this world, beneath the heavens, moral, mental, or physical, which brings spiritual bondage, but disobedience of these very precepts and doctrines. I will defend the Old Testament so far as to say, it is the word of God. And I complain of Clarke's Commentary for saying that it brings spiritual bondage. And I exhort people everywhere, as they value religious truth, to repudiate and disbelieve Clarke's Commentary, and all other books, so far as they teach such doctrines. He says, "Messiah's reign was to be a reign of liberty." Not so by any means. It was not to be, but then was, and always had been, as it always will be, a reign of liberty.

199. Matthew Henry (*Com.*, Gal. v. 1) says, "Christ has satisfied the demands of the broken law, and by his authority as a king, He has discharged us from the obligation of those carnal ordinances which were imposed on the Jews."

The error here is palpable when once pointed out. By his authority as a king, the Saviour did nothing on that subject. The cessation of the ritual observances here alluded to, was by no means the subject of legislative authority. They ceased on the coming of Christ, by their own inherent nature and constitution. They were always and naturally restricted to the state of Christianity prior to the incarnation of Christ. Being instruments to teach the principles brought more palpably to view in the incarnation, they of course ceased when the events occurred. When and where, I inquire, did the Saviour, by his authority as a king, discharge us? There is not a hint of such a thing in Scripture. On the contrary, He always explained that He taught nothing but what was read in the Old Testament. Will any man say otherwise?

200. Dr. Scott (*Com.*, Gal. v. 1) speaks of "the method of justification revealed in the gospel," meaning the New Testament; and by necessary implication contrasts it with a previous method.

Does the New Testament reveal a method of justification? Does divine revelation recognize two different ways of justifying men? How strangely men write!

201. "For then the Jewish Church was abolished, and the Christian entered in its stead; then the law of Moses ceased, and that of Christ and his gospel commenced."

So wrote Prideaux in his Preface to vol. ii. of *Connection*, one hundred and fifty years ago; and so many have believed, to their great injury, ever since. Lord save the Church from such error!

202. "Judaism was to be superseded by Chris-

tianity — the religion of Moses by the religion of Jesus. The substitution of the gospel for the law was the establishment of 'the kingdom of heaven,' the coming of the Son of man." (*Palfrey's Relation*, p. 90.)

To refute such clerical jargon it is necessary only to cite it.

203. "The introduction of the gospel was gradual. It began when Jesus began to preach." (*Palfrey's Relation*, p. 90.)

When everybody knows it began four thousand years before.

204. The eloquent Cookman was more eloquent than accurate, in remarking in a speech at New Brunswick, before the Bible Society, November 17, 1828, concerning the apostles, that "They were linguists without a lexicon, and preachers without a book."

His meaning is, as the context shows, that the apostles, beginning a new religion in opposition to that of the Old Testament, and the New not yet in existence, they had no text-book to use in preparing their sermons. This error is, I suppose, too palpable to need even a remark in its refutation. Then how comes the Old Testament to be a book for us now?

205. "The platform of Jewish ceremonies sank beneath the simple doctrines of Jesus." (*Cookman.*)

What doctrines? Mr. Cookman would have discovered his error if it had occurred to him to try to point out one.

206. President Edwards, referring to Mark iii. 5, says, "It was hardness of heart that excited grief and displeasure in Christ toward the Jews."

It is remarkable that so many persons make the Saviour speak of the Jews, the whole Church, when He refers only to some few persons then present. Toward the Jews generally, there never was any such grief and displeasure.

207. Referring to the fickleness and instability of the Jews, President Edwards says, "But when Jesus stood bound, it was not 'Hosanna!' but 'Crucify Him!'"

This is a common error, but a clear and palpable one. The cry of "Hosanna!" on the entrance of Christ into Jerusalem, is said of the great and teeming multitudes; nor is there the least intimation that they, or any of them, ever cried anything different. The cry of "Crucify Him!" was the demand of a little handful of rabble and soldiery, different persons altogether, who crowded around the governor's door on the morning of the crucifixion. Mr. Edwards' remark is built upon fashion, and fashion alone, without a historic word to support it.

208. A tract published in 1860, by the Rev. Messrs. Boyce and Quintard — now Bishop Quintard — begins thus: "The Church which Christ formed, and which the apostles more completely established, was, from its first beginning, an organized body of believers."

So long as it is admitted an assured fact, certainly written, that Christ formed or founded the Church as an organized body of believers, I do not see how the claim of a succession of apostolic ordinations can be ignored. At all events, it is this admission that gives rise to the long arguments on that subject. The Bishop, and all other High Churchmen are obliged to make historic facts for their doctrine to rest upon.

209. Dr. Cave (*Lives Apos.*, p. 382) says of Philip: "No sooner had religion taken possession of his mind, than like an active principle it began to ferment and diffuse itself."

The context assumes that Philip's first religious impressions were produced by the interview with the Saviour when he was called to be an apostle. It would be hard to believe, especially without a word of testimony, that the Saviour would choose irreligious men, rather than religious men, for his immediate disciples, and the particular purpose intended. This is stated and explained, it is true, in the peculiar case of Paul; but why infer it gratuitously in the other cases? Paul's case was very different. He had renounced the religion of the Church; but nothing of the sort is intimated of the others. The inference rests upon the strange notion that all the religion of mankind, as well as the Church, had become extinct just then. In the entire absence of all testimony, the most natural inference would be that the apostles were pious from early life.

210. Bishop Latimer, who preached three hundred years ago, frequently speaks of the Jews, wholesale, as the enemies and opposers of Christ, without an intimation that any of them were his friends and supporters. This oversight, perhaps already sufficiently exposed, was far more excusable then than now.

211. Macknight (Pref. to Heb.) says: "Most of the Jews adhered to the law of Moses with the greatest obstinacy." And on the next page he says, "The arguments in it (the Epistle) for supporting the doctrines of the gospel, as we have said, are all taken from the Jewish Scriptures."

That is strange. How can both things be true? The Jews adhered strongly to the Old Testament, the law of Moses; and to draw them away from it, and make them believe something else, Paul urges the Old Testament! Macknight proves the very opposite of what he affirms. He shows that the Jewish Scriptures prove the New Testament; that the doctrines of the one are those of the other. And so, Paul needed nothing better than the former to prove the latter.

212. Macknight says, "The revelation which He (Christ) made to mankind is more perfect than the revelation made to the Jews."

I cannot admit that, because I cannot admit that anything is more perfect than any divine revelation.

213. "After this we read of many thousands of Jews that believed in Jerusalem." (Edwards' *Hist. Redemp.*, p. 349.)

Believed what? Anything different from what they had always believed? I know of nothing believed in the Church then by these Jews, that was not always believed, save one thing, which in its nature could not be believed before, namely, that Jesus was Christ.

214. "For it was the manner of the apostles to go first into the synagogues of the Jews, and preach the Gospel to them." (*Hist. Redemp.*, p. 349.)

That is not quite accurate. This would be better. For it was the manner of the apostles to continue to worship in the synagogues, where they always worshipped, and preach to their brethren the joyful news that Christ had certainly come.

215. Dr. Robt. Hall, in *Brit. Pulpit*, on "The Blessedness of Giving," says, "The world never

knew anything of benevolence till Jesus Christ came."

Into what strange fancies will one blunder lead us! No benevolence in the world until Jesus Christ came, eighteen hundred years ago? Let us read: "And if thy brother be waxen poor, and fallen in decay with thee, then thou shalt relieve him; yea, though he be a stranger, or a sojourner; that he may live with thee." (Lev. xxv. 35.) "Is it not to deal thy bread to the hungry, and that thou bring the poor that are cast out to thy house? When thou seest the naked that thou cover him; and that thou hide not thyself from thine own flesh?" (Isa. lviii. 7.) "If I have withheld from the poor their desire, or have caused the eyes of the widow to fail; or have eaten my morsel myself alone; and the fatherless hath not eaten thereof; if I have seen any perish for want of clothing; or any poor without covering," etc. (Job xxxi. 16, etc.) We could read in this way, I know not how long. And yet no benevolence in the world until eighteen hundred years ago!

216. The Rev. Robt. Philip of England (*Brit. Pulpit*, Ser. 44), on Gal. iv. 45, remarks as follows: "And when you consider that four thousand years elapsed between the giving of the promise and its fulfillment, the question can scarce escape being asked, Why was the promise so long being fulfilled? Why was Christ born at so late a period of the world? Why was Christianity not introduced sooner?"

And then we have a long, lame, labored argument, trying to explain why the world was left so long destitute of true religion. All of which might well have been spared, if it had occurred to the learned author that the only religion known to

Scripture, was furnished at once without any delay.

217. Again, Mr. Philip says, "Infidels have often said with a sneer, 'If Christianity is so valuable, why was the world without it so long? Why were four thousand years allowed to pass without its introduction?'"

In the affairs of life generally, it is far easier to keep out of difficulty than to get out of one. And this will be found to apply with peculiar force to logical difficulties. Let it be once conceded that the world was left four thousand years without religion, and I think it will be hard to answer this question. It has been attempted by men as able, perhaps, as Mr. Philip, but has uniformly ended in entanglement and laborious argument, the infidel generally having the advantage. And why make such a concession? It is neither proper, politic, nor truthful. And notice, too, it is right here, at this starting-point, that infidels have, in various ways, secured far more logical vantage ground than at any other. And it is right here that all popery and all High Churchism find a resting-place.

218. Dr. Young of Edinburgh, in his *Mystery, or Evil and God*, p. 288, says of "the Jewish institute as a whole," "But it was essentially a temporary expedient."

Jewish institute is understood to mean the Old Testament religion. Besides the strangeness of a temporary religion, nobody holds it such, nobody treats it such, neither Dr. Young nor anybody else. It is quoted and preached from by everybody.

219. Again, same page, he says, "Judaism was therefore, at its best, an infantile system."

No. Some of the very highest, sublimest, most exalted and perfect, as well as the most classical and erudite Christianity, both in theory and practice, known to mankind, is read in the Old Testament, and seen in the lives and piety of the men of those times. Infantile, indeed! If these are the rudiments of religion, where are the classics?

220. Again, Dr. Young says of religion before the Incarnation: "It was, throughout, an appeal to the senses, and to the mind, chiefly through the senses."

It embarrasses me to meet such a statement in the hands of a Christian writer. Among the ribaldry and coarse slang of infidels I could dispose of it more easily. As it is, I can do no less, and perhaps need do no more, than to aver, in the face of it, that the Old Testament abounds with the highest strains of pious feeling and deep pathos, the holiest and most touching emotion, the sublimest fervor and most impassioned rapture, ecstacy, and enjoyment known to the religion of the world, either written or felt. Spirit of David, of Samuel, of Isaiah, and the prophets, how shall I defend thee? Throughout, an appeal to the senses? No, no, no! The Book is the law and counsel of Jehovah, throughout an appeal to the heart and the intellect, inciting to deep and holy communion with God; and the response of multiplied thousands of Old Testament saints, was the deep sanctification of soul, and high heavenly communion, which the best Christians of this generation would do well to imitate. Who wrote the eleventh chapter of Hebrews, and for what was it written?

221. Again, on p. 289, the Doctor contrasts the religion of the Old Testament with the New, on this wise: "Shall we expect that the twilight shall re-

veal a single thing which the day has left in darkness? Shall we import the principles of a temporary expedient into the enduring and universal economy?"

The rule is, to put the best construction on everything. The only alternative I see, is to suppose the Doctor misses entirely the whole scope of Hebrew Scripture, by regarding its mere instrumental modes of teaching as the religion itself. This might relieve the Doctor personally, however little relief it might afford him as a theologian. But we are dealing with his book.

222. Again, Dr. Young says, "Shall we explain by Judaism the higher doctrines and laws of Christianity?"

I answer, I think we should. And my reason for so thinking is, that I see the Saviour and the apostles do so explicitly, expressly, and exclusively, through the whole course of their ministry. And secondly, I see Christian ministers do so now, directly, in one half the sermons I hear, and indirectly in the other half. Thirdly, I know of no other way to explain these higher doctrines and laws of Christianity.

223. The Introduction to the New Testament of *Pratt, Woodford & Co.'s Bible* says, "The Old Testament was partial and severe. It was confined to the children of circumcision, yea, with some exceptions, to a single nation."

Then what business have we with it? No. All revelation was always addressed to all mankind. Revelation, however, as a mere truism, is necessarily confined, in its practical uses, to the circumcision — the baptism — the Church. That is, religion is confined to religious people.

224. The *Testament and Psalms, with Notes*, of the Am. Tract Society, on Matt. iv. 23, tells us that "synagogues" means "the Jewish places of worship."

I think not. It means places of worship, but not in any exclusive sense Jewish. What are now called churches were formerly called synagogues. Everybody worshipped in them. But after the receiving and repudiating portions of the Church became well separate, they must needs be distinguished by different names. This distinction became established in after years in common parlance. Before that time, the true Church was called Jews; afterward, to distinguish the true and false Jews, they were called by different names.

225. Again, we are told in the same book, Matt. xxviii. 13, "The Jews did not deny the resurrection of Christ for want of evidence to prove it."

The Jews did not deny the resurrection of Christ at all. They, and none else, affirmed it. To this day there is no testimony of that great historic fact but Jewish testimony. Nevertheless, some of the Jews did deny the resurrection, as stated in the verse alluded to.

226. And in the heading of the 12th of Mark, we are told that "In the parable of the vineyard let out to unfaithful husbandmen, Christ foretelleth the reprobation of the Jews, and the calling of the Gentiles."

The text makes no mention of these things whatever. If it had so foretold, it could not be true, so some different explication must be found. The Jews were never reprobated, nor were the Gentiles called, in the technical sense here meant and commonly understood. See our former elucidations of these points.

227. Again, in the heading of the 22d chapter of Luke: " The Jews conspire against Christ."

This is one of the most remarkable things I have seen in Biblical criticism. It is stated, just that way, in more than one hundred editions of the New Testament that I have seen. First, the thing stated is in itself an absurdity and a contradiction. A nation or whole body of people, a million, nor scarcely a thousand, could make a secret agreement to do any thing. A conspiracy, in the nature of the thing, is confined to two or three, or a handful of people. Secondly, the text states the very reverse. The Jews, the people, were the party conspired against, not the conspirators. The conspirators were a handful of priests and scribes.

228. The same book tells us that 2 Corinthians iii. 6–11, sets forth " a comparison between the ministers of the law and of the gospel."

Not only is there nothing of the kind in the place cited, nor in any other, but the thing stated is meaningless and out of the question. The law has no ministers. It was never ministered. It is the mere arbitrary command of a monarch. As the law was designed to secure the highest happiness without sin, so the gospel is fitted to accomplish this design, after the introduction of sin. It is well known that the word law is used in Scripture in many different senses, to mean many different things: but when used in juxtaposition with gospel, as when the law and the gospel are spoken of as above, the meaning cannot be mistaken. It means the system of divine government and responsibility under which the world was placed before it needed either a Saviour or a gospel. Of course it had no ministers. We must not tolerate the clumsy idea inculcated above, that the gospel came first to the relief of man only eighteen hundred years ago. It came before any one ever suffered the penalty of the law. Is any man ever damned without an offer of salvation? The law is the rule now, and applies promptly to all who will not seek the shelter of the gospel. But to speak of its ministers, is to mistake its nature altogether.

229. In the heading of chapter iv. of Galatians, we are told that "We were under the law till Christ came."

Whether that is so or not, depends entirely upon what is meant by Christ's coming. If it means till Christ came to be our Saviour, which, however, very few would be likely to understand by the expression, then it is all right; but if it meant till Christ came in the flesh, in the time of John the Baptist, as most people would understand, then it is all wrong. This *Testament and Psalms, with Notes*, by the American Tract Society, is full of errors of this sort.

230. Mr. Thomas Olivers, quoted approvingly by Dr. Clarke, says, "The Christian religion was then a new thing in the world," meaning in the time of the apostles.

If that were true, then it follows necessarily, that it is a false religion, and that that of the modern Jews is the true faith. Conceding that the Old Testament is revelation, and that it contains a system of religion, it follows that a system new as to that, must be false. Moreover, the historic fact stated by Mr. Olivers is unquestionably untrue. Both these books are now here, side by side, and everybody knows and sees that the religious faith of the one is exactly the religious faith of the other. Matthew and John are not more akin.

231. The American Tract Society, in its *Notes on the New Testament*, Heb. viii. 4, says that Jesus Christ "could not on earth officiate as a priest, according to the Jewish law, because He did not belong to the tribe from which alone priests could be taken."

A most strange reason, certainly. He himself could not, beforehand, by symbolical pre-representation, teach his own future appearance, sacrifice, and death, because He did not belong to the tribe of Levi! This is one of the theological instructions of the American Tract Society.

232. Leigh, quoted by Dr. Clarke, Heb. iii. 2, says that "Christ's faithfulness consists in this, that He has as fully revealed unto us the doctrine of the gospel, as Moses did that of the law."

Besides the offense of putting Christ and Moses in that category, and of eulogizing the faithfulness of the divinity upon the ground that the Saviour was as good a revealer as Moses, I suppose no one would construe the remark to mean less than this, that Moses and Christ revealed, respectively, two different systems of doctrine, the one in the Old Testament, and the other in the New. And yet I presume that if our infidel writers were to insist plainly upon that fact, none would be more readily offended than Leigh and Clarke.

233. Michaelis, referring to 1 John ii. 7, says, "Now Christ himself had given his disciples a commandment which He called a new commandment, and this was 'That they should love one another.'"

However true this may be literally, this unexplained manner of stating it, both here by the learned German, and in many other places by others, is calculated to give, and does give, a very erroneous impression. It implies that to love one another is a principle in religious morals previously unknown. Whereas it is at least as old in the Church as the controversy on that subject between God and Cain, and had been elaborately taught, and practiced too, since that. Nevertheless, it was then new to those whom the Saviour thus taught, or some of them, just as it would be now new to thousands who had not known, or had not heeded it.

234. Hannah More says that "Previous to the establishment of Christianity, philosophy had attained its utmost perfection."

From this, one would infer that the religious faith, or principles of salvation, did not exist before eighteen hundred years ago. The other error, that philosophy, before the apostolic age, had attained any considerable degree of elevation, much less its utmost degree of perfection, does not properly fall within the range of these criticisms.

235. Again, speaking of Paul, "At all times he showed as much respect for their religion as was consistent with that which he now professed."

The respect he showed for their religion was to advocate it wholly, thoroughly, and constantly. The respect he showed for their religious errors, for their ignorance and mistakes in their religion, was to oppose them firmly, but mildly and carefully.

236. Again, "St. Paul powerfully inculcates that new and spiritual worship which was so condescendingly and beautifully taught by the Divine Teacher at the well of Sychar."

This would be better, because true: Paul powerfully inculcates that old and spiritual worship which was so condescendingly and beautifully taught by the Divine Teacher at the well of Sychar.

237. The Rev. Dr. Thomas Raffles, of England, says: "The first heralds of salvation were fishermen, tax gatherers, and tent makers."

We have no information that Abel, Moses, or any of their contemporary heralds of salvation were either fishermen, tax gatherers, or tent makers.

238. The Rev. H. Melville, M. A., of St. Peter's College, Cambridge, in a sermon, speaks of "the introduction of Christianity, when another state of being is brought into the world;" and explains that it was in the time of the apostles.

But it is remarkable that he should go to the 119th Psalm to find a text that would best elucidate the Christianity so introduced into the world a thousand years afterward.

239. The Rev. Bradford K. Pierce (*Notes*, on Acts iii. 22) says of Moses and Christ, that they "were both lawgivers, Moses of the law of rigid justice, Jesus of the law of love."

This is the way our "Sunday-schools, Bible classes, and private readers" are instructed in Scripture theology! A grosser violation of Scripture could not be written. Everybody knows, and nobody better than Mr. Pierce, that this same law of love, and no other law of religion, is written all over the law of Moses, if he chooses so to call the Old Testament, in a thousand places. Mr. Pierce's book is full of such errors.

240. Dr. A. Clarke, in his *Ancient Israelites*, p. 257, gives a chapter on "True Israelites," in which he notices some "splendid examples of holiness'

among the Jewish people at the time of the advent, and concludes the chapter in these words: "Thus the grace of the gospel being superadded to such holy dispositions, it was easy to make *perfect Christians* of these *true Israelites*." I am always careful to italicize as the author does.

In my judgment, this is the germ, whether in the hands of Dr. Clarke, or others, whence springs most of the distorted and crippled theology of the day. These splendid examples of holiness, with such holy dispositions, needed some other essential thing, it is held, in order to make them Christians. What do they need? We are a thousand times led to suppose they needed conversion. Conversion from what? and to what? I would inquire. Dr. Clarke, above, says they needed "the grace of the gospel." What grace, of what gospel? If they were holy, and had the revealed word of God for their religious theory, then that is the grace of the gospel, and all the grace of all the gospel known to revelation. The Christianity supposed to be made up of something superadded to the Bible creed of splendid holiness, is a myth. There is no such gospel, no such Christianity — cannot be.

241. Dr. Clarke says (*Ancient Israelites*, p. 294), "Sacrificing is the offering up to God a living animal, whose blood is shed in adoration of his majesty, and in order to appease his wrath."

It is impossible Dr. Clarke could think so. That is a good description of the idolatrous sacrificing of heathen people; but it is as wide as the poles of describing any sacrificing known to the Bible. Any sacrifice other than that of Jesus, the Son of Mary, is abhorrent to Scripture anywhere, in any age.

The sacrifices of these ancient Israelites were not, in themselves, "acceptable to God," as the Doctor says on the next page, at all; they were only representatively acceptable. As the Doctor wholly fails to explain, or seemingly to suppose, they were acceptable only when, and in that they represented, typified, the true Sacrifice. Nobody explains fuller or better than Dr. Clarke does in hundreds of places, that Christ is, and always was the only sacrifice for sin. Nobody insists more, or better than he, that the animals had no virtue — that they only typified the real and the true. There is no doctrine nor faith in the bits of type metal in a printer's case; and yet these pieces of metal are essentially valuable sometimes in typing, in figuring, in representing valuable religious truth. "To what purpose is the multitude of your sacrifices to me?" (Isa. i. 11.)

242. On page 360, on "Modern Jews," Dr. Clarke tells us, "There is some reason to fear that many Jews in the present day have drunk deeply into the infidel spirit of the times, and no longer receive the writings of the Old Testament as *divinely inspired.*"

Do any modern Jews, or did they ever, receive the Old Testament as divinely inspired? I answer, Most assuredly not. Right here is a great blunder. They say they receive it, but only and exclusively upon the distinct hypothesis that its Christ is a person other than Jesus. They scout it upon supposition that Jesus is its Emmanuel. Is that receiving it? To receive the writings of the Old Testament as divinely inspired, means to receive its religious faith; that is, to worship its Christ. But if you repudiate the Saviour of the Old Testament, how can it be said you receive it as divinely inspired? Is its inspiration separate and distinct from the Saviour it offer and enjoins? Remove its inspiration, and is it then inspired? Surely nothing can be called receiving it, but accepting its Christ—its religion. Is there such a doctrinal difference and incompatibility between the Old Testament and the New, as that the one may be received, and the other rejected? Can you embrace the religion of Matthew, and repudiate that of Mark? If modern Jews receive the Old Testament, then Dr. Clarke repudiates it, because he receives it only and exclusively in so far as it is brought into oneness with the New, and is rightly explained and expounded therein. Is there any inspired religion in the Old Testament not in the New? Surely we must correct such plain and important blunders as this.

243. Dr. Cudworth, Bishop Pearce, Mr. Toinard, and other eminent English scholars, have, with great ability and labor, discussed the question "whether our Lord ate the passover with his disciples before He suffered." In this debate there are four different hypotheses. "First, that our Lord did *not* eat the passover on the last year of his ministry. Second, that He *did*, and at the *same time* with the Jews. Third, that He did eat it that year, but *not with the Jews* nor at the same time. Fourth, that He ate *a* passover of his own instituting, but differing widely from that eaten by the Jews."

In these lengthy and critical inquiries, it seems to me that much talent and learning are employed to very little purpose. What results are hoped for? What is passover? what is Jewish passover? and what is a passover of his own instituting? Passover, or rather pass-over, is the name of a mode in which professors of religion renewed the profession of their obligation to God for his great mercies and deliverance in Christ, and promised unfaltering fealty to Him in the future. By way of convenient distinction, we call this obligation sacrament. Other obligations and the acknowledging of them we call by other names. Now, the eating of anything religiously and in commemoration, that was ever called passover, was the public and solemn acknowledgment of the obligation we are under to God for his great deliverance in Christ, or the renewal of such acknowledgment. What are we to understand then, when told that the last passover celebrated by the Saviour was not the passover of the Jews, but a passover of his own instituting, differing widely from that of the Jews? Differing in what? There is no place for difference but in the mere external mode of eating. In any possible case, it was a form of acknowledging the obligation. Vary the outward action as you will, and call it Lord's Supper, or by any other name, and it is still the same passover of the Jews. There is nothing instituted, or to which that idea will apply, but the outward mode of attesting the obligation. I do not understand the gentlemen. Determined rightly or wrongly, it amounts to nothing. The discussions are called theological, but I cannot discern the theology.

244. Binney's *Theological Compend*, a small manual of divinity, much used in Sunday-schools, says of the Moral Law, that it is "that declaration of the divine will which relates to the duties we owe to our Maker and to one another;" and then observes, "This law is greatly amplified throughout the Old Testament, and though not formally re-

enacted by Jesus Christ, it is nevertheless as clearly revealed in the New."

No laws, precepts, commands, or anything else in the Old Testament, are ever reënacted in the New, because they never ceased or became void. How could any declaration of the divine will ever be re-enacted? All that class of theology is erroneous.

245. M. Renan, in his *Origins of Christianity*, says, "Nicodemus did not become a Christian."

Very likely. The probability is he remained a Christian, and became a much wiser and better one in consequence of his interview with the Saviour.

246. On page 206, Renan tells us that at this point of time Jesus became perfectly satisfied "that there is no compromise possible with the ancient Jewish religion." Again, "From this moment He takes the position no longer of the Jewish reformer, but of a destroyer of Judaism." Page 207: "When He was pushed to an issue, He put aside all veils, and declared that the law was no longer in force." Again, "Jesus, in other words, is no longer a Jew. He is a revolutionist of the highest grade; He calls all men to a religion founded in the childhood of God."

It must be that every sober-minded man, half-way acquainted with Scripture, must see, that in any of these statements, and many, even hundreds more such, that might be quoted from the same author, there is not the slightest approach to historic truth. These things might just as well — or any of them — be stated of Moses, Judas, or Pope Joan, if there ever was such a pope. But this is not the wonder to which I wish to call attention. The wonder is, that such senseless stuff should, among even quasi

Christians, pass for a single day, for half-way ecclesiastical science and history.

247. Bishop Seabury says (*Ser. on Chris. Unity*), "Jesus appointed the Church's government, introduced its priesthood, and ordained its sacraments."

It is not easy to refer such statements to their proper source. They are in the hands of a highly respectable divine, and yet entirely devoid of historic truth. He no more appointed the Church's government than He did the Roman government. There is nothing in the New Testament referring to such a subject. As to its priesthood, He always constituted it, as He does now, ever since the world needed one. He ordained the forms of administering the sacraments; but the sacraments themselves are not subjects of legislative ordination.

248. Olshausen (Rom. x. 3, 4) says: "The law had not wrought in them (the Jews) any consciousness of sin, and therefore they did not lay hold on the new way of salvation, which offered them that which the law could not bring."

And yet when infidels tell us that they object to our religion, on the ground that it is inconsistent with itself, in that it teaches a system of salvation here, and a new way of salvation there, we complain of them, and say that revelation teaches but one way of salvation.

249. Olshausen paraphrases Rom. x. 5–8 thus: "No man can live by the law but he who keeps it; but no one can keep it; consequently another way of salvation is provided."

Not another way of salvation surely, but a way of salvation. The law is not a way of salvation, but a way of living in strict obedience before salvation was known or necessary. Such scholastic romance is alarming.

250. The American Bible Society teaches some erroneous theology in its *Family Testament*, 1856, from which I quote. In chapter heading of Matt. xxii. 9–12, it says it tells of "the vocation of the Gentiles."

This has been previously demonstrated to be clearly an error. All mankind were always called to be religious. When calmly looked at, the supposition that religion was for these, but not for those, is preposterous. Moreover, the text says nothing about Gentiles, nor their being called. How many families are injured by such erroneous comments!

251. The heading of Mark xii. is still worse. Here we are told that in the text, "Christ foretelleth the reprobation of the Jews and the calling of the Gentiles."

This is most remarkable, seeing the care that has been bestowed on these chapter headings. And the people have become so accustomed to such startling statements, that they are read without alarm or inquiry. This remark is made of the first twelve verses, which relate what is commonly called the parable of the vineyard, in which there is not one word said about Jews, nor about Gentiles. Stripped of fancy and mythology, it foretelleth the reprobation of obdurate sinners, and the calling, or recognition, of dutiful persons. What is the obvious and simple meaning of a reprobation of the Jews? It means that God rejected from all hope of mercy — abandoned and consigned to fearful and final perdition — a whole nation of people, or rather the whole Church, then consisting of six or seven millions!

As to the fate of the posterity of these people, near or remote, or their young children then living, in this awful, wholesale slaughter, the theological teachings of the American Bible Society do not particularly inform us. It tells us only that God reprobated the people then constituting the Church, pious people, children, and all, we would suppose; and this would naturally work a reprobation of their posterity, at least for many generations. To reprobate, would not only condemn them, individually, to perdition, but would withdraw from them all the gospel means of instruction and salvation known to divine mercy! In reply, I repeat that in the text there is not a word said about Jews, or Gentiles; nor, as I think, an allusion to either, as such. Secondly, the thing could not be true, because it is well known, and unquestionable, that for the space of about ten years after the crucifixion, the entire Church, with its various membership, apostles and all, when it must have amounted to some millions, was made up of these very Jews. And the Scriptures inform us of multitudes, multitudes oft repeated — whole cities and countries — myriads of them, who were the most staunch, heroic, and self-sacrificing Christians known to the history of human religion. Reprobated, indeed! And their posterity, with everybody else that would join them, have constituted the Church to this day. Thirdly, the reprobation, wholesale, of a numerous people, is so unnatural, unreasonable, and abhorrent to the whole tenor of Scripture, that it fails to furnish grounds for an argument. Who can suppose that Christ excommunicated every man and woman in the Church without notice, and without cause?

252. In the heading of Acts vii., we are told by the Bible Society that the meaning of Stephen, in verses 44–50, is, that "all outward ceremonies were according to the heavenly pattern, to last but for a time."

In the first place it is obvious, and does not admit of argument, that nothing of this sort is stated in the text. And secondly, if Stephen had so taught, it would have been clearly untrue. What! All outward ceremonies to last but for a time? Congregational worship, singing, praying, preaching, reading the Scriptures, observance of the Sabbath, all outward ceremonies previously in vogue in the Church, to cease then? So we are told by the American Bible Society; so our families are taught, and so our pulpits are misled.

253. In the heading of Rom. xiii., we are told that "Gluttony and drunkenness, and the works of darkness, are out of season in the time of the gospel."

And the converse of the proposition is, that previously to the time of the gospel — the period of the Jews — these things were in season. So the Bible Society teaches our families and our pulpits, though it makes no comment.

254. Mr. Richard Watson is unfortunate in some of his teachings. On the one hand he insists, in many places, both in his *Institutes*, and *Theological Dictionary*, on the specific oneness and identity of the Church in all ages. He will not allow us to speak of the Jewish Church, nor the Christian Church, as though there was a difference between them. They are "not two," he says, but "one and the same." Neither are there two religions, he says; salvation is always the same — the conditions of

pardon are always the same in all ages. This, I suppose, is wholesome teaching. Here Watson is himself. But then on the other hand: —

We are told the apostles and their followers "embraced a new and despised religion." (*Inst.*, p. 73.) "The Christian religion had its rise and began to be propagated in the times of the Roman emperors, Tiberias and Claudius." (Page 74.) "Moses and Christ, the Jewish and Christian religions." (Page 82.) We are "given information on which the divinity of both systems, the Jewish and the Christian, are built." (Page 83.) "The actual effect produced by this new religion on society." (Page 134.) What new religion? "The work of God in the hearts of sincere Jews, which took place in their transit from one dispensation to another, from Moses to Christ." (Page 563.) What transit was that? "The ancient visible Church, as constituted upon the ground of natural descent from Abraham, was abolished by the establishment of a spiritual body of believers to take its place." (*Inst.*, p. 622.)

Here I must remark, that this last expression is exactly and precisely the very sentiment Mr. Watson deprecates and insists must not be allowed. (See *Dict.*, art "Church.") And on the point of "natural descent" being the ground of membership formerly, and spiritual experience and consideration being the ground afterward, I insist there is not, and never was any such difference in the elements or formation of Church membership. It is now as it always was. Most assuredly it was the law, that all the "descendants of Abraham" should remain in the Church. And it was also the law that everybody out should come in. Both parts of this law were partially, but neither fully complied with. "Many of the people of the land became Jews." (Esth. viii. 17.) But not all. And on the other hand, many went out — thousands and millions went out, and so ceased to be Jews. Precisely is it thus now. The law is, that all born in the Church shall stay in, and that those out shall come in. Some people comply with the law, but many do not. Many born in, go out; but surely they go out in violation of the law. And those out who stay out, do so in violation of the law. The law of Church membership has never been changed.

255. "The moral laws of the Mosaic dispensation passed into the Christian code." (*Inst.*, p. 624.)

But according to Mr. Watson, and the Scriptures, there is, and always was, but one code. So, there could be no such passing.

256. "Much light is thrown upon the constitution of the primitive churches, by recollecting that they were formed very much after the model of the synagogues." (*Inst.*, p. 683.)

No; according to Mr. Watson, and according to the Scriptures, there was no forming at all of a Church, or churches. "The Church continued the same," Watson says. Its model was simply itself.

257. "Ordination of elders or presbyters is also from the Jews." (*Inst.*, p. 684.)

No; not from the Jews, but in the same Church — not another. "Such was the model which the apostles followed in providing for the future regulation of the churches they had raised up." But if the Church merely continued the same, then they raised up none.

258. "This change was no other than the abro-

gation of the *Church state* of the Jews which had continued for so many ages." (*Dict.*, p. 351.)

Then the Church did not merely continue the same, but one came to an end, and a new and different one began.

259. "Since the gospel, the true religion is not confined to any one nation or country, as heretofore." (*Dict.*, p. 425.)

And yet nothing is better known than that it never was so confined in any way, or in any sense.

260. The Epistle to the Hebrews "was written to those Christians of Judea who had been converted to the gospel from Judaism." (*Dict.*, p. 468.)

How could a man be converted to the same religion he had always held? How could a Jew, who steadfastly maintained his ancient faith, and in so doing received Christ in the person of Jesus, at the earliest period practicable, be said to be converted to some other religion?

261. "The Jewish religion is, perhaps, more a religion of minute and trifling rites and ceremonies than even the Roman Catholic religion." (*Dict.*, p. 570.)

That is strictly true exactly as stated. The Jewish religion that now is. But this modern Jewish religion is a wholly different thing from the religion formerly called Jewish, from which these modern Jews apostatized. But this is not the sense in which the Dictionary is understood.

262. "The conversion of Cornelius, the first Gentile convert." (*Dict.*, p. 794.)

Esther viii. 17, and many other historic passages, state very differently.

263. "The first Gentile church was now established at Antioch." (*Ibid.*)

Not if the Church continued the very same.

"In this manner Paul prepared the overthrow of two religions, that of his ancestors, and that of the heathen." (*Dict.*, p. 789.)

This is precisely the charge brought against Paul, in his day, after his celebrated journey to Damascus, by all his enemies, in and out of the Church; but which he himself stoutly denied everywhere, affirming on all occasions that he was strictly maintaining the religion of his ancestors. And it is unquestionable that this he did to the day of his death.

264. "We have already quoted the testimonies of Tacitus and Suetonius to the existence of Jesus Christ, the founder of the Christian religion." (*Methodist Catechism*, No. 3, p. 45.)

It is very true that Tacitus and Suetonius regarded Jesus Christ as the founder of the Christian religion. And also the Sanhedrim, and all the apostatizing Jews, charged the same thing against him. But it is strange a Christian catechism should do so, since all the apostles, of whom we know anything, stoutly repelled the charge on all occasions. If Jesus Christ was the founder of the Christian religion, then modern Judaism must be true.

265. "The design of the Christian dispensation was clearly to develop a perfectly different truth; namely, that God had established an immutable economy of grace; that salvation should be a free gift, and all its privileges and blessings conferred as a gratuity; and besides, that faith alone should be the condition." (*Dixon's Meth.*, p. 41.)

And so we have in the New Testament a perfectly different truth from that taught in the Old! What stuff!

266. Bishop Seabury's sermon on *Christian Unity*, (Prot. Epis. Tract, No. 44), assumes in many places that the Christian Church had no existence, in any sense, prior to the time of the apostles. It was then "first organized;" and just so it must continue. It is not "confined to one nation, as the Jewish Church was, but admits for its members, people of all countries and nations."

How errors so glaring could be written and insisted on so plainly by a scholar, and remain year after year among the standards of a Church, is difficult to conceive. And how long the Church is to be hampered and damaged by such teachings is a far more important question.

267. Under the word "Church," the *New Am. Cyclopædia* says: "In the Scriptures the name is also given to the body of Jewish believers; the Jewish Church being composed of all those who followed the law of Moses. The Christian Church is the society of those who profess the religion of Jesus Christ."

But there is no religion of Jesus Christ different from that written in the Old Testament. What is it? Where is it? What is one or more of its tenets? It is a myth. Those who truly follow the law of Moses, the Old Testament, are Christians.

268. *Covel's Bible Dictionary*, art. "Jews," says, speaking of the distresses resulting from the destruction of Jerusalem: "It is hardly possible to consider the nature of their sufferings, and not conclude their own imprecation to be signally fulfilled upon them: 'His blood be upon us and our children.' Matt. xxvii. 25."

The historic difficulties with the above are, first,

that the Jews, as a whole, had no concern in this war with Rome. The revolt consisted only in the anti-Christian portion of the Judean Jews, about forty years after the separation. Secondly, they made no such imprecation. That was made by an irresponsible handful of officials and rabble at the governor's door, perhaps not twenty or fifty in number; certainly very few. The account shows it to have been impossible there could have been but a few. The people knew nothing of it. None but the repudiating party ever even sanctioned the crucifixion.

269. "When Jerusalem was entirely destroyed, and the descendants of Abraham were rooted out of the land," etc. (*McIlvaine's Evid.*, p. 114.)

Such a thing never happened. Nothing like it. The persons here called the descendants of Abraham were not rooted out of the land. On the contrary, "three thousand," "five thousand," "multitudes," "great multitudes," often repeated, — whole cities, countries, "myriads" of them, afterwards called Christians, were not in the revolt of Jerusalem, were never rooted out of the land, only as in common with other Christians they suffered occasional persecutions. How wildly men write!

270. On page 155, Bishop McIlvaine says that all the Jews and heathen were enemies of the Gospel.

No; some of these very Jews, exclusively and alone, composed the entire Church in connection with the apostles, for about ten years after the crucifixion, and remained firm.

271. Page 75, the Bishop says: "It is worthy of distinct remark, that when the books of the New Testament are quoted or alluded to by those whose testimony has been adduced, *they are treated with*

supreme regard as possessing an authority belonging to no other books, and as conclusive in questions of religion."

Then such persons were not intelligent Christians. If they had been they would attach the same importance to the books of the Old Testament.

272. Bishop McIlvaine's Christianity is throughout a system of faith and practice, wholly new to mankind. Frequently it is called a new religion, a perfect novelty to mankind, with many such expressions. I do not remember an intimation in his book, that there is a principle of religion or ethics that is common to both the Old and New Testaments. Such Christianity is spurious and ought not to be received. But it is the only theory that can possibly accord with the Bishop's High Church notions of ministerial authority. Let the Old and New Testaments be put together, and form one system of salvation, regarding the Church as a religious brotherhood common to both, and the Bishop's Church system could not possibly survive it.

273. Dr. Isaac Watts' *Rational Foundation of a Christian Church* was published in London, in 1747. And though, in my judgment, one of the very best expositions of ecclesiastical science in our language, it is long since out of print. It is, however, not entirely free from the hamperings of older and contemporary divines. On page 6, he says we are to look in the New Testament for "what new doctrines God has there proposed to our faith, and what new duties to our practice."

And yet it contains neither new faith nor duties. This truth is inculcated all through the book, with this and a few other unfortunate exceptions.

274. "The Jews have lost their peculiar position in the favor of God, and are now wanderers from the land which is specially their own." (*Melville's Sermons*, vol. ii. p. 298.)

By the Jews is understood the people so known and denominated at and before the coming of Christ. Surely they have not lost the favor of God; only that portion of them, perhaps less than half, who apostatized. The other half have since, — they and their posterity, — been called Christians. As to the land of Palestine being specially their own, I inquire, Whose own? Which half is meant?

275. "Life and immortality had not been brought to light by the gospel." That is, at the period of Ezekiel's vision of dry bones. (Same page.)

Yes it had. I suppose this expression means the bringing of salvation to the world by Christ. And was not that preached by Ezekiel?

276. Gieseler's Church History, one of the most eminent extant, has the comprehensive title of *A Text Book of Church History*. He teaches as plainly and clearly as words can teach, that our Saviour, in the days of his manhood, announced and taught a system of religion, the character, principles, and doctrines of which were wholly new to mankind. Its rudiments, its laws, its faith, its conditions of salvation and means of salvation, were wholly an invention of his own, and now for the first time were announced to mankind. At page 27, volume i., he enumerates the sources of Church History. These are, "1st, the Scriptures of the New Testament. 2d, Ecclesiastical Histories. 3d, All the Christian writers of this period. 4th, The acts of the martyrs. 5th, Certain passages of writers not Christian, namely, Josephus, etc."

The Scriptures of the Old Testament not only do not contain any Church History, but are not at all useful as a source of information on the subject! This is the plain and unequivocal teaching of Dr. Gieseler. Surely its escape from universal denunciation is attributable to the character of the author, and not to the things taught, especially these things.

277. *Gieseler's Hist.*, vol. i. p. 57, under the head of "Christianity in its infancy," makes it attack the "Jewish national religion," and attempt its overthrow. It was far more difficult to "establish Christianity among the Jews" than it could have been with any other people, they being so hampered and prejudiced with so bad a religion.

Now, the difficulty with these historic facts is, that there never were any such two religions. The Jewish national religion, meaning the written religion, and the Christianity, that fought each other so hard, were one and the same identical thing. The fighting was between other parties; between the adherents to this common religion on the one hand, and certain false and mistaken teachers of it on the other; just as it is now.

278. Vol. i. p. 77, Gieseler says, "After they had again abode for a long time in Antioch, Hebrew Christians came hither, who excited divisions in the Church, by the assertion that the recently converted Gentile Christians must also necessarily become Jewish proselytes of righteousness."

The very reverse of what took place. To become proselytes of righteousness, that is, to embrace the true religion of the Church, as it then stood in the Bible of the Church, was the very thing then, and now, necessary in all Christians. These mistaken

Hebrew Christians sought to do the very reverse of this, namely, to get the converts to depart from true, proper proselytism, and embrace some erroneous notions of righteousness, then somewhat prevalent with some persons.

279. Mr. John Wesley (Sermon No. 40, on *Christian Perfection*) teaches that the religion he now recommends was impracticable and unattainable by "all the holy men of old, who were under the Jewish dispensation."

It is a strange notion, which will not bear the test of examination a moment, based solely upon the supposition that our Saviour taught new truths and new principles. Did ever more holy men live than some of the Old Testament saints? Mr. Wesley says not. And again, the same great theologian, far the greatest of his age, very properly teaches, that holy men need no other perfection of a religious kind, than to grow in grace, as is done always, everywhere, by all truly pious or holy people. The pen that never slips is inspired.

280. Dr. George Peck, in his Introduction to Lord King's *Prim. Church*, says, "The truth is, that the details of Church government are not specifically defined in the word of God, but are left to be supplied by the wisdom of the Church. Certain general principles are laid down, under which there is room for some variety."

This has been a thousand times stated; but a thousand repetitions would not make it true. I never knew any one attempt to define what general principles were thus laid down. If there are any, they must fix its legislation, its judicature, and its execution, for these are the general principles of any government. Now which one of these, or which portion of either, is laid down in Scripture? Obviously and palpably, neither. The New Testament no more lays down any general principles for churches — legal principles of Church government is of course meant — than for the State, the family, or a school. All churches make their own laws of government.

281. "But we must not forget that the New Testament, including the Acts of the Apostles and their Epistles, does not profess to give us any minute and regular account of the formation of the Church. Unquestionably such an account may in a great degree be gathered from it — but only by a careful comparison of one part with another, and by the aid of other witnesses, whose writings throw light upon expressions which would otherwise remain obscure." (*Sewel's Hist. Early Ch.*, p. 2.)

This small book, we are told, was written "for the use of young persons." And thus it is that such teaching, page after page, is inflicted upon the tender minds of young persons, fixing upon them the baldest and most wholesale untruths in the cardinal principles of ecclesiastical science. Brethren of the Church, why not let this great fundamental error be arrested? It would dry up a thousand streams of poison which are now injuring the Church, and do much towards removing the bracings from Romanism and other false religion.

282. "The earliest opposition to the Christians arose from the Jews." (*Sewel's Hist.*, p. 6.)

Yes, and the Christians thus opposed were every one of them Jews.

283. Prof. Moses Stuart, of Andover, has given us a treatise on *Traits of History and Doctrine*,

peculiar to Christianity, previously alluded to. In this he represents that Jesus arose in the midst of his nation, an humble, modest, unpretending, but bold and intrepid religious revolutionist; that He declared for the extirpation of the religious faith and principles of mankind, and particularly for the overthrow of "the established religion of his nation." Hear him: "It was a bold undertaking to come out against the whole Jewish people, and specially the priesthood, on the subject of their religion. . . . But what did this young adventurer propose to do? Nothing less than to abolish the Mosaic ritual in the end, and entirely change the whole face of the Jewish religion. A formidable undertaking, most truly. Yet even this was not all. He proposed to teach a new religion, which should pervade not only Palestine, but the whole world." (*So. Meth. Quarterly*, July 1851, p. 329, etc.) Several other such statements could be quoted.

When balderdash and romance is labeled "Balderdash and romance," it is not likely to do much harm. But when printed in religious books, from a Christian minister, and published in a Christianlike way, the case is different. Now if any should deem these remarks erroneous, let the following plain, Biblical, historic facts determine.

1st. When Jesus became a man, He was a member of the Church, the only divinely recognized Church on earth, call it by what name you will. 2d. His Church had a written religion, which we have now, word for word. 3d. There was also in the Church a thing which has always been in it, namely, persons, teachers and others, who more or less misunderstood their written Scriptures; and so taught and believed many things which the Bible did not warrant. 4th. This written religion was divine, and therefore not only true, but immaculate. 5th. Jesus, from the time He was twelve years old, till He was led away to Calvary, approved, believed, recommended, taught, and enforced every doctrine, precept, and rule, of both morals and faith, written in the Scriptures. 6th. He did not announce, propagate, or teach any religious doctrine, principle, or rule of ethics not then and now read in the Old Testament. Nor did He change, or hint at changing, either entirely or partially, any one of them. 7th. As to the religious errors above alluded to, we are not informed as to the comparative extent of them. But, as is the case now, and has always been, they prevailed considerably. 8th. The Saviour always treated these errors as errors, not as religion. He always spoke of them as he must needs do, to speak the truth — not as the religion of the Church, nor any part thereof, but as religious errors, foisted upon the credulity of those who believed them, by ignorant or wicked men. And He exhorted men everywhere to discard, disbelieve, and abandon these errors, and cleave to the true, written religion of the Church, as it had been handed down of old. 9th. He never came out against the whole Jewish people, nor against any portion thereof, unless you would call persuading men to abandon error and do right, coming out against them. He opposed the errors as a teacher and philanthropist, because He loved the people and the Church. 10th. He never sought entirely to change the whole face of the Jewish Church and religion, nor any part thereof. Nor did He propose to teach a new religion, either in whole or in part. He was no more a new teacher than all true teachers are such. His lessons were new to those unacquainted with them. 11th. Nevertheless, the Saviour discontinued the use of such symbolical modes of teaching religious doctrine, as in their nature pertained to that period of the Church before the incarnation. These particular parts of the Mosaic ritual necessarily and unavoidably abated, not however because the Saviour abolished anything, but merely because He was the Saviour incarnate. But no other portions of the then existing ritual of the Church went out of use, in that age, so far as we know, save such unimportant modifications as convenience suggested, and as have been seen at other times. 12th. I have vindicated the epithet "Balderdash and romance," which I applied to Professor Stuart's "Peculiarities of Christianity," seldom as such an accusation ought to be made. His peculiarities, so far as here noticed, are imaginary, fanciful, and not real. The Saviour was precisely what, with his own assent, He was recognized and announced to be, a teacher sent from God; and no more of a revolutionist or innovator than any minister now might be so regarded. I appeal to the Scriptures, and the common intelligence of all men.

284. "A little band indeed it was, which stood opposed to the mass of their own nation." (*Prof. Stuart*, p. 332.)

Not at all; all the history is widely different. It is plain and unmistakable, that on the death of Jesus, at the first reasonable opportunities to do so, and having never expressed themselves differently, so far as we know, thousands upon thousands, multitudes upon multitudes, whole cities here and whole regions of people there, gave in their adhesion to and recognition of Jesus, the crucified, as the Christ they had always worshipped in the most open, public, and solemn manner. And more too: These very same Jews, of their own nation, who thus declared for Jesus, so soon as reasonable information and opportunity warranted them in doing so, and who never did oppose Him in any way, so far as we learn, constituted the entire apostolic Church — that is, the whole Church — apostles and all, up to a period about ten years or more after the ascension, when the Church most probably counted millions. It was not a little band. Moreover there was no time within hundreds of years of that period when the true, divinely-recognized Church, most of them solidly pious so far as we know, did not amount to hundreds of thousands, if not to millions, with a regular ministry, almost all over the then known world. Nevertheless there was a little band, in that day, and a very important one, but not such a one as Professor Stuart imagines. In the nature of things, not many persons could, at the very first, have any reliable assurance that Jesus was Christ. Demonstration of this fact must, at the first, rest on ocular and other sensible testimony, and so must be confined to a few. All other men, then and now, must depend upon their testimony and other subsidiary evidence for the truth of this fact. But among the millions who received this testimony from the apostles there were none, or none of note, who stood opposed to them; much less were they opposed by the whole people. Of the millions so receiving this testimony, we are warranted in believing that they received it gladly. At the same time, those who rejected the testimony — perhaps one half the Church nearly, rejected it — they and they only were opposers of Jesus.

285. " A universal religion! The very idea would have been deemed an absurdity by them." (*Ibid.* p. 334.)

So far from there being truth in this remark, it is well known that their openly confessed, written, and well understood religion was universal — open to everybody — in the broadest and most unlimited sense. Every prophet had so declared it; and so far as we know, every teacher had so taught it. And every minister now so preaches it out of the Old Testament declarations of it. Spirits of David, of Isaiah, of Ezekiel, and your noble and inspired associates, be vindicated from such miserable blots upon your bright escutcheon! Let any man open the Bible now and see what it teaches on this point! Does not everybody know that the Old Testament now contains a universal religion?

286. " As a scheme of general benevolence toward universal man, what is there on earth, or ever was, which bears any comparison with the gospel? Certainly nothing. All the rest is but chaff when compared with this wheat." (*Ibid.* p. 335.)

By gospel he explains himself to mean the New Testament. Well, Professor Stuart may deny inspiration to the Old Testament, and so raise that question; but he cannot deny its fact, nor its chronological antiquity to the New. And that its pages do, everywhere, contain a scheme of general benevolence toward universal man, is as palpable as the existence of the book.

287. "The deluded Jews, having crucified the

Lord of glory, and imprecated 'his blood on their own heads and those of their children,' have met with a terrible retribution." (*Ibid.* p. 336.)

The history is that the Lord was crucified, not by the Jews, but by a few, perhaps not fifty or a hundred. Its millions could not have known of it till afterwards. And as to the imprecation, the account is plain that it was the reckless, unauthorized, and hasty exclamation of the leaders of a little rabble and perhaps a few officials. Scarcely a hundred persons or so could have even heard it.

288. Chateaubriand, in his *Genius of Christianity*, proceeds throughout upon the ground that Christianity, in every aspect in which it may be viewed, began to exist in the lifetime of Jesus. Like many other writers, he assumes everywhere, as a matter well understood, that the religion known as Christianity, and introduced by Jesus Christ, is totally new to mankind in every principle and feature it has. This work was first published in 1802, and is regarded as the masterpiece of the great literary friend of Napoleon. To me it seems strange it did not die still-born under the disregard of Christendom. Hear him a moment: "That Jesus Christ should have chosen for the head of his Church the very man among his disciples who had denied Him, appears to us a most sublime and affecting mystery. The whole spirit of Christianity is unfolded in this circumstance." Now, upon supposition that Jesus Christ made a new Church, a supposition upon which Romanism rests solely, and is thoughtlessly and unfortunately conceded by many Protestants, then it is a little strange that He should have chosen this particular man for its head, if He did so. But suppose no Church at all was formed

by Christ or anybody else, then what about the mysterious peculiarities of Peter's headship? The mysteries of Romanism are the very mysteries of this new Church, and the vitals of Romanism are this very untruth. Strange that Protestants continue to supply those vitals with the breath of life!

289. The controversy about baptismal regeneration is stated in a nutshell by Bishop Philpotts, Bishop of Exeter, in a charge to his diocese in 1842, in which he condemns the Oxford Tract theology, but gives it credit for some things. "They have given the sacraments their due place in the scheme of our holy religion, as contrasted with those who would make them little else than bare signs and symbols, instead of channels of regeneration and sanctifying grace."

Those who regard the sacraments themselves, considered apart from the mere modes of administering them, as new laws of religion, introduced now for the first time, by way of divine legislation, find hard work in attempting to steer clear of at least thus much of baptismal regeneration. New ceremonies, new modes of teaching, are one thing, but new principles of worship imply a new relation between the divine and the human. It is remarkable men do not see that it is not the sacrament itself, the obligation or duty, that is new, but the mode of performing it.

290. I have before me a tract written by the Rev. Leroy M. Lee, D. D., of Virginia, on the *Rite of Confirmation.* I look to see what the argument is, and find it to be, whether confirmation is or is not "a positive institution of the gospel;" that is, whether it belongs to "the organization of the Church as established by Christ."

We have near fifty pages of argument on that

question. Would it not have been well, first, to inquire whether there was ever such a first organization of the Church at all, as is here supposed? And seeing there was not, and so this argument is but an inquiry into something that never happened, it is therefore a very harmless one.

291. Bellarmine's argument about *The True Church* is merely an inquiry whether Jesus Christ, in "forming the Church originally," did or did not establish in it this or that particular law, either of religion or government.

But suppose the Saviour did not form the Church originally, by positive legislation, at all; what then?

292. Soame Jenyns was in his day, the last century, a writer of no ordinary merit. He was a barrister at law, a man of letters, of high cultivation, logical training, and of course very exact in the use of language. One of his best works, by reputation, was on the *Internal Evidences of the Christian Religion.* This essay, first published in England and then in this country, is by some rated among the religious classics of the day. It is one of the official publications of the American Tract Society, and is complimented as a work of great argumentation and strength by Dr. Paley and others. His argument is thrown into three logical propositions, as follows:

"First. There is a book entitled the New Testament.

"Second. That from this book may be extracted a system of religion entirely new, both with regard to the object and the doctrines, not only infinitely superior to, but totally unlike everything which had ever before entered into the mind of man."

In his argument on this second proposition he declares it to be incontrovertibly true. I believe it to be incontrovertibly, and also palpably, false. I hold it to be as well known as any historic fact ever was known, that at and before the making of the New Testament there was in existence another book, which we now call the Old Testament; that this book did then and does now contain a system of religion, the object and the doctrines of which are, at least somewhat, like those of the New; and that there are some things common to both. Nay, I affirm further, that at least some of the doctrines of religion found in the one are found in the other. I believe, for instance, that in the Old Testament are found the doctrines of one God, of human sin, of a divine government, of salvation, and several other things, which are also found in the New. I remember that in a portion of the Old Testament called Exodus, and at the 20th chapter thereof, there are seen no less than ten distinct religious precepts, which go, at least somewhat, to make up the system of religion which Mr. Jenyns extracts from the New Testament. Now if the decalogue, or any portion thereof, has regard to either the object or the doctrines, or any of them, which enter into the system of religion found in the New Testament, then the latter is not entirely new, nor infinitely superior to, nor totally unlike everything which had ever before entered into the mind of man. The simple truth is, that this whole proposition of Mr. Jenyns' is wildly and recklessly erroneous. It is utterly defenseless at every point, with no pretense to truth about it! A higher or more untrue impeachment of the Old Testament was never written. And yet there it remains, in our Church books, reprinted over and over again, for more than a hundred years.

Its lesson of wholesale untruth has poisoned the mind of families and Sunday-schools by the thousand!

293. Dr. Bushnell, in his most excellent treatise on *Christian Nurture*, says the congregation to which Peter preached on the day of Pentecost were sinners.

Of this there is not the slightest historic proof, and it is in the highest degree improbable, while its injury to the Church is, that it inculcates the doctrine that the Church and religion previously existing had become extinct, and that this was a beginning *de novo* to build up a new Church and new religion.

I know of no milder expressions that the language admits of than to say that Mr. Bushnell's argument, or his assertions rather, are absurd and ridiculous. I use the mildest language I can find, that is true. The conclusion that thousands of professing Christians, met for public worship, holding a true faith, about whose piety not an unfavorable word is uttered, are sinners, wholesale, because religious ignorance and irregularity are stated of others, is absurd; and it is more, it is ridiculous. The argument, however, might be made a little more ridiculous by charging those people that they did not know that Christ and Jesus were identical. Neither did Noah, Abraham, Samuel, or Daniel. Dr. Bushnell himself did not know it until somebody told him.

294. It is quite too much for Mr. Watson to call Cornelius "the first Gentile convert."

Both he and everybody else teaches, and the Old Testament everywhere proves, that he was not. Converts from without were common always. Countless thousands preceded Cornelius. The peculiarity in his case was, not that he was converted from without, but that Peter went out after him. Previously, preaching was generally confined to the Church, and outsiders were expected to come in of their own accord. In this instance Peter, on purpose, went out from among the Church to preach to outsiders. It was the first missionary or aggressive act of the Church, of a notable and prominent character.

295. Bishop H. U. Onderdonk, in official Tract No. 47, proves, as he claims, that what he calls Episcopacy must form the substance of the government of the Christian Church, because the Saviour so organized the Church at first.

Without stopping to inquire whether the Saviour ever organized, set up, or established anew a Church at all, or not, it is taken for granted, and the argument of the tract is built upon it. And those who concede that ground to him would, in my judgment, find it difficult to meet all his arguments.

296. "Christianity is that system of religion of which Christ is the founder." (*New Am. Cyclopædia.*)

An essay of fifteen pages in this work opens with this language. Throughout it is plainly taught that the system of religion, as a whole and in detail, which we call Christianity, in its doctrines, faith, worship, all, is a new thing, for the first time introduced to mankind by our Saviour eighteen hundred years ago. It was a "new-born heavenly life." Human religion was brought to light "through the apostles." It was "the new religion." Many other expressions and the entire drift of teaching show that no feature of this new system was ever known before. The difficulty with the essay is that it is fundamentally erroneous. The New Testament is an utter stranger to any new religion, or new doctrines. The

Christianity which it teaches is made up wholly of the faith and precepts of Moses and the prophets, and is but an elaboration of them.

297. *Milman's History of Christianity* is an English work of much classical renown. It is here assumed, without a word of explanation, that Christianity, its faith, doctrines, morals, and precepts, its very being, in every aspect in which it can be viewed, began absolutely to exist in the world, as a totally new thing, in the time of the apostles. Its specific teachings to this effect are numerous. Nor does the book contain a distinct remark, that I remember, to relieve it from such wholesale violation of the history of Christianity as seems apparent. The surprising blunder here, and with many others at this point is, that that which was new in the Church did not relate to either doctrines, principles, or moral teachings, but to modes of teaching, with of course better teachers and better teachings. And this improvement in both teachers and teachings was consequent on the sensible appearance and visibility of such of the atoning acts of the Saviour as were visible. Now they are visible and historic; before they were only adumbrant; though Christ was virtually slain from the foundation of the world.

298. "As Rome had united the whole Western world into one, ... so Christianity was the first religion which aimed at a universal and permanent moral conquest." (*Milman*, p. 22.)

Yes, but this was not the new, mythical Christianity of the recent formation you speak of, but the old Christianity of Abel and Moses.

299. Tacitus says, "The worship of the Jews is purely mental."

This is not strange, so far as I know, for I believe he is not regarded a very safe Christian teacher. But it is strange that Mr. Milman should endorse the statement, and then pass on as smoothly as if nothing had happened. It is strange that such wholesale onslaughts upon the Old Testament should pass for a single day without the promptest denunciation from the religious press. As to truth, everybody must know, on a moment's reflection, that it possesses not a shadow of it. I would gladly say less, but how can I?

300. Fairbairn, in his *Typology*, argues at length, "why it is no longer proper to keep the symbolical institutes connected with the law," and remarks, "It is true that no express authoritative injunction was given at first, for the discontinuance of these services."

At first? No, nor at last, nor ever. They discontinued from the necessity of the thing, just as the date of a year discontinues.

301. Two separate and distinct churches, the Jewish and Christian, with their separate and distinct religions, are in numerous places, in Fairbairn's *Typology*, as plainly set forth as language can state facts. The entire drift of teaching is, that the relation between the two religions is merely typical and historic; but as to religious doctrines, they are as wide as the poles, and irreconcilably hostile. I know of nothing ever written, better calculated to degrade the Old Testament Scriptures. And yet there it lies, in two goodly sized octavo volumes, and counted good Christian reading.

302. Mr. John Wesley (*Notes*, on Acts xxviii. 15) says, "It is remarkable that there is no certain account by whom Christianity was planted in Rome.

Probably some inhabitants of that city were at Jerusalem on the day of Pentecost, and being converted themselves, carried the gospel thither at their return."

I see nothing more remarkable about Rome, in this respect, than a hundred other places where the early Christian history has faded away. It is certain that Christianity, not indeed called by that name, but the same religion afterwards called Christianity, existed in Rome long before the death or birth of Jesus Christ. The Church in Rome began to be called by the name of Christian, not immediately after the day of Pentecost, but some time, we do not know how long, after it began to be so called at Antioch. As to the assumed necessity of these persons from Rome, at Pentecost, being converted then, it is as gratuitous as to suppose the same thing in regard to any other Church members, then or now, of whose personal piety we have no information. No doubt the return of their brethren from Pentecost gave those at home the first certain definitive proof of the incarnation and crucifixion of Christ. Nor have we any reason to doubt but the religious people in that city gladly and fully received this information, and acted upon it at the first practicable moment. But that is a very different thing from planting a Church.

303. There are few authors for whom I have higher respect than Archbishop Whately. And yet I think some of his views are fundamentally defective. Some of these errors, pointed out, cannot be mistaken. His debates with the Oxford Tract men, running through much of his later writings, relate entirely to the question how this new Church, new kingdom, was framed, and precisely what religious and ecclesiasti-

cal doctrines and laws were put into it. They seem not to have stopped to inquire whether those things were done at all or not. On "The Constitution of the Church," it is very plainly and carefully taught, that Jesus Christ formed a society, a personal community, consisting of separate individual men and women, beginning with twelve men, and increasing it by taking in others from among Jews and Gentiles, whoever would consent to become religious. For this social brotherhood He prescribed a government, with, of course, particular laws, and which was to be of perpetual continuance. (See *Kingdom of Christ*, p. 22, etc.)

Now, in the face of all this, I think it is so plain as not to admit of a doubt, when one reflects a moment, that neither the Saviour nor others acting under Him, established, organized, or set up any society, or personal community, or Church, at that or any other time. Jesus was Himself a member of the Church, and recognized all other members, all Jews, making no difference among them, as his brethren. He corrected their errors, instructing, admonishing, and reproving those He met with who needed such teachings and admonitions; but as to any special society beginning in a nucleus of a few persons, such an idea is not hinted at in Scripture. He had twelve special disciples for a special purpose, but quite a different one from that supposed by the Archbishop. The special office of the apostles, and reason for their separation or distinction from other Church members, was not to organize a Church, for this they did not do; but that they should form in themselves an intensified focal centre of faith in the personal Christship of the man Jesus; that this fact, not having anything to do with doctrines or Church rules, might be rationally and authoritatively spread and diffused throughout the Church. This was the peculiar business of the apostles. They neither made a new Church nor preached a new religion.

304. "The Jews expected a Christ who should be a heaven-sent king of the Jews." (*Kingdom of Christ*, p. 17.)

It is indeed remarkable that such a writer should make so prominent an allusion to this oft-repeated assertion that the Jews looked for a temporal Saviour. It is quite a possible thing that there may have been some persons then, as now, who may have had very erroneous notions about the Saviour. If there were any such persons, we know that such belief was contrary to their religion, for we can refer to that *verbatim* any moment. But what is the evidence of any such belief among the Jews? Next to none. There is a very incidental remark in John vi. 15, that some few persons just then, in the excitement of the moment, would have made Him a king. But that such a belief existed to any considerable extent, or amounted to anything, there is not the slightest evidence.

305. "It appears highly probable, I might say morally certain, that wherever a Jewish synagogue existed, that was brought, the whole or the chief part of it, to embrace the gospel, the apostles did not there so much *form* a Church (or congregation: *ecclesia*) as *make an existing congregation Christian*, by introducing the Christian sacraments and worship, and establishing whatever regulations were requisite for the newly adopted faith; leaving the machinery (if I may so speak) of government unchanged; the

rulers of synagogues, elders, and other officers, (whether spiritual, or ecclesiastical, or both) being already provided in the existing institutions. And it is likely that several of the earliest Christian churches did originate in this way; that is, that they were *converted synagogues*, which became Christian churches as soon as the members, or the main part of the members, acknowledged Jesus as Messiah." (*Whately's Kingdom of Christ*, p. 29.)

Coming from such a man, this is most remarkable. I inquire, when a synagogue was thus brought to embrace the gospel, what did any of them embrace? what doctrine, tenet, rule of Church or of life, that they had not always embraced? They embraced nothing. And worship. What new worship was introduced? None. And establishing whatever regulations were requisite for the newly adopted faith. What were those regulations? and what the newly adopted faith? As to the likelihood that several of the earliest Christian churches originated in this way, it is certain that no Christian churches originated at all in that way, in any other sense than they do now. It is equally certain, however, that there was a peculiarity in one vitally important thing in the Church, just at that period, that never could occur at any other. It became necessary for the Church to recognize Jesus as Christ. And this, as any one may see in a moment, necessitated a change in the outward mode of taking the sacrament. That is all there was of it. The synagogues, *i. e.*, the churches, that recognized that fact were true churches. Those that refused were not.

306. George Benson's *First Planting of the Christian Religion* says, "It was almost fifteen hundred

years before this, and on this very day of the year, that the law was given by God from *Mount Sinai*, in the sight and hearing of all Israel, ... and now the new law of grace is given to the apostles."

This lesson, with others quite as bad, is published by the Methodist Sunday-school Union, in a Sunday-school book called "Lives of the Apostles." The title of the book is enough to condemn it. And thus it is that our children suffer.

307. Whately's *Errors of Romanism*, p. 13, says, "In treating of all these points, I shall adhere to the plan hitherto pursued, namely, of contemplating the errors of the Romanists, not with a view to our own justification in withdrawing from their communion."

What does he mean by withdrawing from their communion? These are important words, involving a vital principle. It is to be feared that Protestantism is not well understood by Protestants. In what sense did Protestants withdraw from anybody's communion? Did Protestants withdraw from the Church and set up another Church? Most assuredly I do not so understand it. I understand that Protestants merely protested and turned away from certain practices and doctrines in the Church which they claimed had been surreptitiously foisted upon the Church by certain officers thereof, contrary to the Scriptures, they themselves remaining all the while in the Church, but following Scriptural doctrines and practices. Protestants, most assuredly, did not protest against the Church, but against certain unlawful things in it. This they did, most certainly, not for the purpose of going out, but in order that they might rightfully remain in. The Reformation was a reformation of the Church; and if Papists would not reform and discontinue their unlawful practices, the Protestants could not help it, and were not responsible.

308. The American Bible Society, heading of 1 Cor. x., says, "The sacraments of the Jews are types of ours."

It is in the first place not only a comment, but a very doubtful one, to say the least, I think, to suppose that the first seven verses of this chapter treat of sacraments at all. And secondly, it is impossible there can be any sacraments of the Jews different from ours. The sacraments of religion pertain to religion wholly, solidly, and not to different states and conditions of the Church.

309. *Elliott on Romanism*, two octavo volumes, concedes wholesale, by necessary implication, that the errors he refutes might be true; *i. e.*, he argues the main question of history as to whether the Saviour, in making the Church, incorporated into it this, that, or the other feature. Thus the issue he accepts does not admit of demonstration, because questions of old historic detail never can be settled. His admission that Jesus Christ formed the Church at all is fatal to his whole argument.

310. And so we read, "There could be no other design in writing the books of the New Testament than to preserve the memory of Christ's history and doctrines." (Vol. i. p. 45.)

This would be a legitimate conclusion upon the hypothesis that it is a divine announcement of a new system of doctrines, establishing a new Church. But suppose it does neither of these things; then where is this design?

311. "It is also said, that 'the books of the New

Testament were not written till long after the establishment of Scripture, and therefore Christians had not the Bible for their directory and rule.' But the binding obligation of the Old Testament remained till the crucifixion; and in the interval the Church was favored with the personal presence of the apostles, whose living voice supplied a rule of faith of equal authority with that of Christ." (Page 57.)

Will the reader pause here a little. Right here, not only Dr. Elliott, but I know not how many others, by admitting the Romish excision of Old Testament authority, and the necessary supplying of that of the new Church in its stead, concede all the ground asked for, and all the ground Romanists could need or have, on which to build the doctrine of Church supremacy and infallibility. And all this is done at the expense of the plainest historic truth! If the binding obligation of the Old Testament remained till the crucifixion, and then for near two hundred years, or for any time, the Church had no written guide, then it is for Protestants to show how and when this necessary Church power was removed. But there never was any such interregnum at all. If the Old Testament authority remained till the crucifixion, in what has it since rested? This interval, conceded by such writers as Dr. Elliott, furnishes Romanists the entire ground they stand upon in regard to Church power. Protestant writers must learn better than this.

The Old Testament remained in force till the resurrection; and of course, the meaning is, no longer. Who repealed the Old Testament? and how came the repeal to take effect just at that time? If this was so, it was physically impossible the whole Church, spread as it was over the known world, with no facilities of travel could be informed of it under several years. And for the same reason it was impossible the apostles could supply the Church by their living voice with Scripture direction. Twelve men could see but a small portion of the Church.

Dr. Elliott, in conceding the new Church, gives up to the Romanist everything he could desire. We must maintain the truth at this important point, and let Romanism go down. We have upheld it long enough.

312. "To this we reply, that we find Christ and his apostles continually referring to the written word of God; and though they declared many truths not contained in the Old Testament, in general they only enlarged upon, and more fully, what had been formerly written." (Page 83.)

And yet it is plain there is not such a new truth in the New Testament.

313. *Lives of the Apostles*, a Methodist Sunday-school book (New York: Lane and Scott), teaches children and youths on this wise, page 11: "And how strange, in the view of human wisdom, that such instruments should be employed in establishing a new faith."

This is most remarkable — it is surprising. If the author of this book were asked what new faith or doctrines were there announced, on a moment's reflection he would be obliged to reply, There were none. And yet there the statement stands, year after year, to the great injury of multiplied thousands.

314. "Matthew, before his conversion, was a publican or tax gatherer under the Romans." (Page 94.)

This is a naked assumption, without a particle of testimony or even probability to support it. When was he converted? The supposition of some that the Saviour selected irreligious men exclusively for the peculiar work of the apostleship, since there is not a hint to that effect in Scripture, is in the highest degree unreasonable. Most assuredly such a thing could not be believed, but on the plainest Scripture testimony.

"Among those who were converted were Timothy's parents, who received and entertained the apostles in their own house." (Page 206.)

The Scripture account is widely different. It says they were already pious; that they, as well as Timothy himself, had become converted long before the time here alluded to, through the instrumentality of the Old Testament. We are here told that the Old Testament, without a personal knowledge of Jesus or the apostles, was sufficient to make one wise unto salvation.

315. Bishop Marvin, on *Romanism*, a most superior treatise on ecclesiastical science, p. 79, says, "Eleven men, without prestige, without resources, ignorant and despised, on a mountain of Galilee, received orders to make conquest of the world!"

Just exactly in the same sense that Bishop Marvin received orders, in Missouri, to do the very same thing, and in no other sense. The instructions given to the apostles, as mentioned in the last of Matthew, were in no proper sense a commission. The same authority was abundantly possessed and considerably exercised before, hundreds and even thousands of years before. It was not a commission personal to the apostles themselves; for they had the same authority before. It was such instructions to ministers as might be properly given at any time, but were peculiarly useful and appropriate just then, a brief notice or outline of which is recorded by the Apostle. The eleven men were commissioned to inform and certify and prove to the Church then existing, and to the world, by their personal knowledge, that Jesus was Christ, the well-known Christ of the Church. That was their commission; and, vitally important and signally necessary as it was, it was all that was peculiar in their ministry. As to doctrines, they were to preach those of the Bible, then, before, and now preached by all true ministers. The certain information is, that thousands upon thousands, and myriads of the Church received their testimony about Jesus gladly, and it is likely that these embraced a full half or more of the Church in that age. The other half, refusing to acknowledge Christ in Jesus, apostatized.

316. Rabbi Raphall, in his *Post-Biblical History of the Jews* (Appleton, 1866, vol. ii. p. 373), says, "It was during the administration of Pontius Pilate that the events related in the historic books of the Christian Scriptures are said to have occurred; and it was from before his tribunal that the founder of the Christian faith was led forth to execution. We do not feel called upon to enter into this subject, for at its origin and during its infancy, Christianity has no claim on the attention of the Jewish historian."

This brings out the gist and vital point of our controversy with modern Jews. If Jesus was the founder of the Christian faith, a religious faith new to the Jewish Scriptures, which had then and there its origin and its infancy, then it seems to me the modern Jew cannot be jostled from his position. He claims validity for his faith only on the ground of its identity with the acknowledged Scriptures, and that Christianity is new; and if this is so, then, I ask, on what ground can Christianity be defended?

317. "And thenceforward (after the Babylonian captivity) until the present day, the descendants of Jacob are called Jews." (*Union Bib. Dictionary*, art. "Jew.")

No, the many multitudes, thousands, and myriads of them who acknowledged Jesus as Christ, were called Christians first at Antioch, and their descendants have been so called ever since.

318. Dr. Hales says, "All the legal dispensation was originally designed to be superseded by the new and better covenant of the Christian dispensation."

If the Doctor had undertaken to explain precisely what he meant by legal dispensation, he would have discerned his error.

319. Schöttgen says the proposition of the Epistle to the Hebrews is this: "*Jesus of Nazareth is the true God.* And in order to convince the Jews of this proposition, the Apostle urges but three arguments: 1st, Christ is superior to *angels*; 2d, He is superior to Moses; 3d, He is superior to Aaron."

Then the Apostle was a poor logician. Proof of these things could not prove the proposition. To prove that Christ was superior to angels, to Moses, and to Aaron, would not prove that Jesus was Christ. It would not prove anything about Jesus. No Jew before the great apostacy that occurred at this time, and out of the apostacy, ever denied or doubted the unlimited superiority of Christ. That was not the question now. The only question now was, whether

Jesus was Christ. This was stoutly affirmed and stoutly denied. It was what Paul, or whoever wrote the Epistle to the Hebrews, proves so well.

320. Dr. Lightfoot repeatedly speaks of the Church in Judea in the apostles' days as consisting mainly of "converted Jews."

How could they be converted as Jews, when they had not apostatized!

321. "*As touching the law*, he was blameless, but was an inveterate enemy to Christianity." (*Henry's Com.*)

Blameless, tried by divine revelation, and yet an inveterate enemy to Christianity. So God's law approves of inveterate enmity to Christianity!

322. Bishop Hobart says, "The Christian Church was founded by bishops, because the apostles, who were bishops, were the first preachers of the gospel and planters of the churches."

No; the prophets were preachers of the gospel and planters of, or at least ministers in, the same Church, long before.

323. Fleetwood, in his *Life of Christ*, says Paul was "converted to the Christian faith," and "from the Jewish religion."

But it would be plainer and better to say he was restored to the true faith from which he had apostatized. He was certainly converted back to the faith he nominally professed before.

324. Dr. Sherlock says, "The first promise of God made to Adam was the promise of a Saviour."

Gen. iii. 15 does not promise a Saviour; it proclaims a present Saviour then furnished. The promise referred only to the human appearance and physical or visible work.

325. "Now it was the very essence of the gospel, in the apostolic sense of that expression, — Christ died for our sins according to the Scriptures." (N. Newton, in *Brit. Pulpit.*)

Certainly; but before these historic events, it was just as much the essence of gospel truth that He would die for our sins according to the Scriptures.

326. Dr. Samuel Clarke says, "till the kingdom of Christ shall be gloriously manifested in the final destruction of the nation."

It would be hard to believe, without at least some proof, that the merciful kingdom of Christ could be gloriously manifested in the destruction of a nation.

327. On Matt. iii. 1, Mr. Jacobus says, "Baptism formerly admitted proselytes to the Jewish religion; now it admitted Jews to the gospel religion."

And yet you say there is but one religion. How are we to understand you?

328. Mr. Alex. Campbell, in commenting on Luke xix. 11–15, says, "It was impossible that the reign of Heaven could literally commence 'till Jesus was glorified,' received the promise of the Holy Spirit, was made Lord and Christ, and sat down with his Father on his throne."

Mr. Campbell was a logical debater of high order; but logic, the highest and completest, furnishes not the least assistance to a man with false facts. How does Mr. Campbell know that God could not reign on earth, through the Christship, before Jesus was glorified? Now, I undertake to say, that it is well known to all Christians, and denied by none, not even Mr. Campbell himself, that Jehovah did so reign on earth for the space of four thousand years. The entire doctrine taught by Mr. Campbell is based upon this naked assumption. The visibility of Christ's work and humiliation is intended to produce effects upon us, not to enable God to do so and so. Suppose Jesus had suffered as He did, and the thing, like many other historic facts, had not been known — it was lost to history; what purpose would it have served? None.

329. Bishop Warburton, in his *Divine Legation of Moses*, says, "When Christianity arose, though on the foundation of Judaism, it was at first received by pagan writers with complacency."

The pagan writers of that age saw, because it was apparent, that the separation of Jews and Christians, as the two parties came to be called along in the age succeeding the crucifixion, was in consequence of difference of belief about the true character of Jesus who was crucified by Pontius Pilate, the former holding Him an impostor, the latter a divine personality. They saw it as it was, a separation of former friends, now very hostile to each other as to this matter of separation. They, not believing in a divine Christhood at all, would be about as likely to extend complacency to the one as the other. But it is evidently irregular to say that Christianity arose on the foundation of Judaism. Judaism, as it existed before the days of Jesus, stood firm, and stands firm to-day. It was the new, false Judaism that arose out of, that is, branching off from, Christianity.

330. Olshausen, Acts x. 37, says, "It is not improbable that Cornelius had already heard of Christianity, and that the object of his prayers was to obtain light from above respecting this new religion."

What new religion? Can a thousand repetitions make a falsehood true?

331. *Wesleyan Catechism*, No. 3, p. 5, says, " The Christian religion is also called ' the gospel,' which signifies ' good news.' The Jewish religion is called ' the law.' "

So our children suffer.

332. Again: " The covenant under the law was made specially with the Jews; but under the gospel with both Jews and Gentiles."

So our children suffer.

333. *History of the Christian Church*, by Dr. Hare, says, " The Church was originally founded by the Spirit, which proceeded from Jesus."

Then it is indeed a new Church, with a new, and consequently a false religion.

334. The " first section " of " Ancient Church History " according to Dr. Hare, extends " from Christ to Constantine." (Page 7.)

So, before that time there being no Church, of course it had no history!

335. Lord Lyttleton on the *Conversion of Paul*, p. 142, says, " The sect he embraced was under the greatest and most universal contempt of any in the world."

Everybody knows that the sect he embraced was the regular Church of the Old Testament, the Church of Moses, of the prophets, and of this present day.

336. Mr. John Fletcher (*Checks*, vol. iii. p. 140) says, " God having *then prepared* to take the Gentiles into the covenant of peculiarity," etc.

That implies, and is understood to mean, whether Mr. Fletcher so meant it or not, that up to this period people out of the Church were not called, or required to be religious. Gentiles, those out of the Church, were not till now called to be religious!

And yet everybody knows that the Old Testament Scriptures in many places call upon all men everywhere, in the most unlimited manner, to come and be religious. Does not everybody know that salvation was always offered to all men?

337. Dr. Jenks, editor of *Comprehensive Commentary*, in a note to Preface to Acts, says, "The claim of the Gentiles to admission into the Church was disputed by the Jews."

It is remarkable a man should so write, when everybody knows it was always the law of the Church, and well understood, to take in everybody from without. Still we are bewildered with such wild remarks.

338. *Trench on Miracles*, p. 53, speaks of "a rigid monotheistic religion like the Jewish."

Monotheism is the simple religion of one deity, and is generally used to describe some of the various forms of idolatry. The term is never applied to true religion. I know of nothing ever written, better calculated to degrade the Old Testament revelation.

339. Paley (*Evidences*, p. 489) says, "A religion which now possesses the greatest part of the civilized world unquestionably sprung up at Jerusalem at this time."

On a moment's reflection no Christian can believe it. If admitted, it proves the truth of the modern Jewish religion conclusively. The simple and indisputable truth is, that the only religion that sprung up at this time was that of the denying, apostatizing Jews.

340. Again he says, "The apostles were the original preachers of the religion."

Then what religion did the prophets preach?

341. Again (page 488): "A Jewish peasant changed the religion of the world."

So far from it He always appealed to Scripture, always declaring He changed nothing; as did the apostles also. And the fact, as palpable as the existence of the New Testament, is that it contains not one new doctrine. Paley's declaration is exactly the ground of the modern Jewish religion, and the only polemical ground they claim to occupy.

342. *Knapp's Christian Theology*, p. 469, says, "Christians took the word (Church) from the Jews."

How could that be when the identical persons you call Christians are the very self-same persons formerly called Jews?

343. Dr. Reinhard (*Knapp's Theol.*, p. 339) says, "Jesus Christ taught the people especially the love of God and our neighbor in opposition to Jewish exclusiveness."

Yes, in opposition to any errors He met with, but in accordance with the Jewish religion; *i. e.*, the religion of the Church.

344. "That Jesus might be shown to be the true Messiah or Christ in opposition to the unbelief of the Jews," etc. (*Benson's Com.*, Matt. i. 1.)

But there was no such wholesale unbelief of the Jews. They divided on that question; and while the New Testament says very little about the numerical strength of the unbelieving party, it says very much about the great multitudes of the believing party. The probability is, that the believing party was the larger one. No unbelief was ever attributed to them.

345. On Luke xiv. 24, Benson says, "Many of the Jews became members of the Church of Christ."

As if there were two different churches. Becoming members of the Church of Christ was simply remaining steadfast in the Church where they were born. They continued in the Church of their fathers.

346. Benson says the book of Acts " contains a history of Christ's infant Church."

When it is palpable there never was any such infant Church.

347. Dr. Hunter, of London (*Sacred Biography*, p. 476), says, " John saw the divine origin of Christianity demonstrated by its success."

No, this demonstration was had several thousand years before John lived.

348. Dr. Stier's *Words of the Lord Jesus* tells us about " the infancy of the Church," " the gospel foundation," the " beginning," " new Church," " primitive Church," etc. On Matt. v. 17, he speaks of " the Church or congregation *hereafter to be built*."

Very strange! I hope such errors may be corrected. Let the religion of the Old Testament, call it by what name you will, be identical with the Christianity of the New, as it afterwards came to be called; let religious errors be distinguished from the religion itself; and then, let the Church continue smoothly and uninterruptedly on, without making a new one, in violation of the plain history in the case; and the great sectarian warfare as to how it was made will cease, bigotry and exclusiveness will have but little ground to stand upon, the whole Church will breathe more freely, and religion have a much fairer chance of success.

349. " Such was the constitution of the Church in its infancy, when its assemblies were neither numerous nor splendid." (*Mosheim.*)

Most of the popular error on this subject has sprung from expressions like this from leading historic writers. That the Church had no such beginning is so apparent as to need no more than a suggestion.

350. *Powell on Apostolical Succession* is an English work, written about forty or fifty years ago, and has been several times republished in this country. It is used largely as a text-book by the Methodist Episcopal churches. This last named fact is remarkable, seeing its teachings are so widely at variance with the laws and usages of these churches.

This entire essay of 350 pages assumes, as a matter not questioned, that Jesus Christ organized the Church *de novo* in every respect, and prescribed its law of government, fixing the official functions of its different classes of ministers, etc. It does not question the doctrine of apostolic succession, but only that of Episcopal succession, as claimed by High Church prelatists. This distinction is important. The former claims, in order to a valid ministry, a succession of ordinations from the apostles down; the latter, that it be confined exclusively to bishops.

Page 59: "Now, it must *clearly* appear to an unbiased mind, from Acts xx. 17–20, that the Church of Ephesus was governed by a NUMBER OF PRESBYTERS, identical with *bishops*."

Suppose it was, what does that prove about churches now? The inference intended is, that therefore Jesus Christ, in framing the Church law, gave presbyters the same powers as bishops, and so all churches must be so governed. But suppose we have no divine law on the subject, then what does it prove? It proves a historic fact of no more importance now, than the geography of Ephesus, nor so much.

Page 70: "It is remarkable that, in the constitution of the Christian ministry, and in the government of the Christian Church, our Lord seems *studiously to have avoided* introducing anything like the *priesthood of Aaron* and the *Mosaic dispensation* and ritual."

This old song of new ministry and new Church is on nearly every page of this book, in some form, and is the basis of every argument in it. Then, if it is wholly based upon a myth, might it not be well to ask, of what use is it?

351. Page 86: "Bishops and presbyters have the SAME QUALIFICATIONS. Bishops and presbyters have the SAME DUTIES. Bishops and presbyters have the *same power and authority.*"

Whether these rules are the law in Mr. Powell's church, or were when he wrote, I may not be presumed to know; but everybody knows that none of these rules have, or ever had, any sort of application to any of the Methodist churches in America. In these churches, bishop and presbyter, or elder, as they are generally called, are as distinct, both by law and usage, in qualifications, in ordinations, in duties, and in power and authority, as are class-leaders and bishops.

352. Page 88: "However, all the difference certainly appears in favor of the divine right of the superiority of presbyters over bishops."

Any sort of divine right, in these premises, of course means that Jesus Christ prescribed these things for the government of all Christian churches in all time. Then I know not where you would find a true Church. Certainly not among the Methodist churches of America. He proves vastly too much.

353. Page 299: "The New Testament lays down GENERAL *principles*, but gives NO PARTICULAR FORM of Church government in detail."

Will any man state any one of these general principles of Church government laid down in the New Testament for the entire Church? The thing is ridiculous, because it supposes and means a new Church.

354. "The people RULING the *minister*, is the SHEEP RULING the *shepherd!*" (*Ibid.*)

And yet nothing is more common in most, if not all the Christian churches around us. Several of them have an equal number of laymen with ministers in their general legislature.

355. On pages 300, 301, and many other places, we are told much about "Scriptural Episcopacy," "Scriptural Church polity," "divine right of all true ministers," etc., always meaning that these things are enacted in the Church government then framed by the Saviour for the entire Church! The book abounds, by scores and by hundreds, in such errors as these.

356. It will be noted that all Roman Catholic and High Church writers of all classes plant themselves fundamentally on the assumed formation of a new Church by the Saviour. This is of course their only pedestal. Later writers copy from older ones. So we hear Bishop Taylor, High Churchman in 1642, in *Episcopacy Asserted*, say, "Christ did institute apostles and presbyters." He then goes on to explain the precise power conferred on each, in governing the churches. How much power He thus con-

ferred upon laymen, I do not see stated. Might it not be well for those who have laymen in their Church legislatures to inquire?

357. So, Dr. Hicks (*Dignity of Epis. Order*, p. 191, London, 1707): "Bishops are appointed to succeed the apostles, and like them to stand in Christ's place and exercise his power," etc.

358. So, Dr. Hook, late vicar of Leeds, in *Two Sermons on the Church*, etc.: "Some persons seem to think that the government of the Church was essentially different in the days of the apostles from what it is now," etc.

Then we have long explanations, showing that as the Saviour first planted the Church and fixed its government, so it must ever remain!

359. All Baptistic, prelatical, and Romish High Church writers stand right here. This is obviously the only place where they can stand. But for lack of time, they could be quoted by hundreds. All High Church arguments are of course drawn from this point. A Church in the nature of a corporation, established by outside authority, under a prescribed law of government, is, and nothing else is, the essential High Church idea. This is apparent by a glance at the Romish or other High Church arguments anywhere.

360. *Scott's Bible*, Pref. to Acts, says of the apostles: "They had all the wisdom and folly, the learning and the ignorance, the religion and the irreligion of the whole world to encounter."

Such extravagance in a sober, theological book is beyond the pale of excuse. So far from being true, everybody knows on a moment's reflection, that up to the time of the death of Jesus, there was nothing like general or popular opposition to either the Saviour or the apostles in any way, or about anything. The only opposition they met with was local, slight, transitory, and numerically feeble. They all professed exactly the same religion. After that event, when the Church divided by the apostacy of those who denied Christship in Jesus, there is no pretense of opposition to the apostles, except by the apostates. Among all those millions, formerly called Jews, now called Christians, there is no pretense of opposition at any time before or after the separation. Outside, among heathen people, there was always opposition. The whole world to encounter, indeed! There was not a day in that age, that the whole Church, numbering millions, were not the fast friends of the apostles, so far as they were known to the Church.

361. Again, "The Old Testament is all types and shadows, and prophecies to be fulfilled."

And Baron Munchausen was the greatest traveller of his time.

362. *Smith's Dictionary of the Bible*, art. "Church," says: "From the gospel, then, we learn that Christ was about to establish his heavenly kingdom on earth, which was to be the substitute for the Jewish Church and kingdom, now doomed to destruction."

It is impossible such a statement can bear the least touch of sober examination. The kingdom of Christ on earth, which I suppose means the divine system of government and salvation, has, naturally and necessarily, some features since the divine incarnation different from what it could have before; but that this kingdom or system began, or was about to be established, in the days of Jesus, is preposterous. No

Christian ever believed it. It is the regular built hobgoblin of infidelity. And as to the Jewish Church, that is, the Church of God on earth, being doomed to destruction, the thought looks as impious as mythical. Let the reader be reminded that there is not an expression in Scripture that gives the least license to the supposition that the Saviour, the apostles, or anybody else, had anything against the Church, call it Jewish, then and theretofore existing. Did Jesus excommunicate Church members by the million and depose ministers by the thousand, against whose piety nothing is intimated; persons whom He never saw, who had never, or but barely, seen or heard of Him? Did He turn out of the Church pious men and women wholesale, without their knowledge, without a reason or pretense of reason? Most of the Church, or at least much of it, lived a long way from the little province of Palestine where Jesus travelled and preached; and we are asked to believe that hundreds of thousands, nay millions of people, many of whom we are obliged to believe were pious, came to learn that years ago they were all turned out of the Church! And for what? No man can assign a reason, good or bad. The supposition is recklessly extravagant and wildly fabulous, to say nothing of its high and intemperate injustice.

363. And so we have, in hundreds of places through this recently published Dictionary of Dr. Smith, the natural offshoots of this fabled new Church in such expressions as "Mother Church of Jerusalem," "Future Church," "The birthday of the Christian Church," "Infant Church," "Infant Society," "One hundred and twenty members at first," with many expressions of the sort, all calculated to mislead, and

giving direct support to the Romish High Church ideas of the Church.

364. Mr. Alex. Campbell, in setting up his exclusive system of High Church immersion, lays his cornerstone in this dual idea of the Church or kingdom of Christ. On almost every page of his *Christian System* he makes this doctrine prominent. The system under Moses was a distinct and exclusive system. It terminated, and the new kingdom was ushered in, on the day of the ascension, and at the precise period that Jesus got " out of sight." " They lived under a constitution of *law*, we under a constitution of *favor*. . . . . Under the government of the Lord Jesus there is an institution for the forgiveness of sins." (Page 180.)

This is naked mythology, without the pretense of even historic appearance.

365. Page 171, we are told, " So soon as He received the kingdom from God his Father, He poured out the blessings of his favor upon his friends ; He fulfilled all his promises to the apostles, and *forgave three thousand of his fiercest enemies.*"

When there is not the slightest historic pretense that any of them ever had the thought of opposition to Him or his Messiahship in any way.

366. " The temple was the house of God to the very close of the life of Jesus. For it was not till the Jewish ministry conspired to kill Him that He deserted it." (Page 165.)

Mr. Campbell is not the only one who has committed this blunder about the temple. He means the old Solomon's temple at Jerusalem. But in that age of the world this temple and this Jewish ministry had no connection with the Jewish Church as a whole, though no doubt it claimed to have. It was the place of festive worship of the Judean portion of the Church only. The Samaritans, ignoring it, had their temple on Mount Gerizim. And the Hellenists, supposed to be larger than both the others, ignoring it, had theirs in Heliopolis in Greece. These three portions or denominations of the Church in that age were related much as the Romanists, Methodists, and Baptists are now.

367. "Judas Iscariot was dead before the apostolic commission was given. Judas in all probability never heard of a gospel ministry. He did not live in the gospel dispensation." (*Abbey's Eccl. Constitution*, p. 299.)

This is most remarkable, since it is quoted from a book the main object of which is to repudiate this very idea of a new system of religion introduced by Jesus Christ. This very book claims to find the true ecclesiastical law in the several churches themselves, and not in any general prescribed law; and that the religion of the Church, its doctrines and morals, were always the very same since a Saviour was furnished in the days of Adam. It is strange then that a man holding such sound doctrines should be guilty of the above expression. It shows, at least, what most of us have not learned, that it is hard to get out from under the influence of early teachings. Educated to a dogma, though a fallacy as palpable as the sun, it is hard to get clear from it. This, then, no doubt is really the case with most of the authors herein quoted.[1]

[1] When this was written a few years ago, it was expected to be published anonymously; and on changing its form in this respect, I have thought it best, as well as most fair, to let it stand. On looking back twenty or twenty-five years, I find my own emancipation from the early teachings of the errors here complained of has been slow and grad-

368. Dr. Chapman, of Lexington, Ky., 1844, in *Sermons on the Church*, says: "I cannot but flatter myself that the last discourse delivered upon these words presented the most clear and invincible testimony from the primitive fathers of the divine origin of our Episcopal ministry; a ministry comprehending the three distinct orders of bishops, presbyters, and deacons."

Now, it is not pretended that any testimony is brought forward here to prove this point other than historic testimony that such was the case in the churches in and near the time of the apostles. All the High Church arguments on this question are of this character. I say all. Then upon the hypothesis that Jesus set up the Church anew and prescribed the functions of its ministry, *i. e.*, the government of the Church, historic proof of this fact would go very far, if it would not be conclusive as to the government a Church must have. But it is easily seen that this assumption is necessary to give any force at all to the testimony, however much of it there might be. The proof proves nothing without this assumption. This point is sweeping as well as vital. Take away the assumption that Jesus made a new Church and new ministry, and in all the scores and hundreds of volumes written to prove what High Churchmen call Episcopacy, there is not one word of argument or testimony, or pretense of either, on the subject.

369. The closing chapter of nine pages of *Powell on Apostolic Succession* is an attempted refutation of Dr. Hook's remark that the Church, as in the hands of Protestants, remained the same after as before the Reformation.

ual. No large stride seems to have been made at any one time. I sincerely hope and pray that others may learn more rapidly.

Some debaters think they have only to deny and denounce everything stated by an opponent. How could Protestants claim to be a Church of God on any other hypothesis? Did Luther and his associates set up a new Church? If this is Mr. Powell's notion of Church organism, then indeed not only was the Church in the hands of those Jews called Christians first in Antioch, and their successors, a new Church, but every modification of Church government makes a new Church. And then the Presbyterian Church under Calvin, the Methodist Church outwardly improved by Wesley, were new churches; the Methodists of America make a new Church every four years; and so of all other churches; and so we have a thousand new churches everywhere. And the Church of God is anything or nothing, with no identity or test of validity!

370. *Evidences of Christianity*, by Mark Hopkins, D. D., is a school book somewhat used as a textbook. The "Christianity" of which it gives evidence "was an aggressive uncompromising religion. It attacked every other form of religion whether Jewish or pagan and sought to destroy it." (Page 44.)

We are not concerned to know what some hypercritic might construe Dr. Hopkins to mean by the Jewish religion. We know what everybody else understands by that expression. The religion of the Jews at the period alluded to is not equivocal. We have it *verbatim*. What anybody then or now mistook it to be is another matter. So we teach in our schools, that Jesus and the apostles were uncompromising in their aggressive attacks upon the religion of the Old Testament! They sought to destroy it!

371. At page 66 we are told that "the religion of Christ" was "heralded by prophecy."

No; it was taught by all the prophets.

372. "We defy him to point out a single duty, even whispered by nature, which is not also inculcated in the New Testament." (Page 102.)

Why this slur upon the Old Testament?

373. "Several of the fundamental principles of Christian morality, such as if adopted would change the face of society, were original with Christ," — meaning Jesus. (Page 104.)

No man can point out one. Had Christ better morality than that which is divine? What principle of Christianity is original?

374. He says Jesus Christ had "no education." (Page 105.)

Where does he get his information?

375. At page 169 we are told this new Christianity "imposes upon man some new duties."

What ones? He cannot answer.

376. "The Jews were divided into three great sects, the Pharisees, the Sadducees, and Essenes. (Page 190.)

Such historic ignorance in a man pretending to teach is disgraceful.

377. "The New Testament contains a fair and plausible account of the origin of the Church." (Page 244.)

It is wonderful how men come to believe a thing from mere repetition. There is not the slightest allusion to such a thing. The New Testament contains an account of the human appearance of Christ in the person of Jesus. And this fact, in its very nature, necessitates some important modes of teaching the same things previously taught; a very different thing from a new Church. You might as well say the introduction of globes and telescopes originates new geography and astronomy.

378. "Eleven men, without learning, wealth, rank, or power, subverted the divinely appointed institutions of Judaism, and overturned the superstitions of ages." (Page 344.)

We are at no loss here to understand what he means by Judaism. It is the divinely appointed institutions of religion as seen in the Old Testament. Those divine appointments were subverted and demolished by Christian people! We also learn that the superstitions of ages were divinely appointed. And our youth are taught to believe it!

379. This school book, by a Protestant college president, inculcates, all through it, the clumsy idea, pernicious and hurtful as it is clumsy, that the religion of post-messianic Jews is the same, intact, as that of the Old Testament. No modern Jew could or need say more. It repudiates Christianity wholesale, and declares the modern Jew to have the true religion. The only fundamental question between Christians and modern Jews is, which party maintained and still adheres to the Old Testament.

The very first and most rudimental thing that Christianity does is to affirm that the Jews, who refuse Jesus as Christ, do by that very act repudiate every vestige of religion known to the Old Testament. I repeat, every vestige. If any one imagines that modern Jews retain any of the religion of the Old Testament, let me ask him, Suppose you wholly exclude Christ from the Old Testament; have you any true religion left in it? Every Christian, yea, and every Jew, will answer — Not a particle. Modern Judaism affirms that Christians abandon the religion of the Old Testament by foisting an impostor into its Christhood; while Christianity says that Jews abandon the Old Testament by repudiating its true Christhood. Then the whole question is settled in a moment by ascertaining whether Jesus is Christ or not.

380. In the *Comprehensive Commentary*, Supplement, p. 87, we read of Luke: "That he was a convert to Christianity from Judaism, however, is upon the whole sufficiently evident both from his style, and the intimate knowledge which he displays of Jewish doctrines and customs."

Of Luke's youth and early history we know but little. That he was of Jewish parentage is quite probable if not certain; but that he was a convert to Christianity from Judaism is next to impossible; at least there is no probability of it. A convert to Christianity from Judaism could only mean one who, like Paul, denied Jesus, and then was converted from the apostacy. Of this there is not the slightest intimation in the case of Luke. The faith called Judaism before the apostacy was and is Christianity. The faith of the Old Testament is the faith of the New. It might be asked when John the Baptist, or James, or Peter, was converted to Christianity. They were converted before the true faith or Judaism, of the Old Testament, began to be called Christianity.

381. Again, the *Comp. Com.*, on Galatians, says, "What these false teachers chiefly aimed at was to draw them (the Galatians) off from the truth, particularly in the great doctrines of justification, which

they greatly perverted by asserting the necessity of joining the observance of the law of Moses with faith in Christ in order to it."

That is to say, in other words, To follow the religion of the Old Testament in respect to the great doctrine of justification is to greatly pervert the doctrine as Paul taught it. Then we need to be told which is right, the Old Testament or Paul, that we may discard the wrong one. No, it is a mistake. Plainly stated, it cannot be believed. Paul and the law of Moses, as the Old Testament is here called, are both right, and both teach the same thing. The doctrine of justification, as taught by Paul, is written in many places in the Old Testament, and it is because it is there written, and for no other reason that we know of, that Paul taught it. Paul taught the doctrine of justification out of the law of Moses, just as everybody does now. He did not therefore complain of those teachers for teaching the Old Testament doctrine, but for not teaching it. Paul ought to be vindicated against this charge of teaching in opposition to the Old Testament; and revelation ought to stand consistent with itself.

382. Mr. Watson (*Conv.*, p. 194), speaking of the apostles and others who were early convinced of the truth of revelation, says, "The most honest and sincere would, in proportion to their honesty and sincerity, require powerful proofs to induce them to venture their eternal interests upon a new religion, and to renounce that of their fathers."

What! Does Mr. Watson undertake to teach that the apostles renounced the religion of their ancestors? If the apostles renounced the religion of the prophets, why do not we? Do we not receive their teachings as infallible? If they renounced the Old Testament, what right have we to continue it in our Bible?

This was not intended as a thrust at religion, for we have no truer Christian in the books than Richard Watson; and yet a more deadly blow against revelation could scarcely be made. And that it has injured religion, as far as it has been noticed and believed, cannot be doubted. The context to this remark affords it not the slightest relief. The faith they renounced was the Old Testament wholesale! And this has passed, for lo, these many years, for theology! And the Church to-day is suffering from the effects of such blunders.

383. Dr. Schaff says (*Hist. Apostolic Ch.*, p. 137), "Our religion indeed, like its founder, is of strictly divine origin. It is a new supernatural creation; a miracle in history. Yet its entrance into the world is historically connected with the whole preceding course of events. It took four thousand years to prepare humanity to receive it."

The Almighty is the founder of religion, if that term can be properly applied to it; but in what sense God can be said to be of divine origin is difficult to understand. Nor is it easy to see how religion can be called a creation, either new or old. It is simply a revelation. As to its having required four thousand years, or any other number, to prepare man to receive it, this is a transparent error. It is some of Dr. Schaff's Christologic mythology. Abel, Moses, Abraham, and millions of others, would tell us otherwise. Revelation tells us that our religion was revealed to, and received by Abel.

384. Dr. Schaff (page 139) says, that "Judaism

and heathenism were the great religions of antiquity which served to prepare the world for Christianity." And in the next paragraph he says that "Judaism is the religion of positive, direct revelation."

Now I think it is clear that heathenism never did anything to prepare the world for Christianity, or did anything in any way promotive of true religion, but was always, as it is now, its deadly enemy. Indeed, it is impossible, in any view, that heathenism could prepare anything for Christianity, since Christianity is older in the world than heathenism. And as to Judaism — or call revelation by what name you may — that *is* Christianity. True, ancient, ante-messianic Judaism is certainly Christianity, though false, modern Judaism is not. What a blind doctor! creating and aggravating religious disease with one hand, while he tries to cure it with the other.

385. Mr. Sawyer, in his *Organic Christianity*, says, "All men agree that Jesus Christ organized the Christian Church; but the precise constitution He gave it, the offices He established in it, and the powers attached to those offices, etc. — all these and other points are matters in regard to which there is great diversity and contrariety of opinion."

Mr. Sawyer, in his Preface, tells us he writes for the "defense of Church democracy." Conceding, then, that the above proposition is true, he has certainly an easy task to perform. Concede that, and it is almost infinitely easy to prove either Church democracy, Church aristocracy, or Church monarchy. One form of government is as easily proven as another, and nothing can be more easy than to prove either.

But Mr. Sawyer did not reflect that the above proposition could not possibly be true, because it is a contradiction. Either member of the sentence might be true, but both cannot, because one denies what the other affirms. He says we know that Jesus Christ organized the Church, but do not know what offices He created, nor what powers He gave to them. To organize a Church means to organize its government. There is nothing else to organize. And to organize a government means to fix its offices, or at least the principal ones, and prescribe their powers. Government consists in Legislation, Judicature, and Execution; and so, to organize a government, is to establish the offices, and prescribe the functions thereof in these departments. To know that a government was established is to know the very things Mr. Sawyer says are not known. He says we agree upon a certain thing, but disagree as to all the component parts of it. That is a contradiction.

It is granted that a government once formed might be modified indefinitely; that is, its legislature might be added to indefinitely, or reduced to one person; and the mode of keeping up the succession might be changed. And so of the other elements. But to say we do not know of any legislative functions established in the Church by the Saviour, nor any judicial functions, nor any executive functions at all, is merely saying, in other words, that we have no knowledge of his having organized the Church. To know He did the thing is simply a knowledge of having done the several things which constitute it.

Now, as Mr. Sawyer's entire argument of near

five hundred pages, setting up the theory of Church democracy, is built upon a fiction, a thing he says we do not know ; the exposition of the fiction, the removal of the single pedestal on which the entire theory is built, will be the destruction of the argument. There, I hold, is a complete answer to his book.

It is precisely as if one should say that Marc Antony founded the government and city of London, and go on with a book full of particulars thereof to the present time. Now, if I were to show that Marc Antony was never in Britain, that he established no government there, then in a single paragraph I have answered the entire book. Moreover, in this supposed government, there was no legislation, no judicial or executive departments established. Then how do we know there was a government ?

386. Harbaugh says, " In the New Testament, we see on almost every page, that Christ came into the world to establish a Church or kingdom." (*Union with the Church*, p. 76.)

Yes, if you mean that Christ came into the world in the days of Adam. It was to establish his kingly rule ; and a Church, *i. e.*, the association of Christians, was the natural consequence.

387. Bishop Stillingfleet, in the *Irenicum*, suffers himself to be drawn into the inconsistency of supposing that the Saviour instituted a new Church. He speaks of its " first institution," of the Saviour's " instituting his Church," of " setting his Church," etc. And on page 201, he concludes the Church was under no obligation to form its government according to that of the Jewish Church. On page 281, he says, " There was nothing in the model of the synagogue at all repugnant to the doctrine of the gospel,

or the nature of the constitution of the Christian churches." He then copies Tertullian's description of the Christian Church and worship, in detail, and says he could not have chosen words which would better describe the synagogue.

Then what are we to understand when told that the Saviour, or the apostles, formed a new Church? I respectfully submit that if a full and exact description of the one is a full and exact description of the other, then they are not descriptions of different things, but of one and the same thing, under different names merely. If from some local cause, either a good one or a poor one, the adherents to Jesus in this great Church trouble choose to disuse the word synagogue as the name of the Church, that does not in the least iota necessarily change the Church's character. The Bishop shows that the thing — the Church — continued the same. Very well, then the change was only in the name of it. Nothing could be more natural than the continuance of the name synagogue by the repudiating party, since, denying the incarnation, they continued the ante-incarnate modes of teaching. And so the other party must needs disuse it to avoid confusion and uncertainty. They must needs call their assemblies by some other name. The word Church was, however, not used for many centuries after. But the thing continued uninterruptedly, with no other change than the discontinuance of a few modes of teaching, or forms of ceremonial worship, which, in their nature, were ante-incarnate.

388. Mr. Henry (*Com.*, Acts iv. 32) says, "Multitudes believed even in Jerusalem; three thousand in one day, five thousand on another, besides those added daily," etc.

To this it might first be replied, — Believed what? Is it meant that they believed anything contrary to, or different from any former belief? Surely not. They now believed that the incarnate appearance of the Saviour, formerly anticipated, had been realized. This was the belief, and the sole belief, of those eight thousand, and other multitudes then spoken of.

But if Christianity began with eight thousand and more, probably ten times that number, how is it said that the twelve apostles, almost or quite alone, began the Christian warfare with the entire world against them? Hundreds of thousands, or a million or so, is a pretty good number to begin with, for almost any popular movement. Is it said that these thousands and oft-repeated multitudes, great multitudes, and myriads, were the early converts from the opposition? The reply then is that there is not the least information, or intimation, in Scripture, that they, or any of them, ever entertained or put forth sentiments in opposition in any way to the teachings of the apostles, or the Church now, about the questions then agitating the religious world. Indeed, the thing was impracticable in any view. Whatever doubts, fears, hopes, or expectations may have been entertained by any before, it is certain no one could or did believe truly in Jesus, as Christ, before the resurrection. No one could believe in a crucified and risen Saviour, until Jesus was crucified and rose. Nor was it practicable then, at the very first, for many to believe, because not many could know of it. Like other matters of fact, there must be time for the information to disseminate. The resurrection was seen by but few; probably less than a thousand altogether. Those at a distance could not know it, until they had reasonable opportunity. They must not only hear of it, but it must be well verified. This could not be done in an hour, a day, or a year, nor in less than ten or perhaps thirty years or more, to all the Church.

Now the evidence is clear that those Jews, who in that age accepted the Christship of Jesus at all, did so at the earliest period reasonably practicable. And there is no intimation that they ever evinced or entertained any opposition to the teachings of the Church then, or now. To this general rule, Paul was an exception. Quite likely there were others in the same category, though none others are mentioned. These eight thousand gave in their adhesion immediately, almost as soon as the apostles themselves did.

389. Macknight (Pref. to Romans) says: "The Judaizing Christians contended that there was no gospel Church different from the Jewish, ... and on the other side of this great controversy stood the apostles and others, and all well-informed brethren, who, knowing that the Jewish Church was at an end, and that the law of Moses was abrogated, strenuously maintained that a new Church of God was erected."

It is unfortunate that such ecclesiastical romance was ever written, and still more so, that it is put forth by men of talent, learning, and piety. We are admonished of the facility with which the truth may be perverted by a mere thoughtless copying from others. A moment's reflection will convince any one, even moderately acquainted with the New Testament, that there is not the slightest semblance of, or pretense to truth, in anything stated in the above extract. If any one doubts this, let him read the New Testament from beginning to end, keeping the above statement prominently in view. There was not only no such controversy, great or small, in those days, but there is not in Romans or elsewhere an allusion to any sort of controversy, debate, or difference of opinion between anybody about the Church at all, or relating to it. There is not a word of history to show that anybody in those days saw anything in the then existing Church, call it Jewish or what you may, that needed modification or change. And as to a new Church of God, such a thing was not dreamed of. I appeal to the book.

Now this is not a matter of opinion but of fact. Then, if I am correct, as any one may ascertain with certainty, I ask, who has perverted or misrepresented the Scriptures more than Dr. Macknight? He has not done it in this place only, but in hundreds of places in his work on the Epistles. I say hundreds, and mean hundreds.

390. "A new commandment I give unto you, That ye love one another." (John xiii. 34.)

This passage has been subject to a singular fortune. Mr. R. Watson (*Conversations*, p. 213) explains it without any explanation, merely calling it the new commandment. Dr. Clarke says the former commandment on the subject required only that we love our neighbors as ourselves, and this new one requires that we love our neighbors more than ourselves. Doddridge says that "mutual love is peculiar to the Christian dispensation," when everybody knows it is part of the decalogue.

Those who look for a new Church, new religion, new terms of salvation, new creation, etc., will naturally find support in this simple remark of the Saviour in his teachings. But we are also told there is no new commandment. This is all easily understood, it seems to me. The divine constitution is stable, consistent, and harmonious. What is called the giving of the Law at Sinai was only the publication of a grand constitution of immutable principles making up the relation between man and his Maker. It is a brief outline of the moral nature of things. It belongs not to times, places, or circumstances, but to God and the race of man. But this law is imperfectly understood. To many it is new, at least portions of it. At this present day the great law of neighborly love is new to many.

391. *Scott's Com.*, Pref. to Acts, says, "Eleven men, obscure and unarmed, with the whole world to encounter, produced the most extraordinary revolution that ever took place in the moral and religious state of the world."

That would be marvelous if it were true. But it is marvelous in this, that there is no truth, nor pretense to truth, in or about it. In the first place, instead of eleven men to produce this great impression, there were at the first thousands upon thousands, great multitudes, even myriads, acting with the apostles, of whom there is not the slightest intimation anywhere that they ever encountered the apostles, or opposed them or the Saviour in any way whatever. And in the second place, instead of producing a revolution, or essaying to do so, that is the very thing and the only thing charged against them at the time by their enemies. This was the thing charged against them by the mistaken Saul of Tarsus, and by the infidel writers of that age, Porphyry, Julian, and such men. And this same complaint, and substantially none other, was continued against Paul after his conversion. And how did they meet it? Always by a prompt and unqualified denial. They declared they were sustaining the old religion of their fathers without change. Strange, that modern writers should make the same charges!

392. Dr. Paley (*Evid. Chris.*, p. 488) says, "A Jewish peasant changed the religion of the world."

The very reverse of what is notoriously known to be true. The Jewish peasant, meaning our Saviour, held firmly and finally, and the apostles after Him, to the religion of their fathers, the regular written religion of the Church. The only thing He sought to change was the religious errors into which many had fallen. Who but his enemies ever charged that He taught contrary to the teachings of the prophets? I aver that a statement more untrue, or more notoriously untrue than the above, could not be written! The voice of Christendom proclaims it untrue in that it recognizes that very identical Old Testament as a part of the Christian Bible. It is venerated and preached everywhere.

393. Dr. Stephen Olin (*Works*, vol. i. p. 259) says of Christ, that "He has fulfilled and abolished the law of ceremonies."

That is strange. Why fulfill a law He intended to abolish? and why abolish a law after He had fulfilled it? In the former case He must have set us an example He did not intend us to follow! And in the latter He prohibited us from following the example He intended!

394. *Alexander's Evidences of Christianity* is a school book, and goes out under the broad endorsement of the Presbyterian Board of Publication. In it our children are taught that the Jews were rejected,

and the Gentiles were called in their room. The teaching is not that individual Jews were rejected for personal wickedness, but that Jews as such, because they were Jews, were wholesale, and for that reason, cast off utterly from all hope of salvation.

This doctrine is abhorrent to Christian theology. The well known truth is, that hundreds of thousands and most probably millions of Jews, all the best portion of the Church at the time alluded to, were always, so far as we know, in good and pious communion with God and his Church. Indeed, they solely, for a number of years after the resurrection, constituted the Church. They were peculiarly heroic, pious, and self-sacrificing Christians. Rejected, indeed! Nevertheless many were rejected, but surely not as Jews, — not because they were Jews, — but for personal wickedness, just as men are always rejected, because they reject Christ.

As to the Gentiles being called, the children would be likely to learn from this teaching, in the unqualified manner in which it is stated, that all Gentiles are now brought into the Church. The misteaching on this subject is great, and ought to be corrected.

395. "All the various forms of religion existing now, or that have existed in the world, are comprised under four denominations, namely, *Paganism*, *Mohammedanism*, *Deism*, and *Christianity*. I do not reckon Judaism among them, because, in its original form, it was a part of the true religion, and identified with Christianity." (*Newcomb's Chris. Dem.*, p. 8.)

If Dr. Newcomb had undertaken to point out what part of Christianity is found in Judaism, he would have discovered his mistake. It is difficult to see what the Doctor means by Judaism in its original form. It has never changed its form. The Penta teuch is now as it was first written; and it was first written as the oral teachings of the Church first were

396. Dr. John Dick (*Theology*, p. 78) says, "In the Christian dispensation there are four particulars by which it is characterized; a greater degree of light, a new system of worship, a more abundant affusion of the spirit, and universality."

Two of those particulars are true, and two are not. Since the advent of Christ, and because of his advent and teaching, the Church has a greater degree of light, and likewise, for the same reasons, it has a more abundant affusion of the spirit. But it has no new system of worship, nor any universality it did not always possess. The Church has never had any fixed system of worship. It has always varied in different ages and different countries. There were incidental modifications in the times of the apostles, but not greater than at other times, and as to universality, it was always unlimitedly universal. It is a mere Irish bull to suppose that the Church, prior to the incarnation, was confined to Jews. Of course it was; how could it be otherwise? When outsiders went in they were now Jews, and their posterity after them, if they stayed in. It was always just as it is now, religion is confined to religious people — to the Church.

397. Dr. John Dick (*Theology*, p. 19) says, "The ceremonial law was connected with the ministry of Aaron and his sons, and prescribed the mode in which they were to conduct the services of the sanctuary; but as soon as they were superseded by the new Priest it became obsolete, and circumstances demanded a different ritual."

It has been already explained that there never was

any special, legal ceremonial law in the sense here meant. There always were, and are now, Church rules about ceremonies, that is, external modes of worship. And also that before the incarnation, some of these ceremonies, pointing forward to the incarnation, must necessarily cease on the occurrence of that event. But how any one could suppose that the Aaronic priests were superseded by the new Priest is strange indeed. Although Dr. Dick says so in this place, in so many words, and in many other places substantially, yet no Christian ever did or could believe it. No man would repudiate the idea more peremptorily or more scornfully then Dr. Dick himself. Everybody teaches everywhere, that revelation knows but one Priest.

398. " Under this dispensation true religion consists in repentance toward God, and faith in our Lord Jesus Christ." (*Fleetwood.*)

Under this dispensation? And did true religion under any other dispensation ever consist in anything else? May we not hope to see Christianity rescued from the entanglements of such teachings?

399. " Of what sect the Apostle Peter was, sacred history hath not informed us." (*Fleetwood's Life of Christ.*)

By sect is here meant the little schools of Pharisees, Sadducees, and Essenes; as if it were a matter of course that he belonged to either. Perhaps not one in five hundred of the Jews then had any connection with any of them.

400. Fleetwood's *Life of Christ* is not the only book that teaches that the Sanhedrim, in sending Saul to Damascus, and other such like acts, did so in accordance with the religion of the Church.

401. But the simple truth is, that in those things they acted in gross and ignorant violation of the Church. These acts were the unauthorized and mistaken doings of fanatics and irreligious men, a majority of whom chanced to rule the great council at this time. But neither the Church nor its religion ought to be held responsible for these acts. Pope Leo X. sold indulgences; but the Scriptures did not authorize it. Moreover, at the time Saul was sent to Damascus on the occasion referred to, the Sanhedrim was not the ruling Church power, though it claimed to be. It was now the ruling power of the apostate Church, recently split off. The Church repudiated the Sanhedrim, and acted independently of it.

402. Paley says: "St. Paul, before his conversion, had been a fierce persecutor of the new sect."

This, if it be true, settles a very important question between Jews and Christians, which has been, to some extent, boldly contested for the last eighteen hundred years. The great question in the days of Paul, between the apostles and their opponents, the Jews who rejected our Saviour, was — which party was the new sect? That is, which had departed from the revealed religion? Whichever party this was, must necessarily have a new, human, and therefore a false religion. Each charged this home upon the other. Each party claimed that it was adhering firmly to the divinely revealed religion, and that the other party was a mere new sect, with a new, and therefore a false religion. Then, if Paley be the admitted spokesman on the part of Christians, it is acknowledged that the rejecting Jews were right, and that Christianity is a heresy.

403. Dr. Schaff (*Hist. Apos. Ch.*, p. 9) says that

"Christ, as Redeemer, is to be found neither in Heathenism, nor Judaism, nor in Islamism."

Very well. Then if Jesus Christ, as Redeemer, is not the Christ so frequently mentioned in the Old Testament, and so often specifically named as Redeemer in Job, Psalms, Isaiah, Jeremiah, etc., be it so; and then we ought to hear no more about Christianity. But for my own part, I can but believe that the apostles were right in claiming that Jesus Christ was and is the Redeemer; that the identical Jesus, and none other, was the Christ of the Jewish prophets. The question is between Schaff and Christianity.

404. And again (page 18): "For us, then, Church history embraces a period of eighteen centuries."

I am unable to conceive of any principle of philosophy, religion, or ethics, upon which we have nothing to do with, or concern in, the history of the Church before that time. A very large portion of the sacred Scriptures is mere history of the Church prior to eighteen centuries ago. And the inspired Word tells us that it is all profitable to us for several valuable purposes.

405. Again, he says: "The *beginning* of Church history is properly the incarnation of the Son of God."

And then, what of the Church, about which we are told so much in Scripture, before the incarnation? Had it no history?

406. On page 140, Dr. Schaff says that "Judaism, along with the pure development of divine revelation, embodied also more or less of human error and corruption."

I hardly know what to say of that remark. In

my mind, it borders closely upon blasphemy, to say the least of it. It cannot, therefore, receive less than an unqualified denunciation. There are some things about which we may not speak mildly. Human error and corruption, in any degree, must not be predicated of divine revelation.

407. On page 143, we are told that "Judaism and heathenism, notwithstanding their essential difference, have some common features and connecting links."

As different systems of religion, the aspects in which they are understood by the author, they have and can have no common features nor connecting links, it seems plain to me. The one is revelation, pure, infinite wisdom; and the other is a wholesale, unmitigated falsehood in its inception and throughout. I cannot conceive of two things in more universal and deadly hostility to each other. In many places the author speaks of them as the great twin preparers for Christianity! This must not be permitted.

408. Conybeare and Howson (*St. Paul*, vol. i. p. 31) say that Christianity "is the grain of which mere Judaism is now the worthless husk."

I do not know what is intended to be meant by mere Judaism, unless the word is used in its proper signification, which is to mean pure, unmixed, entire, or absolute. And so mere Judaism is the written Old Testament. And then the question arises, Is the Old Testament a worthless husk? I put the question directly, and have a right to suggest a categorical answer.

No! It is the precious Word of God. It comprises a large portion of the volume of the Christian Bible. Christianity requires that it be loved, adored, honored, cherished, read, and obeyed. In inseparable connection with the New, the Old Testament is the man of our counsel, a light to our feet, and a lamp to our pathway. To repudiate either is to mar the blessed Scriptures, mutilate revelation, and dishonor God.

409. Mr. Thos. Olivers, quoted by Dr. Clark, says, "The consequence of this opposition, both from within and without, was, that great numbers of the Hebrews *apostatized* from Christ and his gospel, and went back to the law of Moses."

That is to say, they forsook the religion as taught by the apostles, and apostatized to that taught by the prophets. Mr. Olivers did not hear of the millions who apostatized from all revelation, and set up a falsely called Jewish Church ; but he strangely hears of numbers who apostatized from the New Testament to the Old!

410. Again, Mr. Olivers says, "Here *Christ* is particularly compared with Moses, and shown to be superior to him in many respects."

I do not think so. St. Paul never compared Christ to any human being. Such a comparison would be strange. I suppose Paul compared Jesus, the man, with Moses, showing his superiority, and thereby proving that He was Christ.

411. Dr. Clarke says that Philip "preached the gospel to the Ethiopian eunuch."

And I think so too. But then he only explained the 53d chapter of Isaiah in doing so. And then if the author is right here, as he most assuredly is, he is wrong in more than a hundred other places where he inculcates the belief that the gospel was first introduced and preached in the time of the apostles.

412. I am surprised to see a remark of Bishop Watson's defense of the Bible against Thos. Paine, page 36: "The doctrine and prophecy of Moses is true. The law that we have was given by Moses. This is the faith of the Jews at present, ... and no period can be shown from the age of Moses to the present hour, in which it was not their faith."

What! Is the Pentateuch the faith of the present Jews? Then what is the faith we call Christianity? I can conceive of no statement that could be made that would more effectually sweep Christianity by the board. Either Christians or modern Jews, one or the other, have sadly departed from the Old Testament faith; and if the present Jews have not done it, then the Christians certainly have, and Christianity is a heresy. The statement above is precisely what, and precisely all, that modern Jews claim. The Bishop says they have a true faith. Not so; they have a false faith, false because they have departed from the doctrine and prophecy of Moses. The Pentateuch teaches not a Christ, some Christ, but Jesus Christ. If Jesus was not seen when Moses wrote, He has been seen since; and it is now known that He existed then. The Christian faith is true because, and only because, it adheres to the doctrine and prophecy of Moses. Is Bishop Watson a Jew?

413. Again, on page 63, Bishop Watson says: "The books of the Old Testament were composed from records of the Jewish nation, and they have been received as true by that nation from the time in which they were written to the present day."

Now suppose Thomas Paine had rejoined on this wise: "You say the books of the Old Testament contain and teach a true revealed religious system of faith. Secondly, you say, the Jews of the present day receive, hold and possess this true faith so revealed. Then, thirdly, what of this new Christianity of yours which you say is so opposite to the faith of these Jews? If any body believes the Old Testament, he believes it as it is, and not as it is not. Modern Jews believe it as teaching a future Christ; and you say, that is believing it. Then the Christian faith cannot be true, because that believes the Old Testament as holding Jesus to be its Christ. Two opposite and hostile things cannot both be true. Your faith holds Jesus to be the Christ of the Old Testament; and the faith of the modern Jew holds some other and future coming person to be its Christ. And you say this latter faith is true. That is saying that Jesus is not Christ. And then you complain of me for saying the same thing. I am a bad man for saying it in terms, and you a good one for saying it by necessary implication!" What would the Bishop reply to this?

414. "In the law of Moses retaliation for deliberate injury has been ordained." (*Watson's Apology*, p. 208.)

It is painful to see one of the finest and best religious tracts so terribly blotted and disfigured. Where in the Old Testament is such an ordinance to be found? I need not inquire. A far greater than Bishop Watson has examined this specific matter, and we have his exposition. "Ye have heard that it has been said, by ignorant pretenders who understood it not, an eye for an eye, and a tooth for a tooth, that private revenge and retaliation was the law; but, understanding and expounding the Scriptures rightly, I say unto you that ye resist not evil." That is the teaching. The Old Testament indeed enjoins a just return of equivalents, as does the New, and as the civil law does; but where parties cannot agree privately, this must be done by the civil magistrate, and not by private revenge and retaliation. See the chapter in *Ecce Ecclesia* on this subject.

415. Bishop Burnet, quoted by R. Watson (*Inst.*, p. 699) says of the ancient Jews, "And when their sins had provoked God's wrath they were reconciled to Him by their sacrifices with which atonement was made, and so their sins were forgiven them."

And so we are taught that that was the mode and manner of atonement for sin formerly; and now, under a different system, we are reconciled by the atonement of Christ. And so, we are told, this latter is a better mode than the former. I doubt it. I am not able to see the improvement. I would greatly prefer the former mode. And if it were reinstated, I think I could make ten converts to Bishop Burnet's one. What miserable theology! God reconciled by the blood of bulls and goats!

416. It is indeed wonderful how far men of parts suffer themselves to be carried away by the notion of two religions and two churches. I have before me *The Relation between Judaism and Christianity*, by the Rev. John G. Palfrey, D. D., LL. D., late Professor of Biblical Literature in the University at Cambridge, Mass., published in 1854, 8vo. 400 pages. It is really a somewhat scholarly production; but proceeds from the title-page throughout, as a matter never questioned, that the Old and New Testaments present respectively two entirely different religious systems. Moses is the founder of the one, and Christ of the other; and they fraternize, and antago-

nize here and there, so and so, in hundreds of points of relation, just as Christianity and Mohammedanism relate to each other. But that all the books of both the Old and New Testaments conjointly are a reve lation of one identical religious system, is a thing never hinted at by this University Professor of Bibli cal Literature. The two systems are fundamentally and constitutionally hostile to each other, and only agree in minor matters as Christianity and Buddhism might agree. This may seem strange, but there is the book. And the ten thousand times greater evil is, that such is the teaching of others too, that we are not at all shocked at such a book.

417. On page 90, Dr. Palfrey says, " Judaism was to be superseded by Christianity, the religion of Moses for the religion of Jesus. The substitution of the gospel for the law was the establishment of the kingdom of heaven, the coming of the Son of man."

The wonder is not so much that a professed theologian should write such absurdities and contradictions, but that they should be received and read, and be suffered to pass for half-way theology in a Christian country for a single day. To believe it, you must first repudiate the entire drift of apostolic teaching and New Testament history.

418. Bryant, on " The Truth of the Christian Religion," quoted by Paley (*Evid.*, p. 112) says, " The Jews still remain ; but how seldom is it that we can make a single proselyte ! There is reason to think that there were more converted by the apostle in one day than have since been won over in the last thousand years."

If that statement were true it would be strange. But so far from being true, it first, falsifies all history, and secondly, overturns the Christian system completely. The Jews still remain; that is, in the religious faith and status of the prophets; and require to be won over to a different religion. Then the Old Testament is just as far from Christianity as the modern Jews are. They remain together and equally oppose true religion. Any person believing the Old Testament must be won over from it. And then on attempting to believe the New Testament, he finds, as unquestioned matter of fact, the very same system of truths he has just repudiated; and worse still, if possible, the new system everywhere openly professes to draw every doctrine it has directly from the Old Testament!

The fallacy of supposing the three thousand alluded to on the day of Pentecost, and others in that period who never opposed Christ or the apostles, being won over, is abundantly exposed and refuted elsewhere herein. Those who oppose Christ, either in the person of Jesus or otherwise, and they only, require to be won over.

419. Dr. Stier (*Words of the Lord Jesus*, on Matt. v. 17) speaks of "the Church or congregation hereafter to be built."

Yes, certainly, hereafter to be built. That is precisely right if you properly understand the word built. Hereafter to be edified, to be strengthened, to be more and more cemented together, enlarged and blessed. So all Christians are building the Church now. See the Essay on Matt. xvi. 18.

420. Brown's *Epistle of Peter*, p. 73, says: "Final salvation was the subject of Old Testament prophecy." And again, "Final salvation is the subject of Old Testament prediction."

I do not see how the Old Testament, more than the New, can be spoken of as a prophecy or prediction. There are in both many things in the nature of prediction of future events. But that the Old Testament is a prophecy, fulfilled in the New, is a strange fancy. The Old Testament is teaching, didactic teaching. "Thou shalt have no other gods before me." Is that prophecy? "Ho, every one that thirsteth, come ye to the waters!" Is that a prediction of some future Christianity?

421. *Ecce Homo* is a recent publication that has attracted some attention in some places. Its rhetoric and classical style are elegant. Its matter is semi-infidel; its historic basis is utterly and notoriously fabulous. It undertakes to deprive the Christship of Jesus of all and every divine attribute, by showing up our Saviour as a great man. This the Scripture never does. Greatness in Jesus is never predicated of his manhood, but always of his divinity. Jesus Christ was not a man rendered wise and good and great by divine afflatus or extraordinary inspiration. How, as man, He would measure with other men, we have no knowledge. Here Scripture is totally silent. And when we know nothing, we had better say nothing.

Ecce Homo is an elegant romance. The name of its hero is Jesus Christ. He is a new character, now for the first time known to literature. The scene of the romance is the New Testament history, and the plan is to put this wonderful and mysterious man Jesus into the shoes of the true Jesus, and then make him perform wonders which, while in external form they somewhat resemble many things acted by our Saviour, are really things which neither He nor the men of his time and faith ever heard of.

On page 49, we are told as follows: "To deny that Christ did undertake to found and to legislate for a new theocratic society, and that He did claim the office of Judge of mankind, is indeed possible, but only to those who altogether deny the credibility of the extant biographies of Christ." On page 59, we read that "Christ announced Himself as the founder and legislator of a new society." On page 61, the author begins to "deal with the actual establishment of the new Theocracy."

I suppose it is of no use to attempt to meet romance with either truth or argument. No man can read the sacred biographies of our Saviour, with an eye directed to the point, and not be compelled to know that there is neither semblance, nor pretense to historic truth in any of these statements.

The book is a novel, founded on fact, as they say. The name of the hero, the chronological period, the geographical location, New Testament names and circumstances, are mostly familiar, and will be readily recognized as belonging to apostolic history.

Christ was a most remarkable man; in many respects one of the most remarkable, and in some the most remarkable, known to human history. Traits of greatness began to sparkle in his boyhood. Springing from the lower walks of life, and unendowed with either literature or philosophy, He was slow in recognizing his own powers. As manhood began to dawn he felt the slumbering powers of popular control coursing within Him. He had quick and keen perception of men and character. The spirit of the times was propitious. The Mosaic government was feeble with age, and slowness to keep pace with expansion and progress did not escape his keen penetration. Christ saw the opportunity for revolution, and grasped it. Keeping his own counsels, as the horizon of thought enlarged, He planned the total destruction of Judaism, its religion and its civil polity! He began on a small scale the nucleus of an opposing republic. He gathered around Him the right sort of men. He outgeneraled the greatest captains, outplanned the best statesmen, outpeered the wisest philosophers, and in controlling popular sentiment and feeling He outwitted the shrewdest men, and overturned the solidest combinations of his country and times. So Christ demolished and utterly destroyed the Jewish religion and Jewish state, erecting on the ruins thereof a totally new and much purer system of morals, into the belief and practice of which He has drawn some millions of followers. Like other conquerors He lost his life in the struggle, and died in the arms of victory. Such is one of the latest, and, bating its bald Unitarianism and semi-blasphemy, perhaps one of the best late novels.

422. Fleetwood (*Life of Christ*, p. 486) says of Paul: "Having refreshed himself after his voyage, the Apostle sent for the heads of the Jewish consistory at Rome, and related to them the cause of his coming in the following manner: 'Though I have been guilty of no violence of the laws of our religion, yet I was delivered by the Jews at Jerusalem to the Roman governors, who, more than once, would have acquitted me as innocent of any capital offense,'" etc.

We have a most instructing lesson in the last chapter of Acts, from the 17th verse onward. We learn here a very important lesson about Paul's ministry. He called together the chief Church officers of the Jews, the rejecting Jews, and held a conference with them, of which we have a very brief notice. He calls them brethren, and explains that in advocating the Christship of Jesus, he did "nothing against the people or customs of our fathers." He had preached no new religion, changed no customs, either of the Church or of society. He had kept straight forward in the track of his fathers. They then asked him to preach to the people about Jesus; and they appointed a day for this purpose; and he "persuaded them concerning Jesus, both out of the law of Moses, and out of the prophets, from morning till evening;" how many days we are not informed. Some believed, and some did not. As they had "great reasoning" about the matter, Paul must have explained that the Lord's Supper and Baptism were changes of mere form, and not of substance, and that this was from absolute necessity. He declares he had done nothing but hold firmly to Moses and the prophets.

Now the remarkable point here with Bishop Fleetwood is, that after calling particular attention to Paul's declarations on this occasion, he still speaks, and on the same page, of Paul as having forsaken Moses and the prophets, and entered a new Church, and preached a new religion. The contradiction is so glaring, that it is remarkable.

423. Fairbairn accounts for the mistakes of other writers on typology, by saying that "The gospel is read not only through a Jewish medium, but also in a Jewish sense."

I cannot tell what he means by Jewish sense. The Jewish mind, drift of thinking, religious impression, belief and sentiment before the incarnation, and the same thing called Jewish since, are as opposite and antagonistic as any two things can be, and in every respect, too; to which of these does the author refer? He does not seem to discriminate.

424. MacEwen on the Types, quoted in the *Religious Encyclopædia*, says of the types of Scripture: "Some of them afford intrinsic evidence that the Scriptures which record them are given by inspiration of God; the others can be proved to exist only by assuming the fact. But all of them, when once established, display the astonishing power and wisdom of God; and the importance of that scheme of redemption which was ushered into the world with such magnificent preparations."

Revelation was not all made at once, but at many times through a period of two thousand years and more. Neither was it all verbal, though we have it in a verbal and historic form. Very much of revelation, when first seen, consisted in actions, such as the contest between Moses and the Egyptian magicians, the passing of the Red Sea, the performances of priestly actions, the protection of Daniel from the lions, the death and resurrection of Jesus, and many others. Now, that all this revelation had a historic connection, so as to form one solid whole, is very certain; and hence previous ones may be said to be types, or pre-intimations, or pre-representations, or as they often were, fore-symbolizings of later ones. Indeed, they were all, not only historically related, but historically connected.

But it is not true, as Dr. MacEwen supposes, that the revelations prior to the incarnation formed a complete integral whole, and those afterwards a complete whole, and that the former were merely preparations for the latter. This idea grows out of the popular blunder of two different dispensations of different laws and principles of atonement.

The doctrine of a dualistic revelation is not true. And so when he writes about that scheme of redemption which was ushered into the world at the time of Jesus, and that all before was mere magnificent preparations, he writes what I am unable to receive.

This idea of a specific dualistic revelation has given rise to systems of typology, which have been carried to very fanciful and unwarrantable lengths. Everything in the Old Testament, they would teach us, was a mere type or prefigurement of some real principle or doctrine of the real and proper revelation of the New Testament, when Christianity was ushered into the world. There is no such relation between the different parts of revelation. The whole form one complete Christian Bible.

425. Coleridge (*Aids to Reflection*, vol. i. p. 296) says, "Circumcision was no sacrament at all, but the means and mark of national distinction."

That depends upon what he means by sacrament. Circumcision itself is not a sacrament, in the same sense as the same thing might be said of baptism. Both the circumcision and the baptism are modes of administering the obligation to serve God in the Church-state of religion. Circumcision undoubtedly was used as a religious rite. This is elsewhere fully explained. There is scarcely room for difference of opinion.

426. Dr. Barth's *History of the Church upon Scripture Principles* is a brief synopsis of religious history; in many respects an excellent manual of reference for juvenile instruction. It is a German

work, republished in this country by the New York Methodist Book Concern, in 1847, "for the Sunday-school Union of the Methodist Episcopal Church."

He entirely fails to notice the two greatest of almost all the religious facts known to history, namely, the uninterrupted passing of the Church through the scenes and period of the Incarnation of Christ, and the defection and apostacy at that time of the rejecting or repudiating Jews, amounting to probably one half of the Church.

427. Bridges' *Christian Ministry*, first published in England in 1829, and afterwards in this country, is a respectable octavo volume, and treats the subject with fair appearances of learning and piety. But in the first chapter we read, "A separate order of men were consecrated to the great work of laying the foundation and raising the superstructure of his Church. Twelve only were included in the original institution, with a commission, bounded at first within the scanty extent of 'Immanuel's land,' but afterwards enlarged with a tender of the promised blessing to 'every creature.'"

Now I think it is unquestionable, that every minister in the land, as readily including Mr. Bridges himself, as any one else, on a moment's reflection, will say that every part of the above statement is untrue. Everybody knows that his Church, the Church of God, call it by what name you will, was then already in existence, and had been for many hundred years, as Mr. R. Watson and many others say, "the very same Church." Secondly, the twelve only had no directions about any original institution, but were commissioned to tell the Church and the world, that the ancient and then existing

Christ had appeared in the person of Jesus. Thirdly, if by Immanuel's land the author means the land of Palestine, he is mistaken in supposing their commission was so narrowly bounded. If he means the Church, as it was then spread over the known world almost, he is correct. They were first to inform the Church, and the world through the Church. Fourthly, these promised blessings were certainly no new thing in the world. Thousands and millions of Old Testament saints could testify to the same blessings through the same faith.

428. Dr. N. L. Rice, in his *Romanism not Christianity*, at page 17, says: "My first argument against the infallibility of the Church of Rome is, that *there is no evidence by which it can be proved.*"

Waiving the logical point whether that is an argument, it concedes the important point that it might be proved; that is, that it is a thing naturally capable of being proved. Whereas, if the Church did not begin to exist in the way claimed by Romanists at all, namely, by being originally formed by Jesus Christ, then the thing denied by the Doctor is not a subject of proof at all — there could be no such question — there is nothing to prove. Pity the Doctor did not see this point.

429. Again, page 297, he says, "Let us first inquire into the organization of the Church of Christ."

He now proceeds to inquire how, under what constitutional laws, the Saviour organized the supposed new Church; to see whether these laws of organization did or did not establish the infallibility in question. But how much easier it would be to say, He did not establish a new Church at all, with or without infallibility. Then where is the question of infallibility? Thus it is seen the Doctor puts into the hands of his opponents a weapon that historic truth does by no means furnish them, and with which they at least keep him in an interminable and uncomfortable warfare. Why give them the advantage of such a question at all? Truth forbids it, and policy revolts at it.

430. The Rev. John S. Stone, D. D., Dean of the Episcopal Theological School, Cambridge, publishes the *Mysteries Opened*, 1844, a work generally well written, in refutation of the High Church doctrines; but the author greatly hampers himself by essaying to prove that the Low Church doctrine is most consonant with the original Church, as it was said to be first set up by Jesus Christ. Thus he makes the fatal acknowledgment that the present Church originated in that way. That is the very thing, and the impossible thing, he ought to require his opponents to prove.

431. Page 235, we read, "Christ did not cut off the Jews from the hope of salvation, but only from *exclusive* possession and enjoyment of the *means* of that salvation."

That is much nearer the truth than many write on that point. If the remark had been predicated of some mistaken Jews who greatly misunderstood their own religion, instead of the Jews, it would do much better. The Saviour did not cut off anybody from such exclusive possession, because nobody possessed any such franchise. But He taught such as needed the teaching, then or now, that religion was not exclusive. It taught the good old doctrine of the prophets — whosoever will, let him take the water of life freely. He taught then what He had always taught through the prophets.

432. Dr. Collyer's *Lectures on Scripture Facts* is an English book of respectable appearance. At page 272, we read about the reasons why we should regard Josephus' testimony about Jesus Christ as genuine. One was, "A new sect having sprung up, from this very event attracted the notice of both Jews and Gentiles, and boldly, perseveringly and successfully disseminating their tenets," which would be likely to call forth such notice.

Here we are told that the apostles and their followers — half the whole Church — were a new sect that had sprung up, who very zealously disseminated their doctrines. Is this so? Can any man name one new doctrine that they taught? Will Dr. Collyer, or anybody for him, attempt to name one? Surely we might suppose that among their doctrines, the doctrines of a whole new sect, one or two could be named. And if not, then is it not a shame to Christendom that our pulpits, our families, and our little ones, are thus constantly cursed, wronged, and misled by such grave and mischievous fables! Now a moment's reflection will convince any one that this question of a new sect was the only dispute of those times. The only thing charged against the apostles and those siding with them was, that they were a new sect, perseveringly disseminating their doctrines. Dr. Collyer can take which side he chooses, but it can but be seen that the affirmative necessarily places a man with the repudiating Jews.

433. In his chapter on "The Prophecies of Moses, respecting the Former and Present State of the Jews," Dr. Collyer copies from former writers, as innocently as hundreds of later writers copy from him, the doctrine of the genealogical oneness of the

Jews of the present day, with the Jews of the time of Moses and the prophets.

It is quite certain that either the Christians or Jews of the present day are in ecclesiastical and religious oneness, by descent from the people known as Jews, at and before the birth of Jesus. And the only possible way to determine that question is to ascertain whether Jesus is or is not the Christ of the ancient Jews. That will determine it infallibly. If Dr. Collyer's reasoning is good, then the modern Jews are the true followers of Moses and the prophets, and Christians are apostates from revealed religion.

434. Leland's *View of Deistical Writers* was published in England a little over a hundred years ago, and is considered a good exposition of the subject. But he certainly labors under the inconvenience of holding that Christianity is, and is not, a new and different religious system from that of the Old Testament. On page 374, he says the miracles of the Saviour "brought over vast numbers of both Jews and Gentiles, in the very age in which the facts were done, and when they had the best opportunity of knowing the truth of these facts, to receive a crucified Jesus as their Saviour and their Lord."

That remark has very good application to Gentiles, those out of the Church; but what were those already in the Church brought over to? The Christ they believed in and worshipped was previously invisible to sense; and now for the first time He appears incarnate, and on the first good evidence of the fact, they accept Jesus as their Christ. That bringing over! It is remaining intact.

435. On page 163, Dr. Leland says, "One reason

of the extreme virulence with which he (Lord Bolingbroke) hath attacked the law of Moses and the Scriptures of the Old Testament seems to be the near connection there is between this and the religion of Jesus, which he represents to have been originally intended by our Saviour as a system of Judaism."

Well, that is better than the teachings of Paley, Barnes, Jenyns, Dr. Stuart of Andover, and many others, who declare that there is absolutely nothing common to both. Leland admits a near connection. I do not see that his infidel lordship was at fault in insisting that objections would lie with equal force against the Old and the New Testament. Dr. Leland undertook the unequal warfare, with the great and shrewd infidel, of defending Christianity as a system of religion new and different from that of the Old Testament. This wrongfully admitted difference and even antagonism, as it is often said, is the great support of infidelity.

436. Not a little discussion has been had about the origin of priesthood. Fairbairn (*Typology*, vol. ii. p. 220) opens his discussion of the subject, which is both long and learned, on this wise: "It is somewhat singular that the earliest notices we have of a priesthood in Scripture refer to other branches of the human family than that of Abraham." He then notices that the first mention of priest is of Melchizedek; then Potipherah. "Not till the children of Israel left the land of Egypt, were they placed under that particular polity." Then comes the question, "How and when did it originate?" and, "How did they make their approach to God, and present their oblations? Did each worshipper transact for himself

with God, or did the father of a family act as priest for the members of his household? Or was the priestly function among the privileges of the first-born? This last position has been maintained by many of the Jewish authorities, and also by some men of great learning in Christian times."

I understand the subject differently. First, there never was any priest, any atoning or real priest, mediating between God and man in reference to sin and salvation, but CHRIST. You could not speak of Jesus before He lived. The atonement of Christ has no special reference to times, peoples, circumstances, or chronological periods, but is unlimitedly comprehensive and plenary, relating to mankind. How much of divine, priestly atonement is comprehended in visible acts, cognizable to our senses, we do not know. But we do know that those acts which date eighteen hundred years ago, had, before that time, a prospective reference, as they since refer retrospectively. How well this or that person understood this theological subject, in the period before the incarnation, is the same kind of a question as might be asked of persons since. What the divine plan of atonement was, and is, is one thing. How well somebody understands it is another and different thing. The general rule is, the more light the more vision. A child three years old is taught to pray and worship, and yet he knows very little of the theology of salvation.

It follows, therefore, that those who look for the priestly function, or privilege, or franchise of atonement, or the origin of priesthood, among such men as Melchizedek, Potipherah, Aaron, etc., whether they be Jewish authorities or men of great learning in Christian times, are searching for that which does not and never did exist. There never was, nor could there ever be any such origin, privilege, or franchise, so long as it remains written that there is "no other name given under heaven" for priesthood and atonement but the one name. Then let these speculations about priestly functions cease.

Then, what was the function, calling, or office of those men called priests in the ancient Church? If they were not real priests, what were they? They were teachers, teachers of the doctrine of priestly atonement. Their peculiar business was to inculcate the principle and truth of priestly forgiveness. How did they perform these teachings? By actions addressed to the eye. Why not do as teachers of this same doctrine do now, teach with words addressed to the ear? For the reason that before such atoning acts as were intended for the cognizance of our senses became visible and historic, that was impossible. In the nature of things such teaching can be performed in no other way than by adumbrant pre-representation.

Before the events of Calvary, it was impossible to teach the doctrine of atonement in any other way. Our instruments of teaching are historic and sensible; theirs were prospective and theoretical. They taught a truth; we teach a fact. The men are called priests, metonymically, as we frequently call a book by the name of the man who wrote it. They are called priests not because they possessed any atoning franchise, not because they stood any nearer to God than other men, not because they possessed any atoning ability, not because the blood they offered, the blood of bulls and goats, had any atoning efficacy, but because they acted the forms of atonement visibly, as mere instruments of instruction. They did, in the only possible way then, what historic lessons now do by didactic means.

Let a man try to describe something he has never heard, nor seen, nor felt, nor smelled, nor tasted, and he may have some faint appreciation of the reasons why the people of those times did not teach the doctrine of priestly sacrifice as we do now. They were shut up to the necessity of teaching in the manner they did.

437. "The Church of Rome, however, erroneously believe their *priests* to be empowered to offer up to the Divine Majesty real, proper sacrifice, as were the priests under the Old Testament." (*Buck's Dictionary.*)

And why not? I know of no reason why the one may not be as readily believed as the other. The mistake here is, first, in supposing that the priests under the Old Testament were empowered to offer up to the Divine Majesty, real, proper sacrifice. There is no sacrificial virtue whatever in the blood of bulls and goats. The next error is in not distinguishing between Christ and Jesus. Jesus was only the human manifestation of Christ. Jesus had his origin and life like other men at his chronological period. He lived and died. Christ is immutable. Or, without raising any question as to the eternity of the Sonship, He was at least here, in the full exercise of all the functions of Saviourship, in the time of Adam and his sons. And this leads to the third error of supposing that Christ became a sacrifice for the sin of the world, only at the period of Jesus' life. And hence the misinterpretation of Paul, in supposing him to speak of a new principle, or law of sacrifice, whereas he means only new and better facilities for teaching and understanding it.

438. "With the beginning of Messiah's reign on Pentecost, the law of Moses was abolished, and the gospel in its elements, and with its conditions of salvation, first proclaimed."

In one of the recent public debates in Kentucky, on ecclesiastical science, of which there have been quite a number, the above is the carefully prepared proposition of Mr. Brooks of the Christian Church, so called, one of the debaters. The law of Moses is here explained to include, in the largest sense, all that is preceptive or obligatory in the Old Testament. It has no more to do with true religion, with salvation, or the conditions of salvation, than the Koran or the books of Confucius. And as God is unchangeable, it never had!

439. I regret to see that Dr. Lange's Commentary, recently published, fails to notice the uninterrupted continuance of the Church through the period of the New Testament history; and so, on page 4 of his Introduction, he says, "The history of revelation may be divided into the pre-Christian, and the Christian (not post-Christian) era." And elsewhere he speaks more elaborately of the "pre-Christian era," etc.

These expressions are certainly understood to mean what the scholarly author could not have intended. Pre-Christian may be proper enough if it have reference to the mere name of the Church, but to have application either to its religious faith, or the outward organization of its fellowship, is out of the question.

440. Dr. Lange says of Matthew: "Before his conversion, he was employed in collecting toll and custom by the Lake of Gennesareth."

This is entirely unknown. There is not a word in Scripture as to Matthew's early religious history, when or where he was converted. The history of his early acquaintance with the Saviour is exceeding brief. It merely says that he was a collector of custom; that Jesus, after more or less acquaintance with him — we are not informed — proposed to him the mission and calling of his after life; that he complied promptly, entering upon those duties after reasonable time to disengage himself from his former pursuits. But to assume that he was then converted is entirely gratuitous. There is not the remotest intimation, even inferential, of such a thing. We know he was a member of the Church, and that his written creed, or faith, was that of the Church now. It certainly might be that, like Saul of Tarsus, his faith was only nominal, and he then unconverted. But there is not the least intimation that it was so. It would be clumsy and absurd enough to suppose a man was unconverted, because he held the faith of the prophets and believed the Old Testament. All the presumptions are in favor of early piety in the apostle. He accepted the Christship of Jesus at least as early as Dr. Lange did, that is, so soon as he was informed of it.

441. It is certainly a great blunder of Dr. Lange, to speak, as he does in several places, of "the esoteric religion of the Jews." The meaning is, that all true religion prior to the incarnation was esoteric. Used as that word is here, it means private, private teaching, or private religious faith. It is used in contradistinction to exoteric, which means outward, public, or not restricted.

Before that period was there no religion for mankind? Let a man reflect a moment on the idea of a mere private offer of salvation. Many Christians object to ordinary Calvinism; but this is tenfold more objectionable. Are "Whosoever will, let him come," and more than a thousand other expressions of the same general import, esoteric lessons? Are the Ten Commandments esoteric? We have no esoteric Scriptures. If the Old Testament was formerly esoteric, how and by what authority did it become exoteric? We are told the Old Testament was abolished by Jesus Christ. Did that abolition give it exoteric authority? It has been heretofore explained that as true religion, from the early occupation of Palestine by the Hebrews to the incarnation, was called Jew, or Jewish, it was a simple truism that religion was confined to Jews; that is, religion is confined to religious people.

II.

THE APOSTOLATE.

WHAT office did the twelve apostles hold in the Church? What power, duty, franchise, or function was peculiar to them, or, including Paul as the thirteenth, what pertained to them especially, as apostles?

First. It was not to introduce or teach any new religion, or new doctrines, tenets, or principles of religion, or any new rules of morals not already known to the Scriptures, and more or less taught by ministers everywhere. This they certainly did not do. They were not, as we are told in *Smith's Bible Dictionary*, "sent forth first to preach the gospel," if by gospel you mean the universal offer of salvation to all men through Christ. This had been done for hundreds and thousands of years, by thousands of other ministers, and was then being done every Sabbath day by other thousands.

Second. It was not a peculiar function of the apostolate to "found churches," as we are told by the same authority. This they undoubtedly did, but only in common with other ministers. Thousands did the same thing at the same time, as well as before and since. Thousands of churches then existed, not only throughout the little province of Palestine, but over the entire known world almost. The general rule then was, and had been for hundreds of years, to extend and establish churches wherever there were ten persons of leisure. So this extending of churches, however much or little of it was done, was neither new nor peculiar. It was always so.

Third. Neither was it the apostles' business to set up, or assist in setting up a new general Church, as Romanists suppose. This, we may conclude has been pretty well proven, was not done at all by anybody. This, then, was not their office. There was no kingdom of heaven, to introduce and set up anew in the world, either in the form of doctrines or principles of salvation, or of social Christianity manifested in outward religious communion.

Fourth. Neither was it an apostolic function to govern the Church, to administer its laws, ordain its ministers, or supervise its affairs. This was at least physically impossible. Look at the facts, and it is utterly out of the question. It is the notion of many, but will not bear the least touch of sober inquiry. In that age of the world, the Church never numbered less than several millions, spread over the known world. With their means of travel, it was physically impossible they could see it, even once in their lives, much less govern its affairs. The notion that these twelve men governed the whole Church for some years is inseparable from the Romish doctrine of a new Church being then formed in Jerusalem, beginning in the nature of a corporation, with twelve, twenty, or a hundred members. Such a Church, if there had been such a thing, might have been governed by twelve superintendents or bishops, for a time. But there was no such Church. The only Church known to Scripture, or to history, never, in those ages, numbered less than several millions, with probably ten thousand preachers at the very least, and spread over the known world. The travel was on foot. What practical government could they exercise?

Fifth. It is said the apostles were bishops. Perhaps they were, if there were any bishops in those times, *i. e.*, what is now commonly called bishops. Of this, however, there is no mention in Scripture. If the Church then had what we now call an Episcopal form of government, there must have been several hundred bishops.

Sixth. Then if none of these things furnish us with the peculiar apostolic function, what was it? This must be an easy question to answer. Let us look slowly at the condition of things at that period. Christ, as the second person in the divine Trinity, had existed and been in the Church since the days of Adam, but was not to appear and be seen as a man until now. We see also the mode of this appearance. And we see also, not an unlikely thing, that there were false pretensions to the Christship. Hence the necessity of some certain way of identifying the true Christ. Now how was this to be done? His miracles would do something toward it, but we see that these alone were not sufficient. It required the best possible evidence, and of every possible kind. His death and resurrection was the best conceivable, but even that had to be verified.

Let it be borne in mind that this simple question of fact, whether the man Jesus was or was not the Christ, was the only mooted question of any importance in the Church in those times. There were no serious questions about doctrines, or Church government, or anything of the sort. The Christship of Jesus was the only question. The resurrection was the highest proof, but to whom was this presented? Necessarily to a very few. The great mass of the Church was at a distance, and could not possibly see or know these things. They could not even hear about them for months or years. At this time perhaps three fourths, or for aught that we know, nine tenths of the Church, had never heard of Jesus. But a small part of the Church lived in Palestine. And of these, but a few hundred, or at most a few thousand, had had opportunity to learn much, conclusively, of these great matters, or had made the best use of the opportunities they had. The resurrection was known to but a handful.

Now the question arises, How is the Church, and through it the whole world, to be authoritatively informed of the human Christship, with such certitude that it may at once be accepted as a conclusive matter of faith? This question must be settled wherever and whenever fairly presented. There must be no unreasonable delay. Jesus being the Christ, He must be accepted at once. And the question must be presented to the whole Church as soon as practicable. Those few just there, in and around Jerusalem, who were in favorable circumstances, could know and decide. But beyond this handful, how are the millions to know?

Here we see the necessity for the apostles. This was their great office. They were witnesses. They were to testify to the Church and the world that Jesus was Christ. It was first necessary that they themselves be convinced by the highest possible sanctions. Now look at their training for several years, fitting them for the office. At the time of the ascension they not only knew the fact themselves, but were impressed with the necessity of publishing it to the Church and the world, of course "beginning at Jerusalem." This was the natural place to begin; and then in the synagogues, everywhere.

Christ crucified could not be preached until He was crucified; and not even then by those not well and authoritatively informed of the fact. None could know it at first but the apostles and a very few others. The world must be informed. The apostles were the special heralds of this great fact. But in this they certainly preached no new doctrines, they introduced no new religion, they set up no new kingdom.

It was impossible that Jesus could be known as Christ, even after the resurrection, for months and years, by large portions of the Church. So they could not preach what they did not, and could not know. The high apostolic office was, to make this fact known. They were the messengers specially appointed to carry the intelligence speedily to the churches.

Imagine ourselves living a hundred, or a thousand miles from Palestine. We are devout, pious people, trusting for salvation as the prophets trusted, to the merits of Christ. The Old Testament is our Bible, its God is our God, and its Christ is our Christ. We hear strange rumors from Palestine. We are bewildered with these statements. Some of them seem plausible, others almost or quite incredible. Enemies are likely to misrepresent; while friends are not always free from exaggeration. Our piety, if nothing else, forces upon us an intense anxiety to know the truth. The Scriptures favor the general statements, but cannot be conclusive because we do not know whether the facts precisely fulfill the prophecies. Nothing could be more welcome to our pious ears than to hear, in solid, reliable certainty, that Jesus was and is the very Christ. Most of our information comes roundabout and through many hands. O, for something direct and certain! But as we value truth, we must receive this information slowly and cautiously, hoping it may prove true, but fearing it may not.

Now this was, it must have been, the case with hundreds of thousands of pious people then living. Jesus was unknown out of Palestine, nor are we warranted in believing that many in Palestine knew much about Him.

Under these circumstances, O, how welcome a messenger was an apostle affirming, "We tell what we know, and testify what we have seen!" They would tell the churches: "We know Him well; we were with Him almost every day for several years; we saw Him in his ministry, and in his death; yea, we saw Him forty days after his death. We conversed with Him repeatedly and freely after we saw Him die, and in his tomb." O, the thrilling scenes they would relate! O, the responses they would receive!

And then they not only related what they had seen, but they were well backed up with the Holy Ghost, by which they compelled belief in all who were willing to hear the truth. So, while the piously inclined multitudes heard the apostolic messages with delight, and by them were filled with the Holy Ghost, the proud scoffed, and the worldly turned away.

How natural was all this! How true both to reason and to Scripture!

Watson's Theological Dictionary, art. "Apostle," says it means, "One of the twelve disciples of Jesus Christ, commissioned by Him to preach his gospel, and propagate it to all parts of the earth."

This, which is all he says about the peculiar apostolic function, is certainly no description at all of apostle. If he had said they were "men who lived in Palestine," the statement would be true, but would be no description of the twelve apostles, because it would apply just as well to thousands of others. So there were in that age, as well as in this, many other disciples of Jesus Christ, commissioned by Him to preach his gospel, and propagate it to all parts of the earth. The description describes nothing.

Sometimes we are told they were messengers sent to proclaim the gospel. So were Abel, Noah, and every other preacher to this day.

Their office was to proclaim and prove the great fact, and then to explain, where they could, the necessary discontinuance of those religious ceremonies that pointed forward to the visible work of Christ.

Peter and the other apostles seem to have understood their office as here stated. "Beginning from the baptism of John unto that same day that He was taken up from us, must one be ordained to be a witness with us of his resurrection." (Acts i. 22.) There is stated the true apostolic function: to be a witness with us of his resurrection. They were to witness his resurrection, and consequently, of course, his Christship, first to the Church and then to the world. Nothing is said specially about their governing the Church, here or elsewhere.

What is meant, therefore, when we are told, "They were his *messengers*, sent forth to proclaim his kingdom; and after his resurrection, they were specially selected to bear witness of that event?" (*Scott's Bible*, Matt. x. 1.)

What kingdom were they to proclaim? Surely, nothing but what prophets and preachers had always proclaimed. And as to his resurrection, it looks like a very diluted expression to say, they were specially selected to bear witness of that event. Not the mere event surely, but the great, vital truth which this event, taken in connection with other events, proves to be true, namely, the divine Christhood in the man Jesus. The Christhood was the question.

"The apostles were unlearned men, brought up in obscurity, and not used to speak before public assemblies." Dr. Scott writes that just because other men do, and for no other reason. There is not a word of testimony to justify the statement. If I should write that they were mostly learned men, preachers of considerable standing, accustomed to public speaking, the statement would look a little more reasonable, and would at least be difficult to disprove.

"As regards the *apostolic office*, it seems to have been preëminently that of founding the churches, and upholding them by supernatural power, specially bestowed for that purpose." (*Smith's Dict.*, art. "Apostle.")

Where there is difference of opinion about either the meaning of Bible language, facts, or doctrines, one can tolerate, and even have high respect for that which he does not believe. But that is not the case here. There is no rational difference of opinion here. Did the apostles found churches? Where is such a thing intimated in Scripture? Churches already existed all over the land, the very identical churches, hundreds and thousands, no doubt, that merely continued uninterruptedly. What churches were founded, beyond such ordinary extension of churches as has been always going on?

Mr. James Anthony Froude, in a recent address to the University of St. Andrews, says, page 31: "I am not about to sketch the rise of Christianity. I mean only to point out the principles on which the small knot of men gathered themselves together, who were about to lay the foundations of a vast revolution."

Let the blunder here be pointed out, and neither the learned Professor, nor any one for him, would for one moment undertake to defend the language. Here the twelve apostles are represented as being about to lay the foundations of a vast revolution. I will not argue the question how irreligious the Church was, at the period in question; but I must insist, that to sweep out a house is a different thing from removing it and building a new one. The former is reformation; the latter is revolution. The religion of the Church of that day was not revolutionized, for it is our Bible, *verbatim*, to-day. The apostles, and those acting with them, improved it as much as they improved it. If it had been told Isaiah, that the Christ he worshipped, and of whose appearance he prophesied, was going to overthrow his religion, and raise up a new and different one, he would have taught his informer better.

To say that the apostles set on foot a revolution

means that the religion of the Church, that is, the Old Testament, in its religious teachings was radically and thoroughly erroneous, and so had to be destroyed, and replaced by new Scriptures. This is too wild and fabulous to think about. Everybody knows that, holding the Scriptures intact, the Saviour and apostles, and all those coöperating with them, labored to improve the piety of the Church, just as men do now. They did not change, nor seek to change one of its minutest doctrines or shades of doctrine. They introduced such new modes of teaching as the divine incarnation rendered necessary.

As to the government of the Church, there seems to have been no trouble or material change on that score. It is scarcely alluded to in the New Testament. It is nowhere the prominent subject of remark. The Sanhedrim seems to have discontinued, not however, because of anything wrong in its constitution, but because its members mostly apostatized, and thus left the true Church; and so this made it the governing body of another, a different, an apostate Church. The Sanhedrim, though never necessary just as it was formed, was, no doubt, a very useful means of exercising the higher functions of government. In its later history, it was much abused. Something much like it has nearly always been in the Church. It is the mistake of many who suppose that this council, so frequently alluded to in the New Testament, pertained to the entire Church at that time. It had no recognized jurisdiction, beyond the Judean portion of it. The Hellenistic and Samaritan portions of the Church had, no doubt, their respective legislative and judicial councils, more or less similar to, or differing from that at Jerusalem.

The disruption of the Church and apostacy of a large portion of it about Jesus, with the terrible strifes and animosities that ensued, seem to have destroyed the sectarian jealousies between these three denominations. The great and vital question of the Christship overrode and absorbed everything.

But these matters of Church government had no essential connection with the apostolate. That referred to the far higher, and infinitely more important matter of ordaining forever, at the very first moment possible, the great and fundamental fact of the divine Christhood in humanity, the world-wide pedestal upon which all human salvation rests.

III.

MATTHEW XVI. 18.

THE expression here cited, "On this rock I will build my Church," is relied upon primarily, or, with its supposed surrounding supports it might be said almost wholly, to maintain the doctrine of a new and different Church for Christians from the then existing Church. And it is at once obvious that this must be understood as a settled starting-point, before you can begin to consider either Romanism or any other branch of High Churchism. All forms of High Churchism claim only to have ascertained the manner in which this new Church was formed, and the legal principles which were interwoven in it.

That such a construction has been given to this passage is indeed remarkable; and that it has been generally conceded, without debate or question, may be regarded astounding. It is not less than wonderful, that the only important question here has generally been passed over, and a mythical question about Peter substituted in its place. The question about Peter, so much debated between certain Romanists and Protestants, is called mythical, because it inquires only whether Peter, the apostle, acted this part or that, in the formation of the new Christian Church, when there was, in truth, no such formation of a new Church. It inquires how a thing was done, without first stopping to see whether it was done at all, and when the thing never was done.

"On this rock I will build my Church." It has been generally understood in the books, and until lately has not been seriously and widely questioned, that the words, "I will build my Church," were equivalent to his saying, "I am about to begin and set up a new Church, distinct and different from the one now existing." And then the questions have run as to the newly enacted laws of the new Church. No other Scripture except this has been cited, as direct proof of the new Church.

Now, it must first be conceded that this passage does relate to a new Church formation, before any question can arise as to the agency of Peter, or any other agency in it. So a reply at all about Peter's primacy, headship, or office in this new Church, of course concedes that there was such a Church.

This expression of Scripture, "I will build," etc., is made to mean the very reverse of what it does mean. Properly understood, it means that no new Church was to be made, but that the Church then existing was to be improved. Now this shall be made so plain, that there shall not be room for either doubt or objection.

Jesus said that "on" something He would "build" his Church. Now what is *build?* What is the meaning of *build?* See Webster's Dictionary (ed. 1857): "In Scripture, to increase and strengthen; to cement and knit together; to settle or establish and preserve. Acts xx. 32; Eph. ii. 22; 1 Sam. ii. 35."

Now as there is no authority or pretense of authority differing from this definition, one would suppose it might be allowed to settle the question. When the Saviour said He would do to or for the Church what is here rendered build, He said He would increase and strengthen the Church, He would cement it together, He would settle, establish, and preserve it. These words in such a connection, all mean about the same thing. The definition is slightly different in verbiage, in different editions of Webster, particularly those published since the death of the author, but there is no authority in the English language, differing materially from this. Edify, also, means the same thing. Milton, in "Paradise Lost," referring to the return of the Israelites from their captivity in Babylon, and their rebuilding the temple, says, —

"The house of God
They first reëdify."

A building is an edifice. Though of late years custom has mostly discontinued the use of the verb in this sense.

Now, repeating that there is no English authority opposing these definitions, can anything be more certainly understood? What is the use of a spy-glass to see a thing a yard from you, or an elaborate argument where there is nothing to argue about?

This word build, with its derivatives, is used in the New Testament about seventy times. Sometimes — according to the subject and sense — it is translated *build*, *builder*, *building*, etc., and sometimes *edify*, *edification*, etc., as sense, taste, and idiom may seem to require. But here is an important fact necessary to be specially noted: whenever the act is referred to the Almighty, as in this text before us, in all Scripture, it invariably applies to some well known thing already existing, and never to a new thing brought, or to be brought into existence. So when the Lord is said to build, the meaning is that He strengthens, enlarges, makes better, edifies. Any other meaning will make the Scripture appear ridiculous.

This text, therefore, clearly establishes the doctrine of a then existing Church, which the Saviour said He would enlarge, support, build up, and edify. Surely He has done, and is still doing all this.

And then the Saviour said He would do this building, this enlarging, and edifying "on" something. Now what is the meaning of *on?* Let us go again to the Dictionary.

On means "in consequence of, or immediately following;" or in pursuance of; as we would say, "*on* payment of the money, I will deliver the goods." Now, there is one vitally important thing we know with unmistakable certainty, about the Saviour's future intention to edify, enlarge, or build the Church, whether He said so on that occasion or not. We know that whatever was done, or to be done thereafter, in truth, to, for, or about the Church, was to be done *on*, *i. e.*, in consequence of, in pursuance of, or immediately following the fact just then stated by Peter, that Jesus was Christ. This was now the great and fundamental question of the Church. Supposing that Jesus was, and is Christ, it necessarily follows that everything done in, or for the Church, must be done hereafter,—but could never be done before,—on, or in pursuance of that great fact. Now and thenceforward, everything in the Church rests on that rock, on that fundamental fact, Jesus is Christ.

The language of the text looks too simple for difference of opinion. Then to what purpose are these lengthy discussions about Peter — what powers or prerogatives were or were not conferred upon him? What is to be gained by the success of either party? If the Church was then and there made a new religious corporation or society, to have perpetual succession from that time, and work under its then prescribed charter, who cares whether the first president's name was Peter or something else? If Peter was not the first president, or bishop, then somebody else was, and who cares? The supposition that the conferring of some powers of government upon one or more leading Church officers then, fixes official or legal rules for Church government now, rests upon the supposition precedent that Jesus Christ then made anew this Christian Church. And this seen to be a palpable figment, the whole argument, both sides alike, is a palpable figment. The argument is about nothing.

Those who have no better use for ink and paper, may debate whether "Peter was thus honored to lay the first foundation of the Christian Church," or "be the foundation thereof;" and who cares which may be judged the winning side? The question itself being fictitious, how can the answer be anything more?

If the Church is not a corporation formed in such way at all, as we have perhaps abundantly shown, then let that truth answer every conceivable question about High Church doctrines, Popish, Episcopal, or what not. The entire range of ecclesiastical science is thus reduced to a unit, and the Church literature is relieved of vast burdens of polemical rubbish.

IV.

THE ANCIENT PROMISE OF A SAVIOUR.

Closely connected with, and growing very naturally out of the great blunder of an entirely new system of divine administration in the moral affairs of mankind, sought to be rectified in these pages, is the idea that very early in the history of men, God promised a Saviour to the world, to be furnished in some future age. And this idea they claim to get from Gen. iii. 15, where we read, "It shall bruise thy head, and thou shalt bruise his heel." And then, as if to make the matter sufficiently ridiculous, the divine promise is regarded as being announced to mankind in this precise form of words; so that the entire sum of human knowledge for four thousand years was these exact words spoken to the devil; and it would seem presumable, though it is not so stated, that the words were spoken in the hearing of Adam or Eve, or perhaps both.

From these words alone it would be impossible for rational men to come to the conclusion that the world at some future time was to have a Saviour, and if so, what that Saviour was to do for mankind. From this teaching we learn that the seed of the woman would bruise the head of Satan. But when, where, how, to what end, for what purpose, and several other things easily conceived as necessary to a rational understanding of the declaration, are not alluded to. So of what advantage could such a declaration be to mankind?

Moreover, it could not be very consoling to men then, to be informed that the world, away in future ages, perhaps some thousands of years thence, would have a Saviour. It reminds one of the child who came crying with hunger to his father, who replied, "Never mind my son, I'm going to plant some beans to-morrow." The promise was sadly inadequate.

God never promised the world a Saviour. On the contrary, He furnished the world a Saviour, full, complete, adequate in all the functions of Saviourship at the very first. From the first, Christ, our only Saviour, was in full sympathy and activity. Then, there, and not four thousand years afterward, He undertook our cause. He began at the beginning, at the right time, at the right place, and in the right way. And He will finish it, not partially, but fully, completely, in the shortest time possible. The bruising of that head was a far greater work than many seem to think. A little has been done towards it already, and the prediction will be fulfilled. In four or five thousand years, or thereabouts, Christ manifested Himself to men, continuing his work uninterruptedly.

What we read in Genesis is the language of Moses; what he wrote, in exceeding brief, laconic language, many hundred years afterward, about God's early teachings to mankind. How voluminous or extensive in detail these teachings were, or indeed exactly how they were communicated, we are not informed; but we are obliged to believe they were quite sufficiently voluminous to be fully intelligible and practical. They were wisely and mercifully communicated to rational and intelligent beings for their practical advantage. It is impossible to suppose they, as a whole, fell short of making up a complete, intelligible, rational, religious system, in full accord with everything else revealed in Scripture. The supposition that it consisted wholly in this expression, "It shall bruise thy head, and thou shalt bruise his heel," looks exceedingly Lilliputian. That was the sum of it. Moses wrote history. His history of the antediluvian age, and particularly the fore part of it, is very laconic. What occurred, in full detail, is one thing; what Moses wrote to us about it is quite another. This is the nature of all history. If Moses had written ten thousand times more than he did, which certainly might have been, it would probably be of but little benefit to us. He wrote what he wrote, and no more.

But he certainly did not write that God promised that we should have a Saviour in some future age.

V.

THE FIRST CHURCH COUNCIL AT JERUSALEM.

THE 15th chapter of Acts contains a very brief notice of some misunderstanding or disturbance in the Church at Antioch, about the necessity or propriety of continuing the rite of circumcision, and no doubt other such obsolete ceremonies in the Church, which seems to have been quieted by referring the matter to the brethren at Jerusalem. Much more has been made out of this affair than was ever dreamed of by those who participated in it. It was not at all unnatural or unlikely that such a question should arise, nor that it should be quieted in the way it was, without supposing any legal jurisdiction over such questions to have resided with "the apostles and elders" at Jerusalem.

Those who raised this question and favored the continuance of the rite, were believers, — they "believed." Believed what? Evidently they were members of the Church, and believed that Jesus was the Christ. This was the only question then rife in the Church.

Let it be understood that the ceremonies that discontinued in that period were exclusively those which, in their external aspects and teachings, pointed forward to the only atoning sacrifice of Christ; and the discontinuance was because that sacrifice had now transpired. Christ had now made Himself visible to the eyes of men; not that He now began to atone for sin, for He was no more a Saviour now, than He had always been. But He had now appeared; and so those teaching ceremonies that adumbrated the appearance must, of course, cease.

But it was not perfectly easy for every one, at the first, to see and understand this necessity. Habit had very deeply established these ceremonies. Many, no doubt, did not well understand the reason for them, and so, of course, they would be still more slow to understand a reason for their discontinuance. There was certainly no authoritative abrogation of them, else it would be easy to point to the decree, and there would be no necessity of sending to Jerusalem, to consult apostles and brethren about this question, nor any necessity that the brethren at Jerusalem should come together to consider this matter, nor give opinions or sentence about it.

How both these things can be believed, is indeed strange. And yet we are, in hundreds of places, taught, first, that the whole "Ceremonial Law," as they call it, of course including circumcision, was formally and authoritatively abolished by our Saviour; and then, that twenty years afterward, a Church council was convened to consider, and give sentence, whether circumcision should be continued or not in the Church. But if you understand this Church council in any sort of proper sense, it is as easy to believe both things, contradictory as they are, as to believe either.

Nothing is more easy now to see, than that the discontinuance forever of circumcision, passover, etc., was a necessary consequence of Christ's human appearance and visible work ; but it does by no means follow, that all would readily see it then. These were great and important matters, more new then than now. It would naturally take some time for the mind of the Church to settle and adjust itself. Some would see more readily than others. This, and all such like disputes, in those times, for there were many, were very natural.

But why was this question referred from Antioch to Jerusalem ? Why not refer it to any other Church ? There were scores, hundreds, yea thousands, all over the country.

A Romanist would answer this by saying that the newly formed Christian Church had its headquarters, its president and council, in that city, and that there only could an authoritative decision be had, for these apostles only could dispense the new religion.

But suppose there was, or had been, no new Church or new religion, then how stands the case ? Then and in that case, there was no more of Church authority in the Church at Jerusalem, than at Antioch, Cesarea, Damascus, Joppa, or churches of Macedonia, or elsewhere. Who made James, or Peter either, a supreme president of a supreme Church council ? And what becomes of the question whether the name of the first president was Peter or something else, since there was no such first Church or first president ?

It is seen therefore at a glance that this whole notion of supreme authority in the apostles and elders at Jerusalem, is inseparable from and rests wholly upon the Romish fiction of a new Church and new religion. Let this be reduced to sober truth, and the whole fabric is reduced to ruins. And then, also, this great question, great in the estimation of some, whether Peter or something else was the name of the supreme bishop, is disposed of without any great logical crash, by seeing that the entire story is a fiction. There was no new Church.

Nevertheless, nothing is more natural than the rise among honest Christians, at Antioch, of this question about the Church rites with which they had all been familiar all their lives; nor than that Paul and Barnabas should "go up to Jerusalem, unto the apostles and elders, about this question," that they should gravely consider it, and give their advice and counsel, and write a letter of greeting to their brethren away yonder in Syria, in Antioch, and Cilicia, about the matter.

They in Syria knew very well that in Jerusalem they would meet, most likely, some of the apostles and other grave elders of age and wisdom who had had much personal intercourse with Jesus, and whose advice would be almost, if not quite certain to quiet the minds of the brethren. In that age much more than in this, learning, wealth, wisdom, and influence of all kinds concentrated in the cities, and especially in the larger ones. Jerusalem was not only much the largest and oldest city in the land, but was the great religious capital, and had been for many hundred years. But the Church, the entire Church, had neither at that time, nor any other, any general acknowledged synod, conference, or assembly. The Sanhedrim we read so much about in that city had no acknowledged jurisdiction beyond Southern Judea, and perhaps more or less at times in Galilee. Samaria, and all Grecian and African countries had their own Church governments. So that it was very natural and proper that these people in Syria should send to the apostles and elders in Jerusalem for ad vice and counsel, but not for any legal decision about this question. Let it be well understood, that the Church in those ages, during every day of those ages, was scattered thousands of miles over the known world; much of it in interior countries, with very slow and difficult intercommunication. Many think and write about it as a thing to be seen at one time and one place, whereas it was so situate and conditioned that, as a whole, it could understand itself about nothing under a number of years. We see that this great question of the Christship in Jesus was not settled in all the Church for a long time, probably thirty years or more.

Circumcision, and these other ceremonies, did not, therefore, cease all at once. It required time, and thought, and habit, for the Church to adjust itself to their entire disuse. Men conformed their thoughts and conduct to the truth and apostolic teachings, as they better and better understood the remarkable circumstances through which they were so rapidly and strangely passing. I say strange because, strikingly unlike all other men that ever lived, they lived both before and after the life and death of Jesus. They saw and felt the Church pass through the most unique and wonderful crisis and period of its history, actual or possible. This period was necessarily brief, and in that country necessarily presented the most rapid succession of thrilling scenes, at times almost bewildering, and of the most vital importance.

The thought would not necessarily occur to every one that such and such particular ceremonies would be contradictory after the death of Jesus. The reason for the non-user was the same then as now, but many did not readily see it ; and though it was constantly taught by the apostles and others, yet, like any other teaching, it was not always promptly and readily received and appreciated. Many do not seem to see its reasons very clearly now.

It was not by any means at Antioch alone, and on this occasion, that this question arose and troubled the Church ; we have frequent intimations of the same thing at other times and in other parts of the Church. Two things, however, are certain : First, circumcision was not discontinued by any formal enactment of abrogation, or decree, as many writers teach ; if so, there had been no disputation or different opinions about it. And secondly, the Church at Jerusalem, its council or its bishops, had no more legal authority or jurisdiction over the question than the Church anywhere else. That Church no doubt had its bishop, but he was no more, in a legal sense, than any other pastor of any other Church. He, no doubt, stood prominently above most other bishops ; but if so, it was because of his age, talents, wisdom, and opportunities for the best information, and not because of any legal authority.

But whether this council, if any one chooses so to denominate it, was presided over by James, or Peter, or somebody else, or why by James, instead of Peter, might be questions of some interest among High Churchmen, who could probably interest themselves in such a debate. But it is clearly impossible that any but a High Churchman could participate in such debate, because all such questions, in every aspect they present, suppose and grow out of the doctrine of a new Church and new religion then and there set up for the first time.

Then let any man understand that the supposition that this council at Jerusalem had any general jurisdiction, is inseparable from, and indeed is but part and parcel of the supposition of a new Church and new religion. And then let him not forget as he passes, that a new Church, at any time, is a natural and philosophical impossibility, with not a word of either Scripture or reason to support it. And that a new religion, or any new doctrines at any time since the days of Adam, is necessarily a false religion.

Let these necessary things be understood, and let it not be forgotten that the people then and there were natural people ; that they thought, reasoned, and acted, much as we ourselves would be likely to do in such circumstances ; and we shall find no great difficulty in understanding this council at Jerusalem.

A hard lesson for many people to learn is that changes, often very considerable changes, in external manners are necessary in order to maintain consistency of principle. This was the case with the Church of that age, in a most remarkable degree.

In understanding the Scriptures, as in construing any other writing, we must be careful not to violate well attested facts, or well settled principles. The introduction of a new religion, and the setting up of a new Church, by Jesus Christ, or under his authority, is, when looked, nay when glanced at, with a sober eye, a transparent error ; and, looked at specifically, it cannot stand for a single moment. It is both historically untrue, and philosophically impossible. While it has been asserted a thousand times, no man ever even attempted to summon proof, or to make an argument to support it. It is not only the pillar, but the sole pillar of all objectionable Romanism.

Scripture must be maintained inviolate, both in its integrity and consistency. Then we must not on any account, for any circumstances of convenience, or for any reasons, construe Scripture so as to make a court, a council, or anything of the sort, suppose, require, or assent to such ascertained error. Some other construction must be found.

Now read all that portion of the chapter before us; and if you read with care and without prejudice, you will be surprised almost at the simplicity and naturalness of the narration. To give anything then at Jerusalem even the tinge of a forensic, legal, or judicial appearance, among those honest hearted apostles and brethren, in their simple, easy, wise, and discreet attempt to reconcile the troubles away yonder in Syria, you are obliged to screw up, force, and hyperconstrue the simple literature, and also imagine and add to the condition of things greatly, before you can make out of it anything of the nature of Church court, or legal council with authority to decree and decide theological questions.

And if that "first council" possessed the judicial authority attributed to it, upon what ground do you ignore similar authority in a similar council, which sat in Rome in 1870?

VI.

THE KINGDOM OF HEAVEN.

IT is written in the third chapter of Matthew that John, called the Baptist, came preaching and exhorting the people to repent, for that the kingdom of heaven was at hand. What we read here, it should be remembered, is the language of Matthew, not of John. Matthew, fifteen or twenty years afterward, writes, historically, about what John did and said. He uses his own language in notes of great brevity. In this place his language is exceedingly laconic, barely intimating the general burden, substance, or at least some of the general things about which John preached. We learn first that John preached. We know what preaching is. And in his preaching, he brought forward the subjects of repentance and the kingdom of heaven. In this we see nothing new, though from the manner in which the thing is mentioned, rather than from the mention itself, we should suppose it probable that John, when he went out into these country settlements to preach, made the subjects of repentance and the kingdom of heaven more prominent than other preachers were wont to do in those times.

The supposition of its being entirely new to preach repentance might, perhaps, be excused in fanciful sophomoric theologians who had been taught so, but it is as well known as anything else in Scripture, that repentance and the kingdom of heaven had been always preached everywhere, by preachers generally, for thousands of years. Certainly Abel, Noah, and all the prophets preached it. And when John preached it, he only preached what he read all·through his Bible. Nevertheless there was, no doubt, just then and there, great need that these things be made prominent in a practical ministry.

The words "at hand," "the kingdom of heaven is at hand," have attracted the attention of some theologians so as to make the words mean that a new kingdom was about to be introduced. And then a lively imagination connects this idea of a new kingdom to be introduced with a prophecy of Daniel ii. 44, where he says, "In the days of these kings shall the God of heaven set up a kingdom," etc. And the two passages are made to support the doctrine of the introduction of a new kingdom of Christ, meaning thereby a new system of religion, that is, new rules and conditions of salvation, and a new Church.

It is evident that this supposed relation between these two passages of Scripture is entirely dependent on the preconceived supposition of a new religion being introduced into the world, at the time of the Saviour's advent. Remove this idea; let it be once supposed that the conditions of salvation in the days of Adam are the conditions always; that Christ, in the days of his advent, introduces no new system of religion; and then it is impossible to talk about setting up a new, spiritual, religious kingdom, for the two expressions mean one and the same thing. A system of religion is a spiritual kingdom. A spiritual kingdom is a system of religion. In this sense the terms are synonymous.

The word *kingdom*, with a large class of words of about the same meaning, such as *throne*, *sceptre*, *dominion*, etc., are used many hundred times in Scripture. They all mean nearly the same thing, namely, the authority, rule, or control which God rightly possesses and exercises over the hearts and lives of men. The temporal idea of kingdom — power, authority, etc. — is seen at a glance; and the spiritual idea, which the same words represent, is easily seen, if we but notice the simplicity of Scripture language, and avoid hair-splitting interpretations.

What is religion? It is obedience to God. It is the promptly accepted, ready, unresisted rule, authority, or kingly control of God through Christ in the heart and life of man. Obedience, unquestioning, implicit, and full obedience, is the utmost any man ever did or can do; it comprehends the whole subject. How easy then is it to transfer the idea of the temporal rule of a king over his subjects to the moral and spiritual rule of the Almighty over his! The loyal subjects of a king obey the laws of the kingdom promptly and readily. They meet fully all their civil obligations. And so, religious people obey the laws of God in like manner. They are loyal subjects of that kingdom. How natural, then, to speak of a religious kingdom, to people so well acquainted with a civil kingdom!

So it is in this figurative sense that religion, or religious people, or collectively the Church, is called a kingdom. The submission to divine authority, as expressed in Scripture, is like the civil submission in the other case. When, therefore, we speak of

Christ's kingdom, or read it in Scripture, the kingdom of God, kingdom of heaven, etc., expressions with which the Scriptures abound, that we are in it, or belong to it, we easily understand the meaning as submission to the divine authority ; the absolute rule of God in the hearts of men, in and through Christ, as this system of rule and dependence is set forth in Scripture.

Now did this divine rule, control, authority, this spiritual supremacy in the hearts of men, begin at the time of the Saviour's advent or at the first? That is the same as to ask, Did God begin to save men from sin through Christ at the first, or at the time of his human advent? Did the prophets teach the same principles of salvation as the apostles? Did Jesus set up a new religion? Does the New Testament contain conditions of salvation different from the Old?

To ask these questions is to indicate the answer unmistakably. They are not debatable questions. No two men can answer them differently. And it would be idle to suggest such questions, were it not for the fact that a number of Protestant authors do teach, unmistakably, the introduction of a new religion entire, in the time of Jesus and the apostles. Strange inconsistency ; as palpable as it is strange !

Right here, exactly here, is the point of divergence between Romanism and Protestantism. Popery supposes a new religion, a new kingdom. And thus arises her teaching as to how this was done ; what new tenets, what new Church authority, what office the first bishop Peter held, etc., to the end of a long chapter. But upon supposition that no new kingdom at all was set up, there can be no debate as to how it was done.

We ought not to debate questions until we get to them. Debates, where there is no rational issue, are unprofitable. The passage in Daniel, as sometimes interpreted, is put to a very great and unnatural tension by supposing it to describe the great Fifth Monarchy. That fable has long since ceased to attract attention. Before any inquiry about it can be set up, it is necessary to suppose that the principles, mode, and means of salvation, in vogue at and before the time of Jesus, came to an end. This, as a specific doctrine, is absurd. It is more than simply untrue. That the world was left four thousand years or more — for we have no certain ancient chronology — without true religion, as true and good as the world has now; or that any part of it was without revealed religion, only exactly as that is the case now; and that a fuller, or better religious system became necessary; all this is so palpably at war with everything taught in Scripture, that it is a wonder that even the cause of Popery ever resorted to such strange fancies.

There is not a word in Daniel, nor anywhere else, that alludes to a new kingdom, or anything new in the principles, conditions, or means of salvation. These were fixed at the first, and always the same. The kingdom of God, the kingdom of Christ, the kingdom of heaven, are always and everywhere spoken of as universal, spontaneous, everywhere present, everywhere accessible, everywhere in force, everywhere available. Chronology and history do not divide or limit it; neither do geography or lines of civil jurisdiction affect or improve it.

There were some few, we know not how many, in the Saviour's time, who had this same notion of a kingdom of God to be set up at that time. (See Luke xvii. 20–27.) And they inquired of Jesus when this was to be done. His reply ought to have been satisfactory both then and now, but it was not. He told them there was, or was to be, no such kingdom as they inquired about. "The kingdom of God cometh not with observation." It is not some new thing to be seen. It is not something historic, something outward, observable, phenomenal, something to occur in these days. It *is* already. "The kingdom of God is within you." It is spontaneous, not occasional. It is universal, not special. It is not something to come, but something that is now. You have only to submit to it.

And if any would understand the Saviour's reply to mean that the kingdom, or a kingdom of God, was indeed about to be set up, as a new phenomenal or observable thing, but not with such visible aspects and appearances as some anticipated, let him understand that that is supposing the absurdity of a new religion and new Church, dating at that time.

The phrase "at hand," as in Matt. iii. 2, does by no means, as many seem to suppose, always refer to something future. Webster says it means, "Near in time or place, either present and within reach, or not far distant." It is used about thirty times in Scripture, and it sometimes refers to something then present, and sometimes to the future. (See 1 Sam. ix. 8; Jer. xxiii. 23; Ezek. xii. 23; Matt. xxvi. 46; Mark xiv. 42; John ii. 13; Phil. iv. 5, etc.)

It is not denied but the prophecy in Daniel has reference to the post-messianic period of the Church; it is only intimated, for nothing is needed but an intimation, that no new kingdom or new system of grace was introduced at the period in question.

The kingdom of heaven, we are told, "signifies the gospel dispensation." That is true, provided you understand the gospel dispensation to signify the dispensation of salvation, or the dispensation of grace, in which God saves men from perdition through Christ, *i. e.*, by faith in Christ, and obedience to the laws of repentance. But the entire teaching and drift of Scripture is ignored, when we are told that this kingdom was about to appear, or shortly to appear, in the days of John. We know very well that the same gospel dispensation we have now, and about which John preached so well, existed four thousand years or more, before he preached. The dispensation of salvation was as fully known to Abel, and Noah, as to John. The light and the facility of teaching were not so great, we all know; but that the same system of grace existed is equally well known. One day may be dark and cloudy, and the next, a bright sunshine. That indicates the removal of clouds, but not the creation of the sun. Before the life and death of Jesus, thousands and millions of men had faith in Christ. Among them are many of the highest examples of Christian faith known to the history of religion. But of course none in that age had faith in Jesus, for Jesus had not been seen. The incarnate did not exist.

Now we all know that after Christ was manifest in the person of Jesus, the favorable results of the manifestation were enjoyed by the Church, and by mankind generally; religious teaching was more facile, more easy of inculcation, more readily discerned. This is a very different thing from the creation and introduction of a new system of religion, with new conditions of salvation. The system of astronomy is the same it always was, notwithstanding the introduction of the artificial globe and telescope. The system of religion now is the very same in Madagascar and in the best theological schools. The kingdom is, and always remains the same, though its spread and inculcation are greatly facilitated by the visible state of its Christ, its king.

But when told, as we are by Dr. Dwight, that, "As the Mediator, Jesus Christ began to exist at the birth of the man, Jesus Christ," we cannot understand the meaning except in violation of the plainest and best settled principles of Christian truth. That the world had no Mediator until the incarnation of the Mediator, is as clumsy an idea as could well be conceived. Again, he says, "This person, it is plain, had received no kingdom, until his ascension into heaven." Then it is by no means plain what person he is talking about.

Salvation was offered to all mankind, in full time for its acceptance, before any man died. The conditions upon which it was offered were one and the same, unaltered and unalterable. These conditions imply sovereignty, rule, or dominion, on the one hand, which is called a kingdom, by a very simple figure; and on the other hand, by the same comparison, the submissive obedience required places the subjects, by similar metonymy, in the attitude of a kingdom. The kingdom of God is within you.

VII.

THE REFORMATION OF THE SIXTEENTH CENTURY.

It was impossible that the fundamental principles of Romanism could be developed and understood from the bottom, at the first, in the sixteenth century, or for a long time afterwards. There was not a man in Europe but had grown up with stereotyped and unquestioned ideas of government, exceedingly unfavorable to such development. The things objected to by the Reformers were not defended on the ground of their usefulness, their merit, or their accordance with either the scope or the letter of Scripture, but on the ground of Church authority. "The Church says so," was a complete answer to every objection. In the habitudes of the people, there was no clear distinction between civil and ecclesiastical government. There was none in practice. The two jurisdictions were but partially separate. The complaints against the usages of the Church which led to the Reformation, exceedingly well put and well sustained as far as they went, were leveled only against the things they saw. They declared that these things were improper, useless, and unlawful. And when it was insisted and reiterated that "the Church says so," it was responded, — "These unlawful acts are those of Church officers, beyond their lawful jurisdiction, outside the Church constitution." And the question between Romanists and Protestants, from that day to this, has been, mainly, whether the primary Church authority did or did not authorize those things specifically objected to, without stopping to inquire whether there was any such primary Church authority or not.

And now it is here held, that this plea of the Protestants, however well put, as far as it lay, against the matters objected to, was nevertheless an acknowledgment of a great and fundamental error in ecclesiastical science in favor of Popery, and amounts to an estoppel to the most important argument in the case. It virtually acknowledges a divine Church constitution, governing the external matters of social religion. And so the Romish party defended themselves by claiming that the government of the Church being divinely framed, the jurisdiction of its officers must descend perpetually; and so, this authority being divine, it cannot, of course, be inquired into by unofficial men.

To this it was replied, that the Church could not have been organized on such basis, because the teachings of Jesus in organizing the Church must harmonize with other divine teachings. The question was not whether Church authority in the time of the apostles was divine authority. This was virtually conceded. The question was, What is this divine Church authority? The Protestants said, The Scriptures, when they are clear, must govern; and so we must presume the original Church constitution to have been framed that way. While Romanists contended that a divine Church constitution must be infallible, and must descend infallibly, and so the

Scriptures must be construed that way, for the Church teachings must be right. Here it is seen that an original Church charter, or constitution, or law of Church government, or the formation or organization of the Church of Christ, call it what you will, as divinely ordained in the apostles' days, is conceded.

It is strange that it did not occur to the Protestants, but it did not, that there was no divine Church constitution at all, fixing either this or that in Church government. But we now see that this was the form in which the argument was mainly conducted, and is still conducted.

The Romanist asserts the authority of the Church, that it is divine. The original Church, he says, has merely descended to our times just as its original framers left it. The Protestant says the Church has diverged from the original model, because it now varies from Scripture. Thus the controversy continues. The formation of a new Church, and introduction of a new religion is admitted; and the question is, how was the former arranged, and what are the principles and constituents of the latter?

When certain usages are objected to by Protestants, as opposed to Scripture, it is replied, "That may seem so to unsanctified, *i. e.*, out of the Church, human judgment, but these things accord with divine revelation; the Church is as divine as the Scripture, and so this is but an attempt to oppose divine doings here, with divine doings there.

This is the disadvantage the Protestant oftentimes labors under. He acknowledges the Church to be a divine revelation, that is, a divine institution, in that the constitution of its government is divinely prescribed; and in opposing Romanism, he is obliged to oppose Church revelation to Scripture revelation. He makes a good argument as far as it goes. He says these things are anti-Scriptural, and therefore erroneous. But the Romanist answers, "How can that be? How can one form of revelation be supposed to conflict with another form?"

The Protestant who says the Church is a "divine institution," or who talks about an "original Church of Christ," original in the days of the apostles, or about a new Church, or any of the thousand expressions of the same import, is hardly aware that he is virtually, by fair implication, affirming the doctrine of Church infallibility. And yet such is the purport of such declarations. If Jesus Christ revealed a Church constitution, or law of government, *i. e.*, instituted a Church, then it must have descended infallibly, or is as likely to have done so as that the writing of Scripture did so.

So it is easy to see the disadvantage or unnecessary weight the Protestant carries, who makes the admission that our Saviour formed a Church. Why admit what is not only untrue in fact, but so greatly damaging in this argument? Why not deny peremptorily, at the threshold, that there is revelation at all, or inspiration at all, or divinity at all, in the laws of Church association? The true course is for High Churchmen of all classes to be required first to prove that a Church was organized in the days of Jesus at all. Who would undertake to face such a question fairly? The suggestion once made, any man must see that it is preposterous.

The question then arises, Why has not this point been made and brought prominently forward long before? This question, it must be confessed, may *not be easily answered.* Perhaps the most satisfactory solution may be found in this, that our ecclesiastical history and thinking comes through England. In England everything is monarchical and hereditary. All public authority is transmitted or transmissive. The inherited thoughts and habitudes of the people were such, that the effort there to get the Church out of this channel of thought was more than could be expected. The Romish Church had interwoven the idea of transmitted Church authority into the very warp and woof of everything ecclesiastical, not indeed as a question, but as a matter not admitting of question. There was no question about apostolical Church origin. It was a well understood axiom from which all Church questions were reasoned. The great question of the Reformation was debated on other grounds, where, indeed, there was no lack of material in the then present state of the public mind.

As in Germany, so in England, the Protestants contented themselves with charging and proving against the Papists, "You have departed from the Church." This they did to their everlasting renown, and the honor of Christianity. But the debates did not necessarily, and did not in fact, raise and make prominent the question of a Church departure, in the sixteenth century, or the seventeenth, from the external usages of the same historic Church of the first century, it having been set up and made working under an infallible rule, and the divine promise of infallible direction. Whether the Church from which Papists had departed was the Church they alleged to have been organized anew by our Saviour, or a Church consonant to the religion of Scripture, is a question which, vital as it is in ecclesiastical science, did not enter prominently into those debates. English Methodists contented themselves with showing that they were not departing from the general ground occupied by the Church of England; while other dissenters showed that they were keeping within the lines of Scripture.

It is a far greater wonder that the question of the apostolic Church, what it was and what it was not, has not been raised in the United States, where these controversies have run high, and where the mind was more free, the scope of investigation more ample.

But it must be confessed, we Americans have not made much use of these advantages. Where is the book on either theology or ecclesiastical science that has been written in America? We have a number compiled here, but where are those written here? They are few indeed. We go to England for all our thinking. Cramped, iron-clad, tight-bound English thought, which was drawn out and shaped under the clouds and pressure of one or two hundred years ago, form the staple of American thinking to-day!

This ding-dong repetition of English argument and English ideas, drawn from the times of the Reformation or near there, when it was impossible there could be much of clear, independent thinking about it, beyond the simple fact that the Church as reformed is inside the Scriptures, and the Popish Church, much of it, outside, may be excusable in European authors. But why in this country, if not in that, has not the argument been carried much farther? Why has not this supposed model Church, this new Church, this divine institution, this embryo Church, in the college of the apostles, why has not all this been long since denied as a Popish fiction and monstrous untruth? Why do writers of the nineteenth century tacitly or plainly admit that the apostles made a new Church, the then existing Church being abolished? Why give Romanists or any other High Churchmen this foothold? It is as untrue in fact as it is damaging in policy.

Mr. R. I. Wilberforce, an English pervert to the Romish Church, says, "Now that a paramount authority was possessed by our Lord himself, and that He committed the like to his holy apostles, is admitted probably by all Christians."

That in Jesus dwelt all the fullness of the Godhead bodily, and therefore that not only all authority, but all power was possessed by Him, is, of course, unquestioned; but that He committed the like authority to the apostles, or to any other men, is unqualifiedly denied. There, right there, is the great High Church falsehood. And not only so, it is the only High Church error I know of that is fundamental. No Scripture underlies it, no deduction of reason supports it. It is a myth. It must be denounced and exposed.

And so, consistent with this erroneous assumption, Mr. Wilberforce speaks of "the *origin* of the Church's powers;" "its action depends upon his authority," etc. And he inquires, "Was the Church then a mere congeries of individuals gathered together, and possessing no collective character except that which is derived from the conglomeration of its parts?"

I answer it is, and always was, a mere congeries of Christian people, gathered together by the gravitating and cohesive force of the religion possessed by the individuals, and making their own laws of external association as the interest of their cause requires. The love of God and of the brethren keeps them together, as conjugal and parental love keeps families together.

Thus it is that the Church results naturally and necessarily from the personal religion of the individuals. The one supposes the other. They coinhere and coexist. The absence of the Church, in any community, is the best evidence there can be of the absence of religion.

The inculcation and diffusion of a principle requires, necessitates, and supposes social combination and union. And then, as the principle, doctrine, or truth is important to human well being, and of general or universal application, the popularity of the union becomes extended, while the bonds of cohesion become more and more definite, exact, and strengthened in their operation. That is, they become more and more a government for the more definite and certain application of labor within the purview of the enterprise. Here, and here alone, is found both the reason for, as well as the utility of civil government, and of military, political, educational, or merely industrial enterprises.

And when you apply this rule to religion, a matter of such intense interest to those who enjoy it, where the anxiety to spread and encourage it is equal to the degree of personal enjoyment, not only popular combination, but regularity of government and submission to rule, are both natural and unavoidable. Religion supposes and necessitates the Church.

VIII.

THE ROMISH CHURCH SYSTEM.

It is by no means my intention to write a treatise, or set down a catalogue of objections against the tenets of Popery. This would raise questions of controversy which I wish to avoid. I wish merely to state the question. This shall be done so fairly and impartially, that it shall not be objected to on either hand.

The difference between Romanism and what Protestants call Christianity, is, in the first place, constitutional, or of a primary and fundamental character; and secondly, in tenets, forms, and modes of worship which seem to grow out of, or be sanctioned by such first principles. The creed of the Roman Catholic is to believe in the Church and all her teachings. This is substantially the sum and substance of it. The creed or confession of faith which is most commonly used among them is that compiled by Pius IV., and is "drawn up in conformity with the definitions of the Council of Trent." This is specifically set forth and recognized as official by Dr. Milner in his *End of Controversy*, as may be seen at page 99. This creed consists of fifteen articles, and sets forth, first, such fundamental things as were never questioned by any people professing Christianity at all; and secondly, refers everything to the

Church. The Roman Catholic believes what the Church believes, and because the Church believes it. This is the sum of it.

Church authority is, therefore, the fundamental principle. This Church authority is claimed to be derived directly from Christ; the frame-work of the Church government being its vehicle of communication. All the peculiarities objected to by Protestants are mainly derived, plausibly, if not necessarily, from this fundamental principle.

If the offices of Church government were divinely created, and the duties, powers, and functions of some of the different officers fixed by divine revelation, then that means that they were infallibly prescribed. And that means that such officers, and, as the Church was to continue, their successors, were to be protected from error in discharging their particular duties so assigned. This protection we may suppose to work in the ordinary way of what we call inspiration for any other particular work. Inspiration does not make the man infallible. Paul said it did not so protect Peter. It only protects men against error in discharging certain duties. And we cannot suppose any greater difficulty in inspiring men to govern a Church, under prescribed laws, than to write a book of Scripture.

Supposing that Jesus Christ organized the Church society, appointing its first officers, prescribing their duties, etc., we would be obliged to suppose that He appointed a head officer, by whatever name he might be designated; and this would suppose that this divine direction would be of the same kind as that given to Matthew and Mark and others, to write the New Testament. And if the first president or chief officer was thus inspired or protected, it would certainly be gratuitous to suppose that thenceforward such preternatural protection would cease. Why should we suppose the Church to be more fallible or less divinely protected in after years, than at the first? Its necessities would be as great, if not greater.

If the Church originated in the way we are supposing, then we can imagine ourselves to have been present at the meeting when it was done. The twelve apostles, or eleven, were present, and perhaps a few others. The Saviour explains to them the wholesale dissolution of the former Church; and He administers to them the constitution of the new one to take its place. We are obliged to suppose the old was dissolved, because it lacked this constant, day by day, divine protection. It is impossible to imagine any other lack it could have suffered. Now we are about to have a permanent Church that shall lack nothing. Now Jesus says: "Here is your charter. Whatever incidental rules you may need as you go along, make them, but do not infringe upon these fundamental provisions. You, Peter (or you, somebody else), are president. When you cease to preside, this is the way the vacancy will be filled. And so of the other officers; and so I now, here, provide for the Church's perpetuity."

The Church was then infallibly organized. Or, as some have it, the Church was organized on the day of Pentecost. This amounts to the same thing, for if so, it was done under directions previously given to the apostles. Any way it can be imagined, it was either inspired or uninspired. And as to its being uninspired, that is not supposable. Inspiration means the support, divine influence, and protection accompanying divine instructions respecting assigned duties to be performed.

Now, when the first members stood thus in the presence of the Saviour, and the Saviour had finished dispensing to each officer the duties assigned him, was it not an infallible Church? How could it be otherwise? It must have been free from defect, because we cannot suppose the Saviour to have made a defective Church. And then the question arises, how did it lose its infallibility? How could divine provision be made for a fallible or defective Church?

All this does not imply human, but divine infallibility; that is, it is divine inspiration, as we call it, in similar matters respecting other official functions, in other assigned duties.

If the Church was made in the way supposed, then it could hardly be questioned that it might have been infallible, that the original infallibility might have been made to continue. We can hardly conceive of a reason why it should not be. The natural presumption would seem to favor it.

It would seem, then, that the Protestant who concedes that the Church originated in this way, assumes the burden of proof as to how the Church lost its original infallibility.

The objection urged against papal infallibility is that men are fallible. But in the condition of things supposed, this is not the question. Everybody acknowledges that sometimes some men are inspired. The apostles were all inspired. Inspired to do what? Merely to write what they wrote? No; their Scripture writing was done ten, twenty, or thirty years after this time. We suppose they were inspired to do all things pertaining to the apostolate. Then we are obliged to suppose the first Church officers, and particularly the first president, to be inspired. Now did the Saviour inspire the first officers of a Church which was to continue forever, in the discharge of their duty, with the understanding that when they would fall, and their offices be filled by others, this protection would cease? Is it too much to ask for some reason, either in Scripture, or the nature of the thing, why it should cease?

I can see very plainly why, outside of apostolic functions, there should not be inspiration, because there need be no apostolic succession of the afflatus covering the apostles in the discharge of their duties. But that is not the case here. Here are men succeeding to, and performing the very same duties which were performed exclusively by apostles. Was it less important, less arduous, less necessary or useful for the welfare of the Church, viewed in any way, that the second or third presidents should be inspired, than that the first should be? If the same duty and same responsibility, a duty and responsibility at one time peculiar to apostles, did not follow these succeeding official functionaries, then it would be unreasonable to suppose the protection of inspiration would follow. But here is a case where the very same functions follow. Here the succeeding men are discharging the very same duties which one year, or one day ago, were especially and peculiarly appropriate to apostles, and none else, and at a time, too, when it is impossible they ever could be more important than now. Then why should we look for divine protection in the one case, and not in the other?

This, then, surely, cannot be a serious or fundamental question between Protestants and Roman Catholics. It lies further back. Let the Protestants deny at the outset that there was any such original Church, or any such first presidency, or any new Church. Let the Romanist first be required to show that there were any such first officers, that is, anything of this nature to descend from man to man. Let it be readily granted, that all functions of the apostolate were covered by inspiration, but let it be denied that governing the Church is, or ever was an exclusive function of the apostolate. If we have not heretofore done so in the highest and most peremptory manner, it is high time we were doing it.

It may readily be believed that there is not a Roman Catholic argument extant that is not based squarely upon this supposed new Church formation. It is either expressed or implied everywhere. One of the best arguments I know of, in support of Romish Church authority, is that of Mr. R. I. Wilberforce. We might look at it again, because it is substantially the same as stated everywhere.

"Now, that a paramount authority was possessed by our Lord himself, and that He committed the like to his holy apostles, is admitted, probably, by all Christians. Authority to organize and govern the Church is here meant." Let that be granted, and it will be very difficult to disprove his argument.

Again he says, "The Church's existence has been shown to result from Christ's coming in the flesh."

So, according to Romanism, the Church had no existence before the incarnation. It could not be said that there was no association of religious people before that time, but there was no Church corporation. The Church, then, is a corporation made at that period, and working under a divinely prescribed charter. This is the fundamental idea of Romanism, and the only idea it has that is fundamental.

Then, I am not able to see the force of the loud and peremptory objections to Church infallibility, nor to a creed that requires mere subscription to the teachings of the Church. Infallibility might be regarded an open and debatable question, with something to be said on both sides. If I had to debate the question on that basis, I would greatly prefer the affirmative. If Christ enacted the Church charter eighteen hundred years ago, giving it the elements of perpetuity, then it is in the same condition now as if He had made it yesterday. Subscription to the Church is subscription to Christ. Obedience to the Church is obedience to Christ. To follow the Church is to follow Christ. The Church is the living, visible, practical, and real legate and representative of Christ on earth.

Dr. Charles Elliott (on *Romanism*, vol. i. p. 129) says, "It is not controverted between them and us whether Christ is the great foundation of his Church, for in this all are agreed." It may be doubtful what he means by great foundation. The figure is ambiguous. He nowhere ignores or denies the Romish understanding as stated above, that Christ is the maker of its fundamental laws of government; that He prescribed its charter in terms.

Then, I inquire, what is the vital, controlling question between Romanists and Protestants? What one question will control and decide all others? Evidently it is the question whether the Christian religion and Christian Church originated at the time and by authority of Jesus Christ. If these two things found their absolute origin then and there, then it follows necessarily, first, that the religion actually taught in the Old Testament is ignored, and should no longer form a part of Christian Scripture. And then we encounter the awkwardness of repudiating Scripture books which teach exactly the same doctrines as the retained books. And secondly, we open the endless inquiry as to how the Church was first formed; that is, how a thing was done which evidently was never done at all!

IX.

ROMANISM AMONG PROTESTANTS.

On a little reflection, if need be, the following propositions will not probably be questioned.

First. There is but one thing in Romanism that is objected to by Protestants, of a fundamental character. All other objectionable things are secondary, and grow out of this one thing. This principal thing is, that Jesus Christ introduced a new system of religion, and set up a new Church.

Second. This remark will apply equally well to prelacy, to Campbellism, so called, and to all other forms of High Churchism.

Third. This new Church and new religion is assented to, nay, it is taught, by many Protestant writers, who oppose not only Popery, but who oppose Campbellism and High Church Episcopacy.

On these points a few explanatory observations might be profitable. The reason, and only reason, why Roman Catholics do not allow private judgment to question the acts of the Church, is certainly not unreasonable, if the Church is what they claim it to be. If Christ organized the government of the Church, set it going, gave it laws, provided for the mode of bringing in new officers, fixed their powers, assigned their duties, etc., all of which and much more is implied in the idea of organizing a new

Church; and if He then, at the same time, set up a new religion, putting its teaching and inculcation in the custody of the Church; then, in such case, both the Church and religion are divine revelations. They are not subjects of rational consideration. We have no more right to interfere with either, or to exercise human judgment about either, than about another revelation that prescribes salvation on certain conditions. We do not judge whether prayer, repentance, keeping the Sabbath, etc., are suitable enactments in religion. We receive them as divinely prescribed or revealed. And so also of the Church; if its laws of government and authority are divinely revealed, what right have unofficial men to say this is erroneous, and that is unnecessary?

On the principle that the Church is, in this sense, a divine institution, it is a complete and sufficient answer to objections against auricular confession, virgin worship, seven sacraments, penance, priestly forgiveness, prayers for the dead, etc., to say, The Church says so. If the Church, in its outward frame-work, is a divine institution, and it says so, how can it be wrong? Is not one form of revelation as good and as infallible as another form? Suppose we stood in this newly formed Church, in the presence of the Saviour, and the president, ruling bishop, or whatever you may choose to call the chief officer, should direct any practice, or ordain any tenet now seen in Romanism, would we not receive it upon his mere dictum — other officers then present assenting — without attempting to set up our judgment, or interpose other revelations in objection? And if Church authority, as such, was good then, is it not equally good now? If the Church was an institution of that sort, and was to continue, then it contained the means of continuance. The succeeding officers stood squarely in the tracks of the first ones, receiving all their authority.

It follows, then, that all the peculiar things objected to in Romanism, rest upon and grow directly out of this supposed divine authority in the Church. Let this be removed, and then the government of the Church being human, other human judgment may properly come in. It is then human judgment here against human judgment there. But if the Church is a divine institution, these objections to it are human judgment against divine provisions.

A Church acting under divine laws, revealed laws, is a very different thing from one framed by the judgment of men. If the latter, then it may be inquired into, modified, and improved from time to time. But if the form and functions of government are divinely prescribed, how can men inquire into it? The Church was not only to continue, but the specific means and elements of its continuance and perpetuity were provided and placed in the custody of the Church. So the government of the Church is as divine now as at the first.

Then what right have men to object to this or that, if done by the Church in this historic succession? The Church says so, is a complete answer and estoppel to any such objections. Church authority, in this case, is divine authority. So this doctrine of a new Church lies at the bottom of all Romish errors. Remove that, and then each particular error must rest on its own intrinsic merits. Their truth or falsity can be inquired into in no other way.

And these same considerations will apply to all

other forms of High Churchism. Every peculiarity of the system rests squarely upon the doctrine of an original Church, with a divinely formed government. High Church Episcopalians say the original constitution provided and enjoined three orders of ministry, the twelve apostles being the first bishops, etc. Their successors must be regularly appointed; hence the so called, and correctly called, apostolic succession, etc.

Now it is clear the moment you assert the doctrine of a new Church and new religion, you virtually give up the question. High episcopal authority and apostolic succession are the most natural, rational, plausible, if not the necessary and logical results of the erroneously alleged facts of a new Church and new religion.

It is seen, therefore, that primary, essential, fundamental Romanism consists in the single, simple idea of a new Church and new religion, and that this is abundant among Protestants. This, therefore, wheresoever, or by whomsoever taught, is rational Romanism. To inculcate the doctrine is to lay a broad Romish foundation; and although practical Popery is not by any means always built upon it, logical Romanism is never built upon any other foundation. There is no other foundation upon which it can be built.

This view of the subject has been practically verified in recent debates with Campbellites, where it was alleged that the Christian Church is the identical Church formed by the apostles. In opposition it was said: "I deny that any Church was formed by the apostles, or in that age. Let it be first proved that a Church was then formed at all." This position, strongly taken, was a poser. It was utterly confounding. Even a reply of any sort could not be extorted. It had not entered into the polemical curriculum. It can but produce utter silence in any argument of this sort.

Now, what is to be done? Will any one say that fundamental Romanism is not sometimes unwittingly taught by Protestant writers and preachers? It is not always the easiest thing in the world to rectify an error. It is hard to change old sayings and old modes, but it is not impracticable. It ought to be done. Protestants ought, at least, to be themselves Protestant. The writer of these strictures confesses to as much error in these premises, as he dares to attribute to others. In earlier years he did not know any better, and thought and wrote as he saw others do. He followed older and better men. In riper years he saw his error, and dared to correct it.

It is easy to see that here is a point where the great principles of the great Protest were not fully followed up in after years. To close up this point is a duty we owe both to ourselves and to posterity. The Church has a right to the promulgation and elaboration of the argument so lightly and feebly set forth herein. A man unwilling to acknowledge and rectify an error, when pointed out, is a shallow thinker and an unsafe man.

It is remarkable how readily we drift into both the thoughts and expressions of others. Very much of what we boastfully call our thinking and opinions is but the almost passive gliding along in the grooves formed by others.

It cannot be expected that these arguments will reach that large class of men who know everything, and never commit a blunder. But there are others less confident and more thoughtful, and with them there is more hope.

The careful, candid reader can hardly fail to see that the entire subject of ecclesiastical science, in all its forms and phases, rests upon the primary question brought forward herein. If Christ formed a new Church, prescribing for it some perpetual laws of government, then to that extent the government is divine, and must not be interfered with; and if not, then the government is in human hands, and men are responsible for it. Hardly any question about the Church can be answered without first understanding this point.

Now, would it be out of the way to say that most of the questions about the Church, discussed nowadays, proceed upon the assumption precedent, that the Church, in its external frame-work, as well as in its faith and doctrine, was original, had its historic origin in the days of the apostles? How can such teachings lead to valuable results? One says the succession from the original Church must be by official investiture in Church officers; while another says it must be in the faith of the body of the Church. I would inquire, succession from what? Evidently from nothing real, but from something merely mythical and imaginary.

We frequently speak of the primitive Church; but it is not the Church that was primitive in those days, but certain aspects of, and facilities for teaching now for the first time found in the Church. A sensible, historic, or phenomenal view of the atonement was primitive in the days of the apostles; but the religious association of religious people was certainly not then first seen. The knowledge and recognition of the crucifixion and other sufferings of Christ were of course primitive, because they did not occur before; but surely the mediation and Immanuelship of Christ were not then primitive, for they existed in all their fullness, thousands of years before.

Dr. Schaff, in his *History of the Church*, says, "The beginning of Church history is properly the incarnation of the Son of God, the entrance of the new principle of light and life into humanity." Again, "But since the Church as an organic union of the disciples of Jesus, came into view first on the day of Pentecost, we take this point as the beginning." And again, "For us, then, Church history embraces a period of eighteen centuries."

Now if these things are true, if this is the proper view of the Church, I am not able to see how we can get clear of the Romish doctrine of entire social, legal, and constitutional separation between the Church and religion of the prophets, and that of the apostles. See where this doctrine carries us! It not only flatly and palpably ignores all the Bible history in the case, but it makes the Church not a mere religious brotherhood, but a new divine corporation. It is no longer a congeries of religious element brought together by the attracting force of its own gravitation, and governed by its own religious principle and integrity, but a special corporation brought into being by power outside of itself, and placed under a prescribed law of perpetual application and force.

Then it is simply absurd, as well as highly illegal and disobedient, to connect the old, abolished Testament with proper Christianity. For in that case, everything religious, as well as ecclesiastical, was abolished and forever set aside. In that case, I cannot see that the religion and Church of historic priority to the life and times of Jesus, had any sort of connection with those subsequent. There may be more or less of external likeness or similarity between them, but they stand related just as Christianity and Mohammedanism stand related; that is, in an attitude of eternal and unchanging hostility.

Protestantism cannot consistently stand before such doctrine at the bar of enlightened public opinion. And as to history, it is unceremoniously put out of doors altogether.

X.

THE JEWS.

ONE of the commonest mistakes of writers as well as readers of the New Testament is in the meaning put upon the words heading this chapter, which are so frequently used in those Scriptures. Who were, and who were not Jews? And then, secondly, does the term *Jews*, in the New Testament, always mean the same thing?

We need not spend time with the etymology of the word. We know it came from *Ju*-dah, and after the separation under Rehoboam and Jeroboam was applied to that branch of the Israelites who held with the large tribe of Judah; and in process of time it was applied, or at least we now apply it generally to the Church, with but little, or at most but very nominal reference to genealogical descent. In the time of the Saviour and previously, there was a well known and distinctly marked people, chiefly in Western Asia and Africa, called Jews. Their numerical strength is not certainly known, but is generally estimated at five to seven millions. They were distinguished from other people by their religion. We know what this was with certainty, for we have it now word for word.

Some writers seem to regard the Jews or Israelites, at the time of the Saviour's life, as wholly pure blood descendants of Abraham. This is a transparent error, which none can fail to see at a glance. There was a historic period, and but a short one, when that branch of the Church, but certainly not the whole Church, was confined to the family of Jacob, the grandson of Abraham. Of other religious people, such as those connected with Job, Melchizedek, Balaam, etc., there is but bare allusion, and we know very little about them. Of the early Israelites we know but little; but the Church in that age and country, which is historically connected with the modern Church, was for a time confined to the apparent posterity of Abraham, though other large branches of the Abrahamic family were not connected with it.

But the Israelites, even in Jacob's family, were by no means pure blood descendants from Abraham. The twelve sons of Jacob were only one eighth pure. And after this, as the twelve patriarchs did not marry their sisters, their children were but one sixteenth pure as to Abraham. And so the blood necessarily dilutes by halves every generation, save when by marriage the posterity is bred in-and-in. It is as likely as otherwise, so far as I know, though we have no information about it, that the grandsons and granddaughters of Jacob, or many of them, may have intermarried; that is, married their cousins. If so, and this course was maintained strictly, then they would continue one sixteenth pure blood descent from Abraham. There was no law that they should so intermarry, nor do we know of any reason why they should, save their civil relation to the Egyptians. But it is distinctly intimated that there was considerable mixture with Egyptians before the exodus. Portions of those who went out with Moses were a "mixed multitude." (Ex. xii. 38.)

This is about all we know of their genealogy, prior to the exodus. How much foreign blood they possessed by inlet from without, we know not with certainty. The purest were one sixteenth pure. From this time on, forty years, until their entrance into Palestine, they bred in-and-in, remaining, not each family, nor yet each tribe, but as a whole, where they were at the time of the exodus.

Now we enter upon a new genealogical era. A greater blunder could never be made than the supposition that from this time on, the Israelitish people maintained a genealogical exclusiveness as to other people. Both the law and the practice was the very reverse. An ecclesiastical exclusiveness was generally maintained. They might continue to marry in the Church, both men and women, and yet, genealogically, as to ancestral blood, its degree of purity might dilute one half every generation. Thus at the end of fourteen generations, David might have been one sixteen thousandth pure blood as to his ancestral progenitor, Abraham. And at the time of the Babylonian captivity, fourteen generations more, Jechonias, though in a direct male line, might have had blood diluted as to Abraham, one part in sixty millions pure. And at the time of the Saviour's advent, or at any other time, there might have been, and no doubt were, thousands and millions of Jews without the least particle of blood descended from Abraham; while there were other millions whose proportion of pure blood from the patriarchal ancestor was almost incalculably infinitesimal. It was philosophically possible, though improbable, that any Jew at the time of the advent could have had blood as pure as one in thirty-two, sixty-four, or a hundred and twenty-eight.

The historic facts bearing upon this point, though greatly overlooked, are easily seen. It is strange that the notion ever got into the books that the Jews, from Abraham to Jesus, were exclusive as to other people, socially, ecclesiastically, and genealogically. If by the Jews in that period you mean the Church, the only rational meaning the term could have, then it is a simple truism that religious people are exclusive as to irreligious people. This was the only kind of exclusiveness we see among the Jews from the exodus to Jesus.

The historic facts are plain. For about fourteen or fifteen hundred years, during the period of the residence in Palestine, the well known law of the Church was as it is now, to take in all who would come in from without; and now when in, they were in, and were in all respects on an equal footing with those previously in. There was to be no difference between those born in and their posterity, and those who came in and theirs. (See Ex. xii. 49; Num. ix. 16; Lev. xix. 33, 34.) After the first generation there could be no difference, for they were intermarried *ad libitum*, and the posterity was common. This influx from without was great and constant. " Many people of the land became Jews." So a Jew was not necessarily a descendant of Abraham. This mixing of blood in a few descending generations goes much more rapidly than one would suppose, until one comes to look at it carefully.

We have seen that a portion of the people who came out of Egypt with Moses were a mixed people; mixed by intermarriage with foreigners. And we know that the Canaanitish population were by no means wholly extirpated, though wholly conquered.

Many remained alive and became incorporated with the Israelites. Many children never knew the difference. And then, besides those who from time to time, in various ages and various circumstances, joined the Jews from proper religious motives, there were captives, fugitives, hired servants, etc., who came in in great abundance. These incomers are spoken of in Scripture generally as "strangers." That is, this term is applied to those who came in, but not to their posterity. They were soon mixed with the whole mass.

In the time of Solomon we see it incidentally mentioned (2 Chr. ii. 17, 18) that there were at that time, of these strangers, able-bodied, working men, not counting women, children, or infirm, 153,600 in or in reach of Jerusalem. There were then, probably, of those who were themselves proselytes from without, not less than half a million of persons. Nor is there an intimation that this is at all unusual. Then it is probable that at that time proselytes were coming in at the rate of about five hundred thousand in thirty-three years, or about fifteen thousand a year. At other times they came in by nations, and in various ways. And although many, perhaps most of these accessions were, as to themselves personally, of a very dubious or unworthy character, yet this was comparatively unimportant, when we consider that it could only attach to themselves who came in, and not to their posterity. The children soon became mixed with the general and undistinguishable mass.

After the captivity, proselyting among the Israelites improved greatly, both as to numbers and characters. The conquests of Alexander, the Egyptian and Syrian wars, the struggles under the Maccabean princes, and the general expansion of the Roman government, all tended greatly to bring the Jews into notice, to spread them abroad, and give them influence in the world. So we see them everywhere in these later ages, and their proselytes very numerous. The distinction made between proselytes of the gate, and of righteousness, is probably more fanciful than otherwise. Things did not proceed in that exact, mechanical way. They were all natural people. There were probably among them as many degrees of righteousness as we find now among similar converts. Moreover, in a range of many centuries, and in different countries, there must have been great variety in all these habits and customs.

And then, too, we must remember, there was not only great and constant influx from without, by which the genealogical blood of the Church became mixed and mingled in a thousand ways, and as many degrees, with the people of the whole East, but also, in these long years, there was great and constant outflow. Only a comparatively small portion of the blood of Abraham ever was among the Israelites. Look at the Ishmaelites, Edomites, Midianites, all Arabia, and many peoples lost to history long since.

Neither Scripture nor reason attaches any importance to mere blood descent from Abraham, beyond a single genealogical line, showing the Saviour's lineage. It is the inheritance of Abraham's faith, not his blood, that makes a Jew or Christian.

Therefore the term Jews, in Scripture, before the separation, means the Church. In the Saviour's lifetime it is highly probable that most of the Church were Greeks, who, so far as we know, never had any connection lineally with Israelites, much less with Abraham. The Church then existed in three branches or denominations, namely, the Judean, the Samaritan, and the Greek or Hellenistic.

When, therefore, "the Jews" are spoken of before the resurrection, the entire Church is referred to, except in places where the sense distinguishes between the different denominations. After the resurrection, when Jews are spoken of, three different significations are to be given to the term. Sometimes these different meanings are specified, but generally they are not. The sense specifies sufficiently. These three senses of the word arise out of the apparent fact, that in this period there were three distinct classes of Jews, or parties in the Church. To understand the Scriptures, therefore, in Acts, the Epistles, and Revelation, you must know which class is meant, or your reading will be to little purpose. To understand this better, let a few suggestions be made.

The only question of importance in the Church at this period, on which the Church was divided, was this, Is Jesus the Christ? Some holding that He was, it necessarily follows that to acknowledge Him is to stay in the Church, to deny Him is to go out. Here the Church, that is, the Jews, divided. Some stayed in, and some went out. Here are now two classes of Jews. Both claimed to be the Church, on the ground that Jesus was, and that He was not, the Christ of the Old Testament. But the whole Church, consisting of several millions of persons, and being spread over much of the continents of Asia and Africa, travel being mostly on foot, it was impossible this separation could take place at a single time. It began soon after the resurrection, in Jerusalem; but as to most ot the Church, they could not take sides for years, because they could not have the necessary information about it. They could not either accept or deny the Christship of Jesus, until they had received the fullest and most reliable information.

Here, then, for the space of ten, twenty, or most likely, in some cases, thirty or forty years, there must have been a third party of Jews. They stood as before the birth or crucifixion of Jesus.

It is obvious that in a few years all Jews then living must either receive or deny the Christship of Jesus finally; so, thereafter, there could be but two classes of Jews. And it is also obvious that one or the other of these classes must cease in common parlance to be called "Jews." All distinct things must have distinct names. And so it was in this case. Naturally enough, the believing Jews took the name of Christian. And as this branch of Jews, gradually of course, took the name of Christian, and so called themselves, the other branch would naturally retain the old name of Jews.

The common error, therefore, of regarding these rejecting Jews as the proper and sole representatives of the Jews as they existed at and before the time of Jesus, is apparent. Historically they are no more their successors than the Christian party are. The succession lineally was, so far as we know, about equally divided. But religiously the Christians are the sole and exclusive successors. This must be so with unmistakable certainty, if Jesus was and is the Christ.

So that while modern Jews, that is, the successors of the rejecting Jews, are called Jews, and exclusively so called, they are by no means entitled to the name. They are not really Jews, but only falsely pretend to be. This we see clearly stated in Rev. ii. 9 and iii. 9. They blasphemously say they are Jews and are not, but are of the church of Satan. They say they are Jews and are not, but do lie. They abandoned the Church of Scripture, setting up a new and false Church.

It is then a great and dangerous error, however popular it may be, to class modern Jews with the people called Jews at and before the time of Jesus, and to regard the former as both the religious and ecclesiastical successors of the latter. Most assuredly they are neither. To suppose that they are is to suppose that the religion called Christianity is a new and false religion, and the Church called Christian, a new and false Church.

Modern Jews are the lineal descendants of about one half, probably, of the Jews in the Saviour's time, but as to both religion and Church, they are wholly and entirely apostates. This does not admit of question, for it is a conclusion both necessary and palpable.

XI.

THE APOSTOLIC SUCCESSION.

To debate a question is to acknowledge that it is debatable. And this means that certain premises are mutually agreed upon; and furthermore, that the conclusion you deny might be so. If two men were to debate whether Washington was the first or the second president of the United States, it would be a virtual acknowledgment that the United States had presidents, and also that Washington was president at either the first or second term. And after joining that issue, it would be incompetent to deny that the United States ever had a president. You have acknowledged that the United States had presidents, and that the first one might have been Washington.

So, to debate what kind of government Julius Cæsar set up in the United States would be an acknowledgment, on both sides, that Julius Cæsar did set up some kind of government in the United States.

Then if it were alleged that the government set up by Cæsar in the United States, in 1776, was republican, with many peculiar details, and not monarchical, and this is the issue presented, there would be two ways in which the allegation might be met. One would be to resort to the history of the country to show that the government was different from that set up in the allegation. The other would be to deny at the threshold that the Roman emperor was ever in the United States at all, or ever set up any government there. If it could not be shown that Cæsar set up some kind of government there, then all possible questions, and proof thereof, as to the kind of government, are at once avoided. No man would think of meeting such an issue in any other way than by cutting off all argument at once by denying that Cæsar set up any government there at all.

This is exactly the character of the debate — thousands of volumes, and millions of sermons — about the kind of government that Jesus Christ set up in Jerusalem for the Church. I asked a little schoolboy at table, what kind of government Marc Antony set up in Mexico. He replied that Marc Antony did not set up any government in Mexico; that he was never in Mexico. I thought to myself it was strange some of our theologians did not make a reply as true, as sensible, and as conclusive, to the many arguments and historic testimony about the kind of Church government set up by Jesus Christ.

The following facts are true, and so notorious they will not be questioned: First, thousands of volumes and tens of thousands of lesser publications have been made to prove, pro and con, the kind of Church government under which Jesus Christ set up and organized the Church at the first in Jerusalem. High Church Episcopalians have published many of these thousands to prove that the new Church government so set up had three orders in its ministry, with prelatical power in the first order, called bishops. This was one of its main features. Campbellites, or "Christians," and other Baptists, have published their thousands to prove that the new Church government so set up by Jesus Christ was on the republican order. This was a fundamental provision in the new Church. Methodists have published as many to prove that the Church so organized by the Saviour and his apostles had two orders in the ministry only, alleging that in the new Church law, "a presbyter was the same as a bishop." Presbyterians of different classes have published their full share of these thousands, to prove that the new Church so set up by Jesus Christ provided in its government for parity in the ministry. Roman Catholics, since the first distinct formation of their Church, in the eighth century, have held that the new Church of Jesus Christ so set up as above was on the high monarchical principle. Various other denominations have taken various other views about the Church government so set up at the first by Jesus Christ, and with the implied understanding, on all hands, that this new Christian Church government was to be perpetual for the Church in all future time.

Second, Jesus Christ, by Himself or his apostles, did not set up, organize, or establish anew any Church, or the government of any Church, directly or indirectly, in Jerusalem or elsewhere. He merely continued, or suffered to continue, the Church of his fathers as it was of old, and is now. He never intimated, so far as we know, nor did any one else in that age intimate, that the old and then existing Church even needed modification or change.

Now are these two propositions strictly true in every particular? Will any man question either, or any part of either? Then they furnish matter for sober reflection. Perhaps no question in ecclesiastical science has been more voluminously debated than the "Apostolic Succession" so called. What is that question? It is how a thing was done, which confessedly was never done at all! It is the same kind of a question precisely, as to inquire what kind of a government Julius Cæsar formed in the United States. Everybody knows he formed none.

The question called "Apostolic Succession" is not a debatable question. Then there has been no such debate. There has been a wrangle about myths and fables, things which never had an existence. I do not see that the man who denies the doctrine is any nearer the truth than he who affirms it. Such an argument at all, irrespective of any sides, rests wholly upon a falsehood. The question concedes and supposes that Jesus Christ organized a new Church government, and the affirmant says that in doing so, in arranging the new Church law, it was provided that the ministerial authority, which at first resided solely in the twelve apostles, must be handed down from them tactually by personal transmission. And the objector to this doctrine of personal transmission simply denies that the first constitution of the Church contained such provision, alleging that it provided for the enfranchisement by mere Church authority. So the one is evidently as much in error as the other.

The arguments on this subject, many of them, affirm, 1st, that Episcopacy was and was not of divine appointment; that is, was and was not so provided in the new Church law. 2d. Episcopacy is necessary to the perfection of Church government, but not its being. 3d. It is absolutely necessary. 4th. Bishops are by divine right superior to and distinct from elders. They have the sole right to ordain ministers, and govern the Church. 5th. Bishops of this order are the sole official successors of the apostles. 6th. Bishops and presbyters are by divine right the same order in the ministry. 7th. All ministers are the same order. This is according to the primitive Church. To prove what a Church must be now, you have only to ascertain what it was in that respect when it was primitive; *i. e.*, when it was fresh and new from apostolic legislation.

Now I ask, what are all these arguments about? Evidently nothing. They begin and end in myth, romance, and error. It is precisely as if we argue the question, What kind of a government did Julius Cæsar set up in America in the eighteenth century?

When therefore it is said there must be a chain of tactual ordinations from the apostles down, in order to continue the proper existence of the Church set up by Jesus Christ, the only reply that can be made, consistently with historic truth, is that Jesus Christ set up no Church of any kind. It cannot be argued what kind of Church He made, until it first be shown that He made a Church of some kind.

XII.

WHO ARE CONVERTED JEWS?

THERE are two senses in which this expression may be understood, and the meanings are very different. Before the apostacy and secession of the unbelieving Jews, after the death of Jesus, the religion of all Jews was nominally the same. Save some occasional lapses into idolatry in their earlier history, there never was any difficulty among them about their creed. It was nominally the same. Nevertheless in that period, as in all other periods of the Church, you would no doubt find unconverted persons in the Church. Indeed, more strictly, then as now and always, all conversion, regeneration, is in the Church, virtually at least. So such persons being Jews, and being converted, might be called converted Jews.

But that is not the sense in which the expression is generally used. Commonly, it means a person converted from Judaism to Christianity. Of course such conversions can be predicated only of the apostate Jews, after the secession. Of such we are informed in the New Testament of but one instance, though quite likely there were many.

Saul of Tarsus left the Church, and went with the apostates, and after a few years he was converted from his apostacy, from this new form of Judaism, to Christianity. He was in the most proper sense a converted Jew. It was not merely the conversion of a Jewish person, but he was converted as a Jew. It was like the conversion of a Jew now.

But the great mass of Jews who acknowledged the Christship of Jesus in that age could not be called converted Jews. They never had any religion but Christianity. They never denied Christ, either in the person of Jesus or otherwise. It matters not when they acknowledged Jesus as Christ, whether on the day of the resurrection, or ten or twenty years after, if they received Jesus at the first opportunity without denying Him. They were not apostates, and so, not converted Jews. Accepting Jesus as their Christ was only a firm maintainance intact and inviolate of their former religious creed. They retained and maintained the religion of their fathers, receiving Jesus when presented. They could not receive Him before.

XIII.

MODERN OR POST-MESSIANIC JEWS.

THE status of present Jews, those since the time of Jesus, and their relation to the true Church, should be noticed in this connection.

We have seen that before the death of Jesus, the people afterward called Christians and those called Jews were together in one religious brotherhood; and when the question arose about Jesus, whether He was or was not the Christ of the Old Testament, some took one side and some the other. This separation began soon after the death of Jesus, and we may suppose that in thirty or forty years it became complete. The scattered condition of the Church, the civil state of the country, and other circumstances, rendered it impracticable that it should become complete sooner.

We see too that this question about the Christship was, in its consequences, absolutely vital both to religion and to the Church. It could but be well understood on all hands, that if Jesus was Christ, then to deny Him was to deny Christ, and apostatize from the common faith. And if He was not the Christ of prophecy, in that case to accept and claim Him as such was to deny the faith, and apostatize. They separated. Both parties were large, but at this day it is impossible to determine which was the larger, and which the smaller of the two. The question on which they separated being in its nature vital to religion, it threw the parties wide asunder. Their hostility was naturally great. It could not be otherwise. Assuming that Jesus was Christ, then it follows that those so holding, afterwards called Christians, held the old faith firm, and the denying party apostatized. Each party claimed to be right, claimed to be the true Church, the mere regular continuance of the old Church. The Jews, as the denying party came to be exclusively called, after the other party came to be well known by the name of Christians, claimed the regular ecclesiastical legitimacy, on the ground that Jesus was an impostor, while the Christians claimed it on the sole ground that He was the very Christ. Everything hinged upon this simple fact. There was no difference between them about doctrines, apart from this.

Irreligious, outside people then, and those in Christendom now, stood on very different ground. Then outsiders were mostly heathen people, idolaters, believed in no Scripture, denied all revelation. They looked down from their wisdom on both parties, and regarded this separation as a party quarrel among fanatics about one Jesus, who being dead, it was affirmed that He was alive. The denying Jews, keeping up those outside forms of worship most prominently seen, and also retaining the old name, would be naturally regarded the regular party, and the Christians as a new sect or secession. And this they would be still the more likely to do, as the Christians held the strange doctrine that a man once dead was alive. And so we hear the heathen writers of that day speak of them as a new sect. On the question as to which party seceded, the Roman officials and the denying Jews very naturally took the same ground.

And then the deifying and worshipping a convicted criminal, one who had been judicially executed, was in their eyes foolishness indeed. So the government officials and leading men among the heathen, whose position and circumstances caused them to know, or care, or think much about Jew or Hebrew people, would very naturally fall in with the rejecting Jews, without taking any interest at all in the religion of either of the two parties.

So the government hunted, persecuted, and punished the Christians, because they were, as they regarded them, a new sect, and not because they cared a fig about the doctrines of either party. The Romans had stipulated to protect the Jews in their worship, innocent and foolish as they regarded it; and here was in their estimation an opposing religious party, and a disturber of the religious quiet. What many theologians call the calling of the Gentiles was the mere putting forth of more of the proper aggressive force and missionary spirit of the common religion of Scripture.

Thus matters drifted for the space of about forty years, with more or less persecution against the Christians, according to the taste, ambition, personal wickedness, etc., of the conflicting and changing rulers of Rome, until the great Jewish revolt, which ended in the siege and destruction of Jerusalem. This Roman war had little to do with Church or religious matters, so far as history informs us. It was a revolt, not of the Jews, but chiefly at least of the anti-Christian Jews of Lower Judea. What other portions of that class of Jews, if any, joined them, we are not informed. The insurgents were routed, cut up, and dispersed. And after some years we find the whole remainder of rejecting Jews holding on in religious ceremony to ante-messianic forms and modes of worship, which ceremonies, of themselves, declared against Jesus as Christ.

Our Palestinian history of those times is very meagre and unsatisfactory, owing, as we may suppose, to the great destruction of literature, centuries afterward, in the Mohammedan wars. The few scraps left us, hardly amounting to anything like consecutive history, show us that the breach between the Christian and repudiating Jews became deeper and deeper.

In the first three centuries, the rejecting Jews continued to be regarded by the Roman government as the true Israelites, and the Christian party as an illegitimate offshoot. Constantine became emperor A. D. 306. Unlike his predecessors, who were mostly mere despotic rulers, he was a man of the people. Of his semi-fabulous conversion to Christianity, much more has been written than is known. His politics were certainly Christian. Thus much we know, that he made Christianity largely and strikingly popular, and gave it large magnificence and patronage. Now the popular tide turned against the Jews, and they, in turn, became the illegitimate offshoot.

From that time to the present, the Jews have been generally regarded a despised, disfranchised, and downtrodden people. Their religion caused them to prefer exclusiveness, and their neighbors compelled it.

One remarkable circumstance in their civil history has generally been lost sight of. For more than sixteen hundred years, up to one hundred or one hundred and fifty years ago, they have not been permitted to live in the world like other people. Their repudiation of Christ, and consequently of all revealed religion, has been so abhorrent to Christians, and their religion so unable to commend itself to other people, that they have found toleration nowhere. So wherever they have gone, they have been compelled by the civil authority to occupy exclusive, assigned districts, and scarcely to change and reside here and there among other people, as they might choose. It is but lately, mostly within the last hundred years or so, that they have attempted to mix and associate with other people. Either choice or compulsion prevented it. The late liberal principles among the nations of Europe and America have been showing themselves only in the last one or two hundred years. Considerable changes in this respect have been witnessed in the present century. But in some parts of the world, these civil hamperings are felt by the Jews even at the present.

What effect such conditions of life would have upon a people in so long a period, we are poorly prepared to judge, for we have no precedent or parallel case in human history. All nations and peoples are more or less clannish and exclusive, and in proportion as this characteristic is more or less strict, and of long continuance, it produces a nationality of physical appearances as well as of habitude of life. This is plainly seen everywhere.

Now the question is, will not this circumstance account for the physical peculiarities which we see among the Jews of the present day? It is worse than useless to attempt to trace these peculiarities beyond the apostolic age, as if the ante-messianic Jews were one and the same people, as to race or nation. We know that at the time of Jesus, many of the Jews, perhaps most of them, were Grecians and others, who never had any sort of connection with Israelites, except in their religion. Why does it follow, either from the nature of the Church, or from anything else, or where is the history to show, to indicate, or to suppose that the members of the Church at that day, any more than at this, were all of one nation, one kindred, or one people, either civilly or genealogically considered? Fancy and fable do not make good history, though repeated a thousand times. All the history we have proves the contrary.

Some fanciful writers affect to trace the physiognomy of Abraham in the Jewish features of the present day. Why not trace it in those of the Arabians, the Moabites, if they can be found, or in the Christians of the present day?

The Jews before the separation, in the apostolic period, were less clannish and exclusive than other peoples of those ages, so far as we are informed. Like the Church of this and all other ages, the policy was to bring in from without anybody and everybody who would worship God aright. This arises from the very nature of the Church and its religion. And we know abundantly that the Church, for more than a thousand years before the incarnation, did, as it does now, extend itself outward everywhere, that is, bring in from without greatly, so as thereby to swell its numbers more or less in different ages.

It is therefore little short of folly to attempt to trace the present Jews, as a nation or separate people, back beyond the separation. They are traceable since that period only on account of their strange religion, and their strange relation to surrounding nations. The people known as Jews since the separation are but an anomalous fragment of the Jews, that is, of the Church before that event.

It is plainly perceivable that in the last twenty or fifty years, the Jewish physiognomy and external peculiarity is beginning to dilute and disappear. It is not always now, more especially in England and America, that a Jew can be distinguished; and many persons are half, quarter, or one eighth or a sixteenth Jewish, as to one of the ancestral lines a few generations back. And the operation of the same causes, namely, the prevalence of liberal principles by which Jews may live and intermarry freely, like other people, will in time, and indeed in no great time, render it impossible to distinguish a Jew; and thus, by the natural but gradual operation of the same cause, in no great time hence, there will be no such people as Jews in the world, in any national, genealogical, or physiological sense, whatever course the present Jewish religion may take.

Then what comes of all those speculations about the restoration of the Jews? Who are to be restored? and to what are they to be restored? The restoration is predicated of promises in the Old Testament, away in early Hebrew history, and in reference to the seed of Abraham through Isaac and Jacob. Then how can it have any more reference to this fragment of Jews now found in the apostacy, than to those who accepted the Christship in Jesus, or those who branched off from the Church in any way?

Still, the posterity of Jacob have performed a most remarkable, nay a wonderful part in the history of the world. They were made wonderfully instrumental in putting down idolatry, and establishing the true worship of the true God among men. For a time they were distinguishable from other people in a genealogical sense, and then only in a religious sense. Modern or post-messianic Jews, a fragmentary offshoot of a fragment of the old ancestral Jews, have had a wonderful history; but in the end have perhaps furnished more material for semi-romance than for historic truth.

XIV.

MODES OF TEACHING IN DIFFERENT AGES.

It has been insisted that the religion of the Old Testament was the religion of the New; that the one is no more spiritual, or suited to mankind in general, than the other; that the Bible knows no religion but faith in Christ, and corresponding obedience; that there is nothing new in the New Testament, as to the Old, except modes of teaching. Nevertheless, historic facts are always in their nature new.

Religious principles and doctrines are inculcated chiefly in two ways: by verbal or didactic lessons, and the performance of ceremonies. These are done, when properly done, and best to purpose, not always in the same way; but in different ages, in different countries, and among different peoples, in different ways.

The difference, then, between the old and the new dispensations, as these two periods are sometimes called, is not in religion, but merely in the modes of teaching it.

The necessity of different modes of teaching arises out of the nature of things, particularly religious things, and the mental constitution. Before the incarnation of Christ was seen, it was impossible to teach the doctrine of faith in Christ, in the mode, and with the instruments used since. This impossibility is peculiar to religion only in so far as religion comprehends moral and spiritual things. I beg just here to remind the reader of a chapter in *Ecce Ecclesia*, on the "Origination of Ideas."

Before the incarnation, the Church could know nothing of the vicarious atonement, except as an abstract doctrine. Now it is known as a practical, sensible fact, as well as a doctrine. Knowledge on all moral or immaterial subjects must necessarily proceed in this way. The improvement in language and advance of human society must proceed together. They are mutually dependent. By long processes and familiar usage, we have brought into our employ a number of words pretty well fitted to convey a number of ideas respecting this general doctrine, which our distant ancestors did not, and could not possibly have. So they must needs use other instruments. But when the lessons or doctrines to be taught become familiarly associated with the words describing them, then the physical means, formerly useful, or even necessary, become a hindrance.

It is the great mistake of those who make it, to suppose that the Mosaic Church machinery was always the same. On the contrary, it was almost always changing. Like the upward progress of thought and action elsewhere, it was constantly evolving, not new principles, but new modes of displaying and inculcating old ones. So we once saw the tabernacle, greatly useful and much used in its time ; but after the location of the tribes in Palestine, we see little or nothing of it. It was not now useful. Thereafter we see more of the verbal teachings of the prophets. So, after the captivity, we see congregational worship much in use. Perhaps there was not much, if any, of it before. The state of things now called for it. And in the later prophets, we see an evident departure from reliance on external forms, and a more open application of the ideas connected therewith. If the condition of mankind had been such at the first, that man could properly use and appreciate the knowledge which was furnished in the historic scenes of the incarnation and visible work of Christ, then there would have been no postponement of the incarnation. But such was not the case. Man has always been natural. And so it was only in the fullness of time, the time wanted by regular and natural processes, that Christ assumed manhood, and appeared in the humanity of Jesus.

These developments do by no means create new doctrines, or new principles of religion to be taught, but only new and greater facilities for teaching the old ones.

Some of the early Mosaic laws seem to us to be almost devoid of religious principle of any kind. Perhaps in themselves considered they are ; but there is a principle in religion, often very much overlooked ; the greatest and most fundamental of all, the foundation and substance of all, that could not fail of inculcation by any of these direct precepts understood to be divine, no matter to what they might relate immediately. That is, obedience. Obedience, full, complete, absolute, implicit obedience to divine command, is religion of the highest type, no matter to what the particular command may relate. Perhaps much of the early Hebrew ritual was of this charac ter ; that is, intrinsically of little or no value, but highly important to strengthen and habituate a spirit of obedience. A thing commanded to be done may be, in itself, unimportant, and yet the obedience put forth in doing it may be vitally important. So, very much of the early precepts given to the Church might be very safely laid aside, after they had answered their end.

But all the principal or important things which went into disuse in the age of Jesus were, so far as we know, not even of this character. They were not laid aside by mere command, or as matter of prudence and expediency. They ceased by the simplest operation of common sense, from absolute necessity, and the nature of things. They pertained strictly and naturally to the ante-messianic period. To continue them, or any of them, would be absurd and contradictory. It would be to declare that Jesus was not Christ; that the appearance was yet to be looked for.

To have clear ideas, therefore, about either religion or the Church, we must distinguish between modes of teaching and the things taught. As to the introduction of spiritual religion into the world at the period of Jesus, all before that time being legal, physical, external religion; it must be treated in no other way than to denounce it as absurd and ridiculous! It is out of all reason, and out of all question. Stated a thousand times, it is dishonoring to God, derogatory to religion, and most signally untrue.

It is wonderful how a man can read in the Psalms, and many other parts of the Old Testament, of the highest and holiest Christian experience, descriptions of the sublimest and most fervid communion with God, and exhortations to holiness the purest and loftiest ever uttered in human language, — and then write that spiritual religion was not known, that repentance was not taught, that faith in Christ had no existence among men before the incarnation! Shall such stumbling blocks remain in the Church? O Lord, how long!

XV.

THE MYSTICAL BODY OF CHRIST.

A NUMBER of writers make frequent mention of the Mystical Body of Christ, without, so far as I remember to have seen, any explanation of the meaning of the curious phrase. How it ever got into religious literature, others may know better than I do. It seems to be sometimes used as another name for the Church. But what there is mysterious about the Church, I have not been able to see.

Dr. Kitto says (*Cyclopædia*, art. "Mystery"), "A most unscriptural and dangerous sense is but too often put upon this word, as if it meant something absolutely unintelligible and incomprehensible; whereas in every instance in which it occurs in the Septuagint or New Testament, it is applied to something *revealed*, declared, explained, spoken, or which may be known or understood."

This is both sensible and important. The author then proceeds to quote and explain the several passages where the word occurs in Scripture. It seems to me there is far less mystery about the Church, than almost anything else in religion.

I suppose we know very little, if anything, about final causes in any of the departments of knowledge. And in the very nature of religious things, standing as they necessarily do, upon the very borders of finite things, and shading, if it were possible, into the regions of the infinite, it can but be that our knowledge is restricted by our constitutional inability to go farther. And when we know so little about many familiar things, we should not be surprised at our lack of knowledge of religious things. Religious teaching carries us as near to the incomprehensible as it is possible. It teaches of God, but cannot carry the mind to God. It teaches of eternity, but cannot conduct the mind to eternity. And so of heaven, of hell, and other things pertaining to spiritual and infinite things.

In all these matters, revelation teaches as far as man can receive the teaching. Things beyond that might be called mysterious. But what are generally called mysteries in Scripture are revealed things, which otherwise we would not be able to know.

But who does not comprehend the idea of the external association of Christian people? There is nothing more mysterious about that, than about family association. Mystery, indeed! I know of not many things more simple or more easily understood.

And yet the Church is the mystical body of Christ; it is mysteriously connected with the Saviour in some hidden, obscure way, with some secret, allegorical meaning, growing, we may suppose, out of the manner of its formation, taken in connection with the destruction, at the same time, of the former Church.

Thus it is that semi-Romanism is propagated among us in an insidious, matter-of-course kind of way. Thus it is that almost if not quite all the mischievous errors in the Church, about the Church, grow out of this popular error of a new Church, of a new dispensation. The dispensation is new in the sense that, according to a distinguished author, "All before was earthly, or animal, or devilish, or all three together ; but now, all is holy, spiritual, and divine." And according to another, "The planting of Christianity was the total abolition of all the religion that preceded it." A third, "The Christian religion is entirely new, both with regard to the object and the doctrines, not only infinitely superior to, but totally unlike everything which had ever before entered into the mind of man." A fourth says that "All the religion of the Jews before the apostles was, throughout, a system of folly and delusion." A fifth, that "The kingdom of God, which is the Church of God, had no existence, no pretense to existence, before the apostles erected it by Christ's command." And a sixth, a tenth, and a hundredth, in like manner.

Now when the tall teachers of religious teachers teach thus, what are we humble assistants to do? What are we expected to teach? We must break through such shackles and teach the truth.

If we set it down as true that no new Church was formed, and no new religion was introduced in the time of the apostles, then we must maintain that ground, and understand all Scripture that way. All Scripture must conform to everything that is true. Truth must not yield to accommodate anybody, or for fear of anybody.

XVI.

THE HUNDRED AND TWENTY DISCIPLES.

ACTS i. 15 reads on this wise: "And in those days Peter stood up in the midst of the disciples, and said (the number of the names together were about an hundred and twenty), Men and brethren," etc. He then goes on, as the history informs us, to propose another apostle in the place of Judas.

A good deal has been said about this hundred and twenty disciples, so alluded to on that occasion.

Olshausen says: "The whole body of the little Church at Jerusalem amounted, at that time, only to one hundred and twenty souls." How he gets his information is a very serious question.

Burkitt calls them the "primo-primitive Church, consisting of a hundred and twenty persons." Neither does he give us the least intimation as to where he gets his information.

Scott's Commentary says, "The whole number of disciples collected together at this time was about a hundred and twenty." That is a very safe remark. It is what Luke had just stated, that the number of disciples at that time and that place was about a hundred and twenty.

Benson paraphrases thus: "That is, who were together in the upper room, were a hundred and twenty." That is very sensible, and is plainly stated without any conjecture or guess-work.

Dr. Clarke is quite as satisfactory. He regards the one hundred and twenty as the number of persons then and there present in that room; and remarks, "It is remarkable, that this was the number which the Jews required to form a *Council* in any city."

To the conjecture of Burkitt and of Olshausen, it might be replied, first, that the words used by Luke as to the number present on the occasion referred to, are merely incidental and parenthetic, forming no part of the staple of the thing he is relating.

Secondly, there is not the slightest intimation anywhere in any history, that this number of persons has anything whatever to do with the number of Church-members at that time. The supposition, as we will see, is a mere conjecture, and a very wild one. Third, it could not be intended to number the Church, for Paul, in First Corinthians, in a remark equally irrelevant to the numerical strength of the Church, says that some time before that, before the ascension, above five hundred brethren saw the Saviour at one time after his crucifixion. And Burkitt, who, as above, says this one hundred and twenty constituted the entire Church, says also that this five hundred were all members of the Church, of the highest veracity and piety. Both things cannot be true, for they plainly contradict each other.

But in the fourth place, before any person can regard this one hundred and twenty as making up the entire Church of God upon earth, he must answer the question, What became of the Church that undeniably existed a few weeks before, amounting to millions? To question that, a few weeks before this, a Church, a divinely recognized Church, call it by what name you will, existed, a little of it in Palestine, and the rest in other countries, amounting to several millions, would be to question a fact that never was questioned, we may suppose. This Church, the Church of God, with our Bible — all of it that then existed — for their Bible, our Christ for their Christ, and our God for their God, had, it is said, over four hundred of its congregations in the city of Jerusalem alone, and thousands more in other parts of the world. Jesus himself was a member of it. It was physically impossible that any large portion of them could have even heard of those then recent, wonderful events at Jerusalem. Not one tenth, probably, could have heard of his crucifixion and resurrection, and so, could not have denied Him. They could not have questioned his resurrection, either as a fact or as evidence of his Christship. Those who denied the Saviour did it after this. At that time, no serious objection is intimated against any portion of the Church, except a few officials and others in Jerusalem, who aided and abetted in the trial and crucifixion. These could not have amounted to over a few hundred, at most. Now, what became of this entire Church, with its millions of members, and tens of thousands of divinely called and divinely recognized ministers? Does any one say — as no one ever did say, that I know of — that they were all excommunicated, wholesale, without impeachment, without their knowledge, and when they could not have heard of it for many years afterward? As there is not the least historic intimation of such a proceeding, the supposition is absurd. Or did divine wisdom set up two rival churches to waste and devour each other? The one supposition is about as ridiculous as the other.

Dr. Schaff, in his romantic, and it might be prudently added, rather fabulous history of the Church's origin, tells us that the Church was not organized by Jesus in person, nor by the apostles, but by this company of followers and friends of the Saviour, consisting of a hundred and twenty, or thereabouts, and including the apostles, on the day of Pentecost. And although he is very minute in his details about everything that happened, either with or without historic warrant, often drawing very largely on his imagination, he makes not the slightest allusion to the formation of a Church, or anything of the kind. But without a word or hint of history, or pretense of history, he tells us that then and there one hundred and twenty persons formed and founded a new divine Church for mankind! This, for a scholar and a theologian, is certainly extraordinary.

Those speculations, many and varied as they are, about this hundred and twenty, have all grown out of a very natural, but very incidental remark of the writer of Acts, that when it was proposed to select a man for apostle in the place of Judas, there were not many persons present, only about a hundred and twenty.

Whether this number present, one hundred and twenty, had any reference to a Church council, an ecclesiastical body with which they must be presumed to be familiar, we are not informed. This is the opinion of Dr. Clarke and other leading commentators. But it would seem strange that the formation of a new and antagonistic Church, one that was to destroy the Jewish Church then existing, should be set up and made to work by a Jewish Church council!

But from the brief historic notes we have of this selection of Matthias, it does not appear that anybody participated in it but the apostles themselves.

Were it not for the old fable that the Christian Church that now is had its absolute, organic beginning at, or just about this time, one would no more think of finding the formation of a Church in this assembly of a hundred and twenty, than in any other historic matter alluded to in the New Testament.

Some find the beginning of the Church when Jesus began to preach; some here and there in the course of his preaching, and some on the last day of his ministry. Others again find it to have been organized by the apostles, some here and some there, after the death of Jesus. If anything could be found anywhere in the New Testament on the subject, or making any allusion even to such a thing, it would relieve the subject of much of its most serious difficulty. As it is, it is not only wholly conjecture, but looked at soberly, as elsewhere intimated, the thing itself is not only historically untrue, but philosophically impossible.

XVII.

THE TRIAL AND EXECUTION OF JESUS.

It is appropriate that a few observations be made here on this subject. It is the foundation of all true religion, and might be justly regarded the corner-stone of the Church. The accounts we have of this transaction are historically exceedingly meagre and unsatisfactory. Indeed, we have nothing that can be called a history, or even a comprehensive outline of the transactions. We have but a few isolated, dis-integrated facts. It is a mistake with those of us who suppose that the four Evangelists, or any one of them, undertook to write a history of anything. The object of writing the New Testament seems to be, first, to make it patent, to the Church and then to the world, that the great Christhood of revealed religion had culminated in actual, historic manhood; and second, in connection therewith, to give authoritative exposition and elaboration to the revealed doctrines and morals. How much of historic detail of occurrences would be useful to such ends is another question. We may presume we have as much as would be useful to us, though it be not at all satisfactory to our wishes.

Moreover, we are but poorly informed as to the jurisprudence of either Jews or Romans, either civil, criminal, or ecclesiastical, in those times. Our information is in isolated scraps, and is very general. Judea, but a part of little Palestine, was a petty Roman province, a sort of property of little hereditary tyrants. The civil government, as compared with almost anything seen in modern times, was disgracefully miserable. It was this way or that way, here and there, as prejudice, passion, bribery, and tyranny chanced to fancy. And it must be remembered, too, in those days human life was cheap. Cruelties and executions were commonplaces.

Again, the very gospel of human salvation, from the very first, contemplated the sacrificial death of the human exhibition of the Godhead. Voluntary sacrifice, the extremest possible, lay at the foundation, and was inseparable from the idea of man's justification before God. Without the shedding of blood there is no remission of sin. Not that the shed blood, or the shedding of it procures or produces the remission, but because nothing short of that, the knowledge of it on our part — could give us the proper sense of benevolence in a benefactor, which would be sufficient to produce the degree of dependence and humility necessary to establish the natural relation of saved mendicant and independent Saviour. The voluntary death of the Saviour-victim, then, lay at the very foundation — nay, it was itself the very principle of human recovery.

How the Saviour-man would die was an open question. Not only the death, but the manner of the death was essential. Suppose Jesus had died of sickness, as other men die. Then it were a failure, because that could not have produced the necessary effect in the heart of man. In such a death we could see, or be made to perceive very little of sacrifice and self-denial. And we must remember that nothing but sacrifice and self-denial, in actually relieving the distresses of the distressed, can give adequate evidence of any considerable degree of benevolence in a benefactor. Benefaction which costs but little gives no evidence of benevolence.

The death of Jesus, then, as looked at by us, must be inflicted — nay, it must be cruelly and wickedly inflicted. In the very nature of things it was anomalous. While, as Peter said on the day of Pentecost, it was the work of "wicked hands," it was but the regular administration of the law of the Church. The immediate legal cause of Jesus' death was that He claimed equality with God; but the real, procuring cause was largely to be found in jealousy and rivalship of the members of the Sanhedrim. To suffer Him to live, they would lose office, place, and position. So that while the Jewish crucifiers were glad to vindicate and execute the law, they needed the law as their own vindication to back up and justify their own conduct.

Blasphemy was a capital offense by the law of the Church. And it is not at all certain that the death of Jesus was the only one of this sort, about this time. Gamaliel, in his speech before the Sanhedrim, as cited in Acts v. 35–39, mentions two others, Theudas and one Judas. Josephus speaks of a Theudas who played a similar part several years later, in the time of Claudius, and others along in periods not far distant. The times were turbulent; the land was frequently overrun by insurrectionary chiefs. The notion prevailed in Judea somewhat, to what extent we are not informed, that the Jewish Messias would be a civil prince, and free Judea, if not Palestine and even much more of the empire, from the yoke of Rome. So the Messiahship seemed usually connected with the idea of civil insurrection.

The execution of Theudas and of Judas were probably fresh in their recollection. And although they claimed the Messiahship, it is likely their civil offenses so far took the lead, that they were disposed of by Roman authority without much, if any, of ecclesiastical complaint on the part of the Jews.

This was the point in Gamaliel's speech. He seemed to have the true idea of the Scriptural Messiah, and so argues — If Jesus is a false Messiah, like Theudas and Judas, He will soon be checked as an insurrectionist by the civil power; but if He proves to be the true Messiah, He will commit no civil offense; and surely you will not oppose God's true Messiah, lest haply you be found to fight against God.

That argument was very good so far as it went; but it did not, and could not go far enough. The ecclesiastical law denounced the death penalty against blasphemy, irrespective of any civil offense. The Jewish doctors said, We prove Him guilty of blasphemy because, being a man, He maketh Himself God; and if He has not as yet committed overt insurrection, He soon will. It is dangerous to the government to suffer a man to go at large who claims supreme power. If He *is* the Christ, let Him disprove the charge of blasphemy. Surely He can do that.

Reasonable as that would seem, it was demanding an impossibility. The true Messiah must be apparently guilty of blasphemy, and so, liable to the death penalty. It is very difficult, nay, we may say it is impossible, to judge *à priori* of the proper proofs of the true Messiahship. It is very certain Jesus did not convince anybody, not even his warmest and best friends, définitively and conclusively, that He was the real Christ. The most He did, and the most it would seem it was possible to do, was to create, in those in the best position to be informed, a high probability that He was what He claimed to be, the very Christ.

The Scriptures everywhere hold, and reason also seems to hold, that a resurrection from the dead, and that alone, can give the final, conclusive proof of the Christship. This evidence is to be presented in the world but once.

It is a principle in evidence, and a sound one, that nothing is conclusively proved until the best evidence the nature of the case admits of is adduced. Then how, in the nature of things, could Jesus while alive prove certainly that He was Christ? He could not. The nature of the case admits of better evidence than anything a live man can do or say. Resurrection from the dead is the highest conceivable evidence, and nothing else is.

Then Jesus being the very Christ, He was shut up by the very providence of God, and his own plan of redeeming the world, to the inescapable necessities of a judicial death. It was in this way that He planned a voluntary death. Much of the Sanhedrim may have voted with reluctance, but the law impelled them. Jesus did not convince his best friends conclusively; and how then could it be expected of rival enemies, or cold, reluctant friends to be convinced?

So Jesus was virtually slain from the foundation

of the world. His death was planned from the beginning. The seeming agents were but instruments. Verily they did, they knew not what. Mostly, no doubt, they were concerned about office, and place, and salary, etc. Jesus could have arrested them and saved his own life, but not without arresting the constitution and course of things; and this would have arrested the entire course and progress of human salvation.

Human salvation is looked at by many too superficially. It is a far greater thing than many suppose. Many of its aspects are no doubt far beyond human thought or conception. It had to meet the necessities of the case. And some of these necessities were the constitution of man, and the circumstances of human condition. To change man's constitution, and place him in different relations to God and nature, would not be salvation. It was man that was to be saved. The mode was planned by infinite wisdom. The instruments were adapted to the ends. A Christhood, supposed and explained, and the thing is conceivable. To be Godlike, salvation must be within reach of all men. Partial salvation, restricted as to times, places, countries, peoples, chronology, — is unworthy the God we adore. A "temporary system," "confined to the Jews," or confined at all, looks Lilliputian. To be Godlike, it must be plenary and world-wide. And so it was, and is. How could the great Almighty measure and dole out salvation by an almanac and a surveyor's chain, or the petty jurisdiction of some ephemeral king or usurper? God deals with man, and discriminates only between those who are obedient and those who are not.

That aspect of the Godhead which we call Christ, the Divine Son, undertook the enterprise of renovating this world. He began at the right time, and in the right way. The time was before any man died; and the way was by the voluntary suffering and denial of his own self. That part of the work which was designed for the sensible observance of men was not, for natural and obvious reasons, performed at the very first, but somewhat later in the world's history. So this event was, of course, chronological; and so, part of the world's history was before, and part after. But the Christship no more began at this period than the Godhead began at some chronological date. Dates and dividing lines refer to human things, not to great, plenary, divine operations.

The death of Jesus was the death of the son of Mary, but did not affect the Christhood. The son of Mary lived but the very brief space of one third part of a single century; but Christ is coeval with the coeternal years of God.

As to the Church, that naturally takes care of itself. Christianity supposed, the Church is absolutely unavoidable. Internal piety, not external laws, makes the Church. Christians associate religiously for the enjoyment and promotion of Christianity from the very necessities of the case. It would be no more of a contradiction to suppose that Christians did not love God and each other, and did not love private, public, and social worship, than to suppose religion without a Church. Social and public worship are as naturally and as necessarily the consequence of individual piety, as that the social constitution produces its legitimate results in any other departments of life. The Church is the confluent result of personal religion, because of the social gravitation which is the controlling religious ingredient. A thing is the result of its ingredients.

And then, Christianity supposes a ministry, and fellowship; that is, personal membership; and so, all the other external machinery of a Church. Christians who do not attend to, labor and participate in these things, are not Christians. Religion and the Church coinhere, coexist and cosupport each other. They are not two separate things, but two aspects of one and the same thing. They are separable only as filial love and duty are separable, in reference to the father and the mother. But filial duty includes both.

Before the actual life and suffering of the Messiah, the pious man looked to these sacrifices and self denials — adumbrantly it certainly was, because it could not possibly be otherwise — from the position he occupied. He had Moses and the prophets. Their teachings are slightly but clearly hinted at in the writings of the Old Testament. After these things transpired, the pious man beholds the very same thing from a different point of observation. Before, the Christian could only speak or think of sacrifice: now he thinks and speaks of crucifixion; still, they are one and the same thing. The cross is but an instrument of vicarious sacrifice and self-denial. We remember what was formerly anticipated. But the great DEATH underlies the whole. In both cases the pious man has something besides mere external information to rely upon as the pillar of his faith. Human knowledge has two sources, testimony and consciousness; the one addresses his senses, the other his mind. So with the Christian; there are the testimonies, here the witnessing Spirit.

Glorious system! God is merciful! Jesus suffered! And the man of faith and obedience is justified!

INDEX OF AUTHORS AND WORKS REFERRED TO IN THE SECTION "ERRORS OF AUTHORS."

www.ingramcontent.com/pod-product-compliance
Lightning Source LLC
LaVergne TN
LVHW020212110826
845151LV00003B/693

* 9 7 8 1 4 2 5 5 3 4 9 5 0 *